All in One®

FINE ARTS

CBSE
Class 11

All in One®

FINE ARTS

CBSE
Class 11

arihant
SUCCESS AND NOTHING LESS

arihant
SUCCESS AND NOTHING LESS

ARIHANT PRAKASHAN
(School Division Series)

卐 ADMINISTRATIVE & PRODUCTION OFFICES

Regd. Office
'Ramchhaya' 4577/15, Agarwal Road, Darya Ganj, New Delhi -110002
Tele: 011- 47630600, 43518550; Fax: 011- 23280316

卐 Head Office
Kalindi, TP Nagar, Meerut (UP) - 250002, Tel: 0121-7156203, 7156204

卐 SALES & SUPPORT OFFICES
Agra, Ahmedabad, Bengaluru, Bareilly, Chennai, Delhi, Guwahati, Hyderabad, Jaipur, Jhansi, Kolkata, Lucknow, Nagpur & Pune.

PO No : TXT-XX-XXXXXXX-X-XX

Published By Arihant Publications (India) Ltd.

For further information about the books published by Arihant, log on to www.arihantbooks.com or e-mail at info@arihantbooks.com

Follow us on

卐 PRICE ₹215.00

PRODUCTION TEAM

Publishing Managers	Mahendra Singh Rawat & Keshav Mohan
Project Head	Karishma Yadav
Project Coordinator	Shivam Gupta
Cover Designer	Rakesh Rawat
Inner Designer	Arjun Verma
Page Layouting	Sundar Bisht, Shivam
Proof Readers	Sundip, Manisha

Introduction to All in One®

All in One Fine Arts Class 11th has been written keeping in mind the needs of students studying in Class 11th CBSE. This book has been made in such a way that students will be fully guided to prepare for the exam in the most effective manner, securing higher grades.

The purpose of this book is to equip a CBSE Student with a sound knowledge of Fine Arts at Class 11th Level. This book will give you support during the course as well as guide you on Revision and Preparation for the exam itself. The material is presented in a Clear & Concise manner and there are questions for you to practice.

All-in-One Fine Arts for CBSE Class 11th has all the material required for Learning, Understanding, Practice and Assessment and will surely guide the students on the Path to Success.

Huge efforts have been made from my side to keep this book error free, but inspite of that if any error or whatsoever is skipped in the book then that is purely incidental, apology for the same, please write to me about that so that it can be corrected in the further edition of the book. Suggestions for further improvement of the book will also be welcomed.

Authors

Vaishali Jain
Rudraksha Tripathi

FINE ARTS

CBSE Class 11

CHAPTER 01

Six Limbs of Indian Painting & Fundamentals of Visual Arts

In this chapter
- *Six Limbs of Indian Paintings*
- *Fundamentals of Visual Arts*

Indian art form consists of variety of forms like sculptures, paintings, textile art and pottery. The origin of Indian art form can be traced from pre-historic cave paintings of 3rd century BC to the modern contemporary paintings of present time. This Indian art form has passed many generations and developed gracefully with time.

Different art styles have developed that have different cultural and religious values based on certain theories and subject matter. These art styles are Ajanta cave paintings and miniature paintings during Mughal, Rajasthani and Pahari schools which reflects the fundamental theme of Indian classical tradition. These fundamental themes are explained in **Shilpgranth**[1] such as Kamasutra, Vishnudhar-mottar Puran, Natyashastra, Chitralaksan, Samrangan Sutradhar, Shilpratnam, etc. One of the text of Shilpgranth known as Shadangas, describes the six limbs of Indian painting.

Six Limbs of Indian Painting

The six limbs of Indian painting were evolved around 1st century BC till the 3rd century AD. The six limbs were actually different points or strokes which were emphasised to give real-life depiction to the paintings. The six limbs of painting are linked together to form limbs of human beings. These six limbs are known as **Shadangas** in India. Shadangas are rules of art written in ancient times. It comprises of two words, **shad** which means six and **anga** which means limbs or parts.

1 **Shilpgranth** A historical book which contains the information about various forms of Indian art and craft, architectural styles, sculptures and stories of ancient India.

Chapter Theory

Contains the necessary study material well supported by Definitions, Facts, Examples, etc. This section is totally in sync with NCERT Textbook and provides all the essentials needed to prepare you for the exam.

EXAM PRACTICE

Multiple Choice Questions

1. What is meaning of the word 'shad' in Shadangas?
(a) Seven (b) Six (c) Eight (d) ten

Ans. (b) Six

2. Which among the following is author of the book Kamasutra?
(a) Vishvamitra (b) Valmiki
(c) Vedvyas (d) Vatsyayana

Ans. (d) Vatsyayana

3. .... deals with accuracy and precision of measurement and structure in the paintings.
(a) Pramanani (b) Roopbheda
(c) Lavanya Yojanam (d) Bhava

Ans. (a) Pramanani

4. Which of the following is not an element of visual art?
(a) Unity (b) Line
(c) Colour (d) Point

Ans. (a) Unity

5. Which of the following is a principle of visual art?
(a) Pramanani (b) Harmony
(c) Gradation (d) Space

Ans. (b) Harmony

6. Match the following.

List I	List II
A. Sadrisyam	1. The feeling on forms
B. Lavanya Yojanam	2. Blending grace in an artistic representation
C. Bhava	3. Resemblance
D. Roopbheda	4. The knowledge of looks

Codes
(a) A-1, B-2, C-3, D-4
(b) A-2, B-4, C-3, D-1
(c) A-3, B-2, C-1, D-4
(d) A-2, B-3, C-1, D-4

Ans. (c) A-3, B-2, C-1, D-4

Assertion-Reason

7. **Assertion** (A) Pramanani principle is governed by certain laws which give capability of portraying something precisely.
Reason (R) Pramanani teaches the exact measurement, proportion and distance of subjects and objects.
(a) Both A and R are true and R is the correct explanation of A
(b) Both A and R are true, but R is not the correct explanation of A
(c) A is true, but R is false
(d) A is false, but R is true

Ans. (a) Both A and R are true and R is the correct explanation of A

True or False

1. The origin of Indian art form can be traced from pre-historic cave paintings of 3rd century BC.

Ans. True

2. Shilpgranth is rules of art, written in ancient times. It comprises of two words 'shilp' which means six and 'granth' means limbs or parts.

Ans. False

3. Roopbheda means, blending grace in an artistic representation.

Ans. False

Very Short Answer Type Questions

1. Which fundamental themes are explained in Shilpgranth?

Ans. The fundamental themes which are explained in Shilpgranth are Kamasutra, Vishnudharmottar Puran, Natyashastra, Chitralaksan, Samrangan Sutradhar, Shilpratnam etc. Shilpgranth also briefly explain about various art, elements and forms.

Exam Practice

Each chapter contains questions in the format in which they are asked in the examination like; Multiple Choice Questions, Assertion-Reason, Source Based Questions, True or False, Very Short Answer Type, Short Answer Type and Long Answer Type Questions. To Facilitate the easy learning and practice, detailed answers to all the questions have been given.

5. According to your observation, how did the people of pre-historic times select themes for their paintings? *(NCERT)*

Ans. The people of pre-historic times selected themes for their paintings on various basis ranging from their daily routine activities to royal and sacred images such as hunting, food gathering, music, horse riding, honey collection, decoration of bodies and other household scenes.

6. In modern times, how have walls been used as a surface to make paintings, graphics, etc? *(NCERT)*

Ans. The various ways in which walls are used as surface for paintings, graphics, etc are
- For providing social message to people, when government promotes a particular message.
- For depicting various tribal arts.
- For mural paintings which are done directly on walls using water colours, acrylic paints, oil paints, etc.

NCERT Questions

All the Questions of NCERT Textbook with their detailed answers are given in Exam Practice

All-in-One for CBSE Class 11th Examination. It is hoped that this book will reinforce and extend your ideas about the subject and finally will place you in the row of toppers.

Explanation of Sculptures

The detailed explanation of each sculpture given in syllabus, is

Appreciation of the Sculptures of Mauryan Period

Lion Capital, Sarnath

Lion Capital was built by Ashoka in rememberance of the first sermon or *dhammachakrapravartana* by the Buddha. This sculpture was made by polished sandstone, through the technique of carving. The Lion Capital or pillar originally consisted of five component parts which are

(i) The shaft which is now broken in many parts.
(ii) A lotus bell base.
(iii) A drum on the bell base with four animals proceeding clockwise.
(iv) The figures of four majestic enthroned lions.
(v) The crowning element, *Dhammachakra* which is a large wheel. However, this wheel is lying in a broken condition and is displayed in the site museum at Sarnath. The capital without the crowning wheel and the lotus base has been adopted as the **National Emblem** of Independent India.

Name : Lion Capital, Sarnath
Medium : Polished Sandstone
Period : 3rd century BCE
Collection : Sarnath Museum, Uttar Pradesh

The Lion Capital is now has been kept in the archaeological museum at **Sarnath**. The capital has four lions firmly seated back to back on a circular stone abacus. The lion figures of the capital are very impressive and massive. The sculpture is monumental (huge). The facial features of the lions are strong depicting muscularity.

The inversed lines of the lips and its subsequent effect of projection at the end of the lips show the sculptor's observation for naturalistic depiction. The lions appear as if they have held their breath. The lines of the hairs of the lion are sharp and follow the traditions that were in practice during that time.

Their curly manes (hairs on the neck) are depicted by extending mass. The weight of the body of each lion is firmly shown by the stretched muscles of the feet. The surface of the sculpture is heavily polished which is the distinctive feature of sculptures of the Mauryan Period.

The abacus has the depiction of a *chakra* (wheel) having twenty-four spokes in all the four directions. The figures of a bull, a horse, an elephant and a lion are carved between every *chakra*. The design of the *chakra* in Lion Capital is significant as it represents the Buddhist symbol of *Dhammachakra*.

SAMPLE QUESTION PAPER
(Painting)

Time allowed : 2 hrs | MM : 30 Marks

General Instructions
1. All the five sections are compulsory.
2. Answers of all the questions are to be written according to the specified word limit given in the questions.
3. Internal choices have been given in some questions.
4. Marks are indicated against each question.

Section A

I. *Answer the following questions by choosing the correct option.* (1 × 6 = 6)

1. Who made the first discovery of rock paintings in India?
(a) Archibold Carlleyle (b) Cockburn
(c) Anderson (d) Mitra

2. At which site do we find the famous artefact 'The Dancing Girl'?
(a) Harappa (b) Dholavira
(c) Mohenjodaro (d) Ropar

3. Archaeologists have discover red thousands of seals from Indus Valley, mostly made of steatite and other materials like agate copper, terracotta, etc. For which purpose seals were used?
(a) Commercial (b) Artistic
(c) Spiritual (d) Educational

4. With which of the following saint was Qutub Minar associated?
(a) Khwaja Moinuddin Chisti (b) Khwaja Qutbuddin Bakhtiyar Kaki
(c) Sheikh Nizamat Ullah (d) Khwaja Pir Mohammad

5. The world famous Sanchi stupa which contains the relics of Gautam Buddha is located in which of the following Indian state?
(a) Gujarat (b) Madhya Pradesh
(c) Haryana (d) Uttar Pradesh

6. Which among the following is author of the book Kamasutra?
(a) Vishvamitra (b) Valmiki
(c) Vedvyas (d) Vatsyayana

Sample Question Papers

To make the students practice in the real sense, we have provided 4 Sample Question Papers, 1 Sample Question Paper of each course in Fine Arts i.e. Painting, Graphics, Sculpture and Commercial Art.

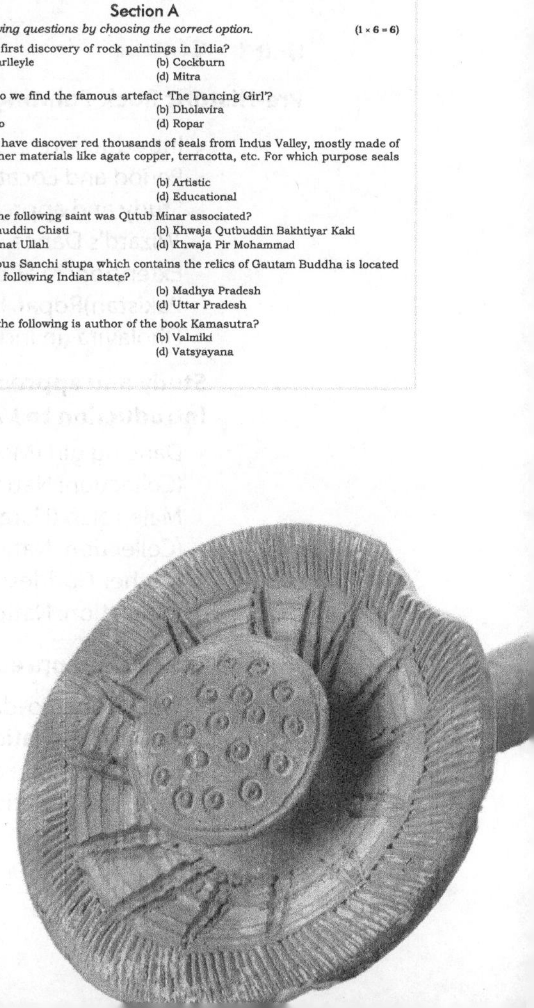

CBSE SYLLABUS

What I have to Study this Year

Painting Code No. 049

Units	History of Indian Art	Marks
1.	Pre-Historic rock paintings and art of Indus / Sindhu Saraswati Civilization (Indus valley Civilization) Buddhist, Jain and Hindu Art	15
2.	Temple Sculptures, Bronzes and Artistic aspects of Indo-Islamic architecture	15

Unit 1	Content
Pre-Historic Rock-Paintings	
1.	• Introduction • Period and Location • Study and appreciation of following pre-historic paintings: Wizard's Dance, Bhimbethaka • Extension: In about 1500 miles. Harappa &Mohenjo-daro (Now in Pakistan)Ropar, Lothal, Rangpur, Alamgirpur, Kali Bangan, Banawali and Dholavira (in India)
2.	**Study and appreciation of following: Sculptures in Bronze and Terracottas: Introduction to Method of Bronze casting** • Dancing girl (Mohenjo-daro) Bronze, 10.5 x 5 x 2.5 cm. Circa 2500 B.C. (Collection: National Museum, New Delhi). • Male Torso (Harappa)Red lime Stone, 9.2 x 5.8 x 3 cms. Circa 2500 B.C. (Collection: National Museum, New Delhi) • Mother Goddess (Mohenjo-daro) terracotta, 22 x 8 x 5 c Circa2500 B.C. (Collection: National Museum, New Delhi)
3.	**Study and appreciation of following Seal:** • Bull (Mohenjo-daro)Stone (Steatite), 2.5 x 2.5 x 1.4 cm. Circa 2500 B.C. (Collection: National Museum, New Delhi). • Decoration on earthen wares: Painted earthen-ware (Jar) Mohenjo-daro (Collection: National Museum, New Delhi).

Buddhist, Jain and Hindu Art (3rd century B.C. to 8th century A.D.)

1.	**General Introduction and understanding of Art during** • Mauryan Period: Mirror like polish (eg. Chauri Bearer from Didar Ganj/Yakshi called Monalisa of India, Iron Pillar of Qutab Minar that has never rusted. Shunga: • Kushana Period: evolution and mutation of Gandhara, Mathura • Gupta Period: Amalgamation of Gandhara, Mathura into Gupta Style
2.	**Study and appreciation of following Sculptures.** **i. Lion Capital from Sarnath** Circa: 3rd Century BCE Period: Mauryan Material: Polished sandstone, Collection: Sarnath Museum, U.P. **ii. Chauri Bearer from Didar Ganj (Yakshi)** Circa 3rd Century BCE Period: Mauryan Material: Polished sandstone, Collection: Patna Museum, Bihar. **iii. Seated Buddha from Katra Mound, Mathura** Circa 3rd Century C.E. Period: Kushan (Mathura Style) Material: Red-spotted Sandstone, Collection: Govt. Museum, Mathura **iv. Jain Tirathankara** Circa: 5th Century Period: Gupta period:5th Century CE Material: Stone Collection: State Museum, Lucknow U.P.
3.	**Introduction to Ajanta Location** Period: 5th Century CE No of caves:30 Chaitya Caves: 5(9,10,19,26,29) subject matter- Buddha meditating Vihara Caves: 25 subject matter- Bodhisattva Padmapani Techniques: Rock cut Architecture, sculpture, fresco painting

Unit 2 Temple Sculpture, Bronzes and artistic aspects of Indo- Islamic Architecture

(A)	**Artistic aspects of Indian Temple sculpture Period: 6th Century CE to 13th Century CE** 1. Introduction to Temple Sculpture Overview of temple sculpture practices in India, with a focus on key periods, regions, and stylistic developments between the 6th and 13th centuries CE.

	2. Study and Appreciation of Notable Temple Sculptures: **Descent of Ganga** • Period: Circa 7th Century CE • Dynasty: Pallava • Material: Granite Rock • Location: Mahabalipuram, Tamil Nadu **Trimurti** • Period: Circa 9th Century CE • Material: Stone • Location: Elephanta, Maharashtra **Lakshmi Narayana (Kandariya Mahadev Temple)** • Period: Circa 10th Century CE • Dynasty: Chandela • Material: Stone • Location: Khajuraho, Madhya Pradesh **Cymbal Player (Konark Sun Temple)** • Period: Circa 13th Century CE • Dynasty: Ganga Dynasty • Material: Stone • Location: Odisha **Mother and Child (Vimal-Shah Temple, Dilwara)** • Period: Circa 13th Century CE • Dynasty: Solanki Dynasty • Material: White Marble • Location: Mount Abu, Rajasthan
(B)	**Bronzes:** 1. Introduction to Indian Bronzes. 2. Method of casting (solid and hollow) 3. Study and appreciation of following South Indian Bronze: **Nataraj** • Period: Circa 12th Century CE • Dynasty: Chola • Location: Thanjavur District, Tamil Nadu • Collection: National Museum, New Delhi
(C)	**Artistic aspects of the Indo-Islamic architecture:** 1. Introduction 2. Study and appreciation of following architecture: • Qutub Minar, Delhi • Gol Gumbad of Bijapur

Graphics Code No. 050

Units	History of Indian Art	Marks
1.	Pre-Historic rock paintings and art of Indus / Sindhu Saraswati Civilization (Indus valley Civilization) Buddhist, Jain and Hindu Art	15
2.	Temple Sculptures, Bronzes and Artistic aspects of Indo-Islamic architecture	15

Note: The Syllabus of Graphics (Theory) for Class XI is the same as that of Painting (Theory) for class XI given earlier.

Sculpture Code No. 051

Units	History of Indian Art	Marks
1.	Pre-Historic rock paintings and art of Indus / Sindhu Saraswati Civilization (Indus valley Civilization) Buddhist, Jain and Hindu Art	15
2.	Temple Sculptures, Bronzes and Artistic aspects of Indo-Islamic architecture	15

Note: The Syllabus of Sculpture (Theory) for Class XI is the same as that of Painting (Theory) for class XI given earlier.

Commercial Art Code No. 052

Units	History of Indian Art	Marks
1.	Pre-Historic rock paintings and art of Indus / Sindhu Saraswati Civilization (Indus valley Civilization) Buddhist, Jain and Hindu Art	15
2.	Temple Sculptures, Bronzes and Artistic aspects of Indo-Islamic architecture	15

Note: The Syllabus of Commercial Art (Theory) for Class XI is the same as that of Painting (Theory) for class XI given earlier.

TABLE OF CONTENTS

CHAPTER 01

Six Limbs of Indian Painting & Fundamentals of Visual Arts

In this chapter
- *Six Limbs of Indian Paintings*
- *Fundamentals of Visual Arts*

Indian art form consists of variety of forms like sculptures, paintings, textile art and pottery. The origin of Indian art form can be traced from pre-historic cave paintings of 3rd century BC to the modern contemporary paintings of present time. This Indian art form has passed many generations and developed gracefully with time.

Different art styles have developed that have different cultural and religious values based on certain theories and subject matter. These art styles are Ajanta cave paintings and miniature paintings during Mughal, Rajasthani and Pahari schools which reflects the fundamental theme of Indian classical tradition. These fundamental themes are explained in **Shilpgranth**[1] such as Kamasutra, Vishnudhar-mottar Puran, Natyashastra, Chitralaksan, Samrangan Sutradhar, Shilpratnam, etc. One of the text of Shilpgranth known as Shadangas, describes the six limbs of Indian painting.

Six Limbs of Indian Painting

The six limbs of Indian painting were evolved around 1st century BC till the 3rd century AD. The six limbs were actually different points or strokes which were emphasised to give real-life depiction to the paintings. The six limbs of painting are linked together to form limbs of human beings. These six limbs are known as **Shadangas** in India. Shadangas are rules of art written in ancient times. It comprises of two words, **shad** which means six and **anga** which means limbs or parts.

1 **Shilpgranth** A historical book which contains the information about various forms of Indian art and craft, architectural styles, sculptures and stories of ancient India.

Thus, Shadanga consists of six limbs of Indian art on which ancient paintings depends. The paintings are called **Alekhya** in Shadangas. During 200-300 AD, a great writer **Vatsyayana** highlighted the importance of painting in his book Kamasutra. He explains that painting occupy 4th place out of 64 art forms in India. He also emphasised about the six limbs of art which are used to add meaning and grace to the paintings. In 11th century, another great artist **Yashodhar Pandit** explained Kamasutra to define art. He named them as Jaimangla which explains six limbs of Indian painting through a Shloka which is

"Roopa Bhedah Pramanani Bhava-Lavanya-yojanam |
Sadrishya Varnikabhang iti chitra Shadangkam" ||

The six limbs or Shadangas of Indian painting are

1. Roopbheda : The Knowledge of Looks and Appearances

It consists of two words, **roop** which means outer form or appearance of subject and **bheda** which means difference. It focused on the classification of the physical appearance of the form (*Rupa*).

It states that to develop painting, an artist must possess sufficient knowledge of different forms that exists. He should know how to depict form of life and death differently. This knowledge is developed with experiences and his vision to create forms.

2. Pramanani : Accuracy and Precision of Measurement and Structure

This principle is governed by certain laws which give capability of portraying something precisely. Pramanani teaches the exact measurement, proportion and distance of subjects and objects. This also provides an understanding about **anatomy**[2] of the object. For example, to know about how blue the sky is, a measurement will be useless as it cannot be depicted on a piece of paper. Similarly one cannot predicts the colour of ocean by few strokes of brush.

3. Bhava : The Feeling on Forms

Bhava means an emotion, intention and feelings. A Bhava is a form which gives motion to a painting. This is one of the most important aspect which can impart life to a painting. Bhava is important in order to represent the inner feeling, thoughts, emotion, affection and sentiments of the subject. Bhava are of two types i.e. **covert** and **overt**. Covert form depict the hidden emotions and overt form depicts the revealed emotions.

For example, in one of Raja Ravi Verma's painting, Shakuntala is shown pretending to remove thorn from her foot (overt form) while she is actually looking for Dushyantha (covert form).

2 **Anatomy** The branch of science concerned with the bodily structure of humans, animals, and other living organisms.

4. Lavanya Yojanam : Blending Grace in an Artistic Representation

Lavanya Yojanam means amalgamation of grace or knowledge in an artistic representation. The Pramanani depicts the rigid proportions and Bhava expresses the emotions. But Lavanya Yojanam represent balance between the rigid proportions and emotions.

Abanindranath Tagore, the famous artist from Bengal, has described Lavanya Yojanam as a 'loving mother', who is also careful about the rules of raising up her child.

5. Sadrisyam or Resemblance

Sadrisyam represent the degree to which a depiction is similar to an artist's vision and subject matter of the painting. It is a way of representing similarity among various elements just like a poet compares a woman's locks of hair with a snake, her elegant face with moon, her lips with rose petals and her eyes with the eyes of a deer.

6. Varnikabhangam : An Artistic way of Making use of Brush and Colours

It signifies the artistic manner of using the brush and colours to draw and paint mersmerising painting. It conveys the knowledge of a colour scheme and to use the colours in an artistic style for creating an aesthetic sense. The use of better combination of colours makes a painting attractive and perfect.

Significance of Shadangas or Six Limbs

The Shadanga is an inevitable part of every great Indian masterpiece. When an artist is creating a piece of art or any critic is assessing a work of art, he must keep in mind the six limbs of art to create or analyse it properly. These limbs are the basic principles on which Indian art was found. These limbs make Indian art exceptional and precious which is visible from the ancient paintings of Ajanta to the paintings created by Raja Ravi Verma, Hussain and many other artists of the modern period. Thus, Shadangas reflects the limbs of art, without which an art work is incomplete.

Fundamentals of Visual Arts

Any art form whether it is painting, sculpture, pottery or textile, depends upon some fundamentals which are known as the elements of art and its principles.

Elements of Visual Arts

- **Point** A point (•) is something which does not have magnitude, dimension or direction. A point is the visual element upon which all other elements are based. In any art form, points are used for marking and shading purpose.
- **Line** A line is a long collection of points extending in two opposite directions. Line is the most basic visual element. Lines can be used to define shapes and figures and also to indicate motion, emotion and other elements. It may be vertical, horizontal, transverse, angular, curved or wavy. The use of lines allows artist to demonstrate delicacy or force.

The upward and downward movement of the curves of lines expresses the twists and turns in the painting. The use of different lines adds various moods and feelings in an artpiece.

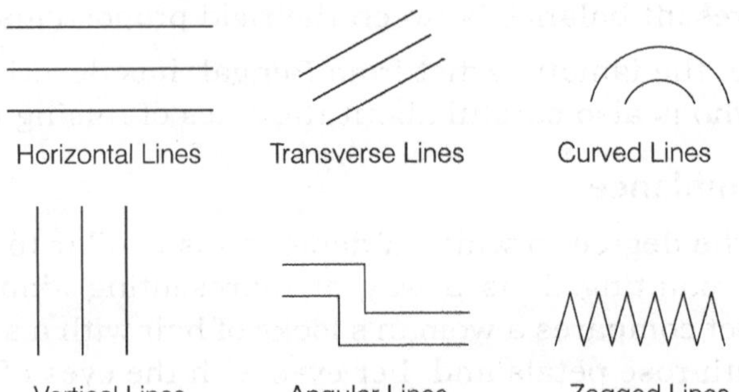

Presentation of Different Lines

- **Shape** It is an element of art that is two-dimensional, flat, or limited to height and width. Shape can also be defined as a two- dimensional area that is determined by a change in value or some other form of contrast. Shapes can help to create complex drawings and paintings. It affects the structure of the paintings and contribute to the balance within a work. A shape can be geometrical or irregular.

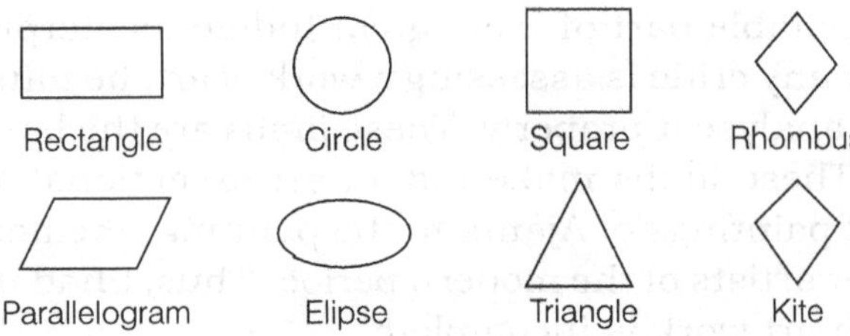

Different Shapes

- **Space** Space in a work of art refers to the distance between the area around and within shapes, forms, colours and lines. The area around the primary objects in a work of art that is unoccupied is known as **negative space**, while the space occupied by the primary objects is known as **positive space**.

  Artists use space in art to create effective imagery, convey messages and meanings, create balance and draw the attention of their viewers. The use of space by an artist can also add depth and perspective to a work, creating the illusion that some objects are bigger or closer than others.

- **Colour** In works of art, artists use colour to depict and describe the subject. Artists utilise their knowledge of colour to portray mood, light, depth and a point of view in a work of art. There are three basic colours i.e. red, blue and yellow. After mixing these colours in some proportion and quantity, secondary colours can be made.

Different colours express different emotions. Warm colours such as red, orange and yellow express feelings of happiness, optimism and energy. On the other hand blue, green and purple are considered as cool colours and they are usually calming and soothing.

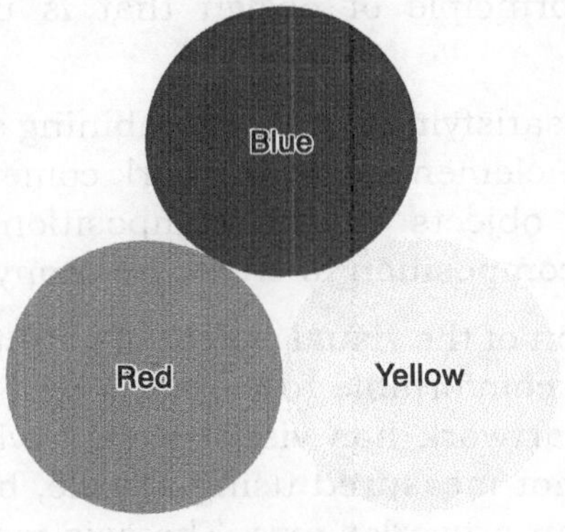

Primary Colours

- **Tone of the colour** Tone of the colour comprises of tints and shades. Tint is the lighter version of the colour that are made by mixing a colour with white. Shade is the darker version of the colour that is made by mixing a colour with black. For example, pink is a tint of red, while maroon is shade of red.

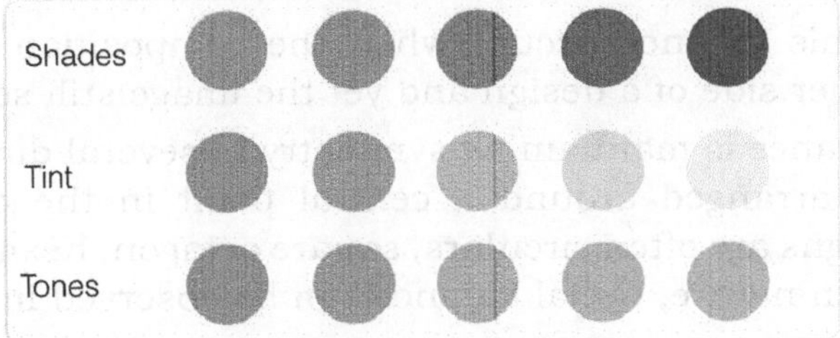

Tone of the colour

- **Value (Gradation)** Value defines the proportion of lightness or darkness of something on a scale of white to black. White colour is the highest value, while black colour is the lowest value. Values are best understood when visualised as a scale or gradient from dark to light. Value is responsible for the appearance of texture and light in art. It may vary due to shading, brush stroke, space between the objects, etc.

Value

- **Texture** It refers to the characteristics of the surface of the material on which an artist paints or draws the picture. The surface could be dotted, rough, smooth, linear, etc. in texture. It is an element of two-dimensional and three- dimensional designs and is distinguished by its perceived visual and physical properties. Use of texture, along with other elements of design, can convey a variety of messages and emotions.

Principles of Visual Arts

- **Unity** It refers to how different elements of an artwork or design give the artwork, a sense of wholeness. It can be achieved through simplicity, repetition and continuation. Unity is an important principle of design that is used by artists to bind the composition together.
- **Harmony** It is the visually satisfying effect of combining similar or related elements. It can be achieved when the elements of an artwork come together in a unified way. To create harmony all the objects in the composition should be well placed. A considerable aspect of a composition to create harmony is the space management.
- **Balance** It is the distribution of the visual weight of objects, colours, texture and space in a composition. It feels comfortable to look at a well balanced composition. Each visual component of an artwork has visual weight which is different than actual weight. Visual weight is not measured using a scale, but must be observed. Visual weight balances around an artwork's axis. The axis may be vertical in which visual elements balances on both sides. Artworks may also balance around a horizontal axis, in which visual elements balances from top to bottom. There are three different types of balance i.e. symmetrical, asymmetrical and radial.
  - (i) **Symmetrical** This balance occurs when the composition has the same visual weight on each side of an axis.
  - (ii) **Assymetrical** This balance occurs when the composition have different visual images on either side of a design and yet the image still seems balanced.
  - (iii) **Radial** This balance is maintaining symmetry in several directions. All the visual elements are arranged around a central point in the composition. Radially balanced designs are often circulars, square octagon, hexagon, star shaped, etc. For example, in nature, radial balance can be observed in the form of flowers.
- **Proportion** It refers to the dimensions of a composition and relationships between height, width and depth. To maintain proportion of each object in the composition, each part of the object must be in exact ratio and in perfect shape. The proportion is maintained when the size of the objects correlates with the distance between the objects in the composition.
- **Rhythm** In art and design, rhythm refers to a relationship between elements that creates a sense of harmony. Rhythm can be seen in patterns, in relationships between colours and shapes and in repetitions of lines and forms. By maintaining rhythm in the composition, a viewer can easily observe the composition as a whole.
- **Emphasis** It is used to attract a viewer's attention to the focal point or main subject of an artwork. For example, in a portrait, the artist usually wants the viewer to see the subject's face first. So, the artist will use colour, contrast, detailing and placement to attract the sight of the viewers.

EXAM PRACTICE

Multiple Choice Questions

1. What is meaning of the word 'shad' in Shadangas?
   (a) Seven (b) Six (c) Eight (d) ten

Ans. (b) Six

2. Which among the following is author of the book Kamasutra?
   (a) Vishvamitra (b) Valmiki
   (c) Vedvyas (d) Vatsyayana

Ans. (d) Vatsyayana

3. .... deals with accuracy and precision of measurement and structure in the paintings.
   (a) Pramanani (b) Roopbheda
   (c) Lavanya Yojanam (d) Bhava

Ans. (a) Pramanani

4. Which of the following is not an element of visual art?
   (a) Unity (b) Line
   (c) Colour (d) Point

Ans. (a) Unity

5. Which of the following is a principle of visual art?
   (a) Pramanani (b) Harmony
   (c) Gradation (d) Space

Ans. (b) Harmony

6. Match the following.

	List I		List II
A.	Sadrisyam	1.	The feeling on forms
B.	Lavanya Yojanam	2.	Blending grace in an artistic representation
C.	Bhava	3.	Resemblance
D.	Roopbheda	4.	The knowledge of looks

Codes
(a) A-1, B-2, C-3, D-4
(b) A-2, B-4, C-3, D-1
(c) A-3, B-2, C-1, D-4
(d) A-2, B-3, C-1, D-4

Ans. (c) A-3, B-2, C-1, D-4

Assertion-Reason

7. **Assertion** (A) Pramanani principle is governed by certain laws which give capability of portraying something precisely.
   Reason (R) Pramanani teaches the exact measurement, proportion and distance of subjects and objects.
   (a) Both A and R are true and R is the correct explanation of A
   (b) Both A and R are true, but R is not the correct explanation of A
   (c) A is true, but R is false
   (d) A is false, but R is true

Ans. (a) Both A and R are true and R is the correct explanation of A

True or False

1. The origin of Indian art form can be traced from pre-historic cave paintings of 3rd century BC.

Ans. True

2. Shilpgranth is rules of art, written in ancient times. It comprises of two words 'shilp' which means six and 'granth' means limbs or parts.

Ans. False

3. Roopbheda means, blending grace in an artistic representation.

Ans. False

Very Short Answer Type Questions

1. Which fundamental themes are explained in Shilpgranth?

Ans. The fundamental themes which are explained in Shilpgranth are Kamasutra, Vishnudharmottar Puran, Natyashastra, Chitralaksan, Samrangan Sutradhar, Shilpratnam etc. Shilpgranth also briefly explain about various art, elements and forms.

2. 'The six limbs of Indian painting were evolved around 1st centrury BC till the 3rd century AD.' With reference to this statement, discuss what are Shadangas.

Ans. Shadangas are rules of art written in ancient times. It comprises of two words i.e. 'shad' which means six and 'anga' which means limbs or parts. Thus, Shadanga consists of six limbs of Indian art on which ancient paintings depend.

3. What information did Vatsyayana provide through his book Kamasutra?

Ans. Vatsyayana highlighted the importance of painting in his book Kamasutra. He explains that painting occupy 4th place out of 64 art forms in India. He also emphasised about the six limbs of art which are used to add meaning and grace to the paintings.

4. Give the meaning of the term 'Roopbheda' with context to the six limbs of Indian painting.

Ans. Roopbheda consists of two words 'roop' which means outer form or appearance of subject and 'bheda' which means difference. It stresses on the physical classification of form. It states that to develop painting, an artist must possess sufficient knowledge of different forms that exists.

5. Why is Sadrisyam regarded as the challenging task?

Ans. Sadrisyam means creating a resemblance. It is regarded as a challenging task as it involves representing the depiction as similar to an artist's vision and subject matter of the painting. Sadrisyam is a way of representing similarity among various elements.

6. Write short note on Varnikabhangam.

Ans. Varnikabhangam signifies the artistic manner of using the brush and colours to draw and paint mersmerising painting. It conveys the knowledge of a colour scheme and to the use the colours in an artistic style for creating an aesthetic sense.

7. Explain briefly significance of Shadangas.

Ans. The Shadangas are inevitable part of every great Indian masterpiece. These limbs make Indian art exceptional and precious which is visible from the ancient paintings of Ajanta the paintings created by Raja Ravi Verma and Hussain and many other artist of the modern period.

8. Describe line as an element of visual art.

Ans. A line is a long collection of points extending in two opposite directions. Lines can be used to define shapes and figures and also to indicate motion, emotion and other elements. It may be vertical, horizontal, transverse, angular, curved or wavy.

Short Answer Type Questions

1. Give a brief history of Indian art form.

Ans. For history of Indian art form, refer to text on pg. 1.

2. Six limbs forms the significant part of Indian paintings. With context to this statement explain any two limbs of Indian paintings included in your course of study.

Ans. For the limbs of Indian painting, refer to text on pg. 2 and 3.

3. Write short note on elements of visual arts.

Ans. For the elements of visual arts, refer to text on pg. 3, 4 and 5.

Long Answer Type Questions

1. Shadanga are rules of art written in ancient times. With respect to the given statement briefly explain any of the three Shadangas.

Ans. For any three of Shadangas or six limbs, refer to text on pg. no. 2 and 3.

2. Explain briefly the principles of visual arts.

Ans. For the principles of visual arts, refer to text on pg. no. 6.

CHAPTER 02

Pre-historic Rock Paintings

In this chapter

- *Period and Location of Pre-historic Paintings*
  - *Material and Methods used by the Earliest Artists for Paintings*
  - *Significance of Pre-historic Paintings*
  - *Examples of Pre-historic Paintings*

The period of time before written records is known as **prehistory** or **pre-historic time.** In pre-historic time, there was no paper or language, thus there was no written records of books or documents. Scholars excavated the places where pre-historic people lived to understand how they lived in the past. Old tools, pottery, habitats, bones of ancient human beings and animals and drawings on cave walls are some of the significant discoveries made by scholars. Through these discoveries, scholars have constructed fairly accurate knowledge about what happened and how people lived in pre-historic times.

After meeting the basic needs of food, water, clothing and shelter, people were needed to expressed themselves. Thus, **painting and drawing were the oldest art forms practiced by** human beings to express themselves using the cave walls as their canvas. There could be many reasons for pre-historic people to drew these pictures. They may have drawn and painted to make their shelters more colourful and beautiful or to keep a visual record of their day-to-day life.

Period and Location of Pre-historic Paintings

Pre-historic paintings have been found in many parts of the world. There is no evidence to know if **Lower Palaeolithic**[1] people ever produced any art objects or not. But by the **Upper Palaeolithic**[2] times, growth of artistic activities started.

1 **Lower Palaeolithic** Lower Palaeolithic time period i.e. 1.5 million to 2,00,000 years ago.

2 **Upper Palaeolithic** Upper Palaeolithic time period started about 50,000 years ago and ended approximately 10,000 years ago.

In India, the earliest paintings have been found from the Upper Palaeolithic times. The walls of many caves of pre-historic times around the world were carved and decorated with paintings of animals which were hunted by the cave dwellers. The subjects of their drawings were human figures, human activities, geometric designs and animal symbols.

The first discovery of rock paintings was made in India in 1867-68 by an archaeologist, **Archibold Carlleyle**, twelve years before the discovery of **Altamira**[3] in Spain. Cockburn, Anderson, Mitra and Ghosh were the early archaeologists who discovered a large number of sites in the Indian sub-continent. Remains of rock paintings have been found on the walls of the caves situated in several districts of Andhra Pradesh, Karnataka, Madhya Pradesh, Uttar Pradesh and Bihar. From Kashmir, two slabs with engravings have been found.

Rock Paintings of Karnataka and Andhra Pradesh

The granite rocks of Karnataka and Andhra Pradesh were the most suitable canvases (a strong unbleached cloth) for the Neolithic man to draw paintings. Some famous sites in these states where paintings are found are **Kupgallu**, **Piklihal** and **Tekkalkota**. Three types of paintings have been found from here which are paintings in white colour, paintings in red ochre over a white background and paintings in red ochre.

These paintings belong to late historical, early historical and Neolithic periods. The subjects depicted in these paintings are bulls, elephants, sambhars, gazelles, sheep, goats, horses, stylised humans, tridents, etc. Vegetal motifs are rarely depicted in these paintings.

Rock Paintings of Uttarakhand

Kumaon hills in Uttarakhand also bear remains of the earliest rock paintings. These pre-historic painting are found on the rock shelters on banks of the river Suyal at **Lakhudiyar**, about 20 kms on the Almora-Barechina road. The literal meaning of Lakhudiyar is one lakh caves. Due to wide diversity, the paintings here can be divided in three categories i.e. man, animal and geometric patterns in white, black and red ochre. In these paintings, humans are represented in stick-like forms.

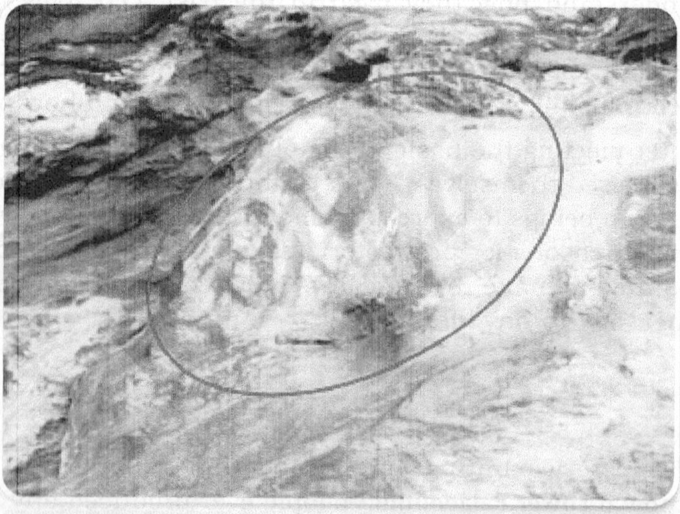

Hand-linked Dancing Figures, Lakhudiyar, Uttarakhand

---

3 **Altamira** Cave of Altamira is famous for pre-historic art. It features contemporary local fauna and human hands.

A long-snouted animal, a fox and a multiple legged lizard are the main animal motifs in these paintings. Wavy lines, rectangle-filled geometric designs and groups of dots can also be seen in these paintings. One of the interesting scenes depicted in these paintings is of **Hand-linked Dancing Human Figures**. There is some overlaying of paintings found in Lakhudiyar. The earliest set of paintings were made in black colour, over that paintings were made in red ochre colour and the last set of paintings were made in white colour.

Rock Paintings of Madhya Pradesh and Uttar Pradesh

The earliest rock paintings are also found from the Vindhya ranges of Madhya Pradesh and their Kaimurean extensions into Uttar Pradesh. These hill ranges consists of many Paleolithic and Mesolithic remains. These hill ranges also include many forests, wild plants, fruits, streams and creeks, hence it was a suitable place for Stone Age people to live. The most notable and largest rock shelter is located in the Vindhya hills at **Bhimbetka** in Madhya Pradesh. Bhimbetka is located 45 kms South of Bhopal. It spread over an area of 10 sq km and have about 800 rock shelters of which 500 rock shelters bear paintings.

The caves of Bhimbetka were discovered in 1957-58 by eminent archaeologist **VS Wakankar**. Wakankar spent several years in surveying these inaccessible hills and jungles to study these paintings. Later on, many more caves were discovered. The themes of paintings found here are of great variety as these range from ordinary details of daily life in those times to sacred and royal images.

These include hunting, dancing, music, horse and elephant riders, animal fighting, honey collection, decoration of bodies and other household scenes. The rock art of Bhimbetka has been classified into various groups on the basis of style, technique and superimposition. The drawings and paintings can be categorised into seven different historical periods. Of these, Period I was Upper Palaeolithic, Period II was Mesolithic and Period III was Chalcolithic.

Upper Palaeolithic Period

The paintings of the Upper Palaeolithic period are linear representations in green and dark red colours. The paintings are of huge animal figures, such as bisons, elephants, tigers, rhinos and boars. There are also stick-like human figures. Some paintings are made through **wash technique**[4] but most of the paintings are filled with geometric patterns. The green paintings are of dancers and the red paintings are of hunters.

Mesolithic Period

The largest number of paintings belong to Period II that covers the Mesolithic paintings. During this period, the themes are multiple but the paintings are smaller in size. Hunting scenes predominate in this period. The hunting scenes depict people hunting in groups, armed with spears, pointed sticks, arrows and bows. In some paintings, the primitive men are shown with net traps probably to catch animals. The hunters are shown wearing

4 **Wash Technique** In this technique of painting, a paint brush which is very wet with solvent and holds a small load of colours, is applied to a paper or raw canvas. The result of this technique is smooth and semi transparent.

simple clothes and ornaments. Sometimes, men have been adorned with elaborate head-dresses and sometimes they were also painted with masks. Elephant, bison, tiger, boar, deer, antelope, leopard, panther, rhinoceros, fish, frog, lizard, squirrel and some times birds are also depicted in the paintings of this period.

The Mesolithic artists loved to paint animals. In some pictures, animals are depicted chasing men. In others, they are beings chased and hunted by men. The paintings also show fear as well as tenderness and love towards animals. There are also a few engravings representing mainly animals. The animals were painted in a naturalistic style, while the humans were depicted only in a stylistic manner.

Women are painted both as nude and clothed. Both the young and old figures were painted in these paintings. Children are painted running, jumping and playing. Community dances is a common theme in these paintings. There are paintings of people gathering fruit or honey from trees and of women grinding and preparing food. Some of the pictures of men, women and children seem to depict a sort of family life. Hand prints, fist prints and dots made by the fingertips are depicted in many of the rock shelters.

Chalcolithic Period

The paintings of this period reveal the association, contact and mutual exchange of requirements of the cave dwellers of this area with settled agricultural communities of the Malwa plateau. In the paintings of **chalcolithic age**[5], pottery and metal tools can be seen. The paintings show the influence of the painting styles of Malwa region.

> **Superimposition or Overlaying of Paintings**
>
> It has been found at many rock art sites that, a new painting is often painted on top of an older painting. In some places at Bhimbetka about 20 layers of paintings are found, one on top of another. There could be many reasons for this. For example,
>
> - May be, the artist did not like his creation and painted another painting on the previous one.
> - The paintings and places were considered sacred or special.
> - The area may have been used by different generations of people at different times.

Material and Methods used by the Earliest Artists for Paintings

- The artists of Bhimbetka used many colours, including various shades of white, yellow, orange, red ochre, purple, brown, green and black. But white and red were their favourite colours.
- The paints were made by grinding various rocks and minerals. The rock of mineral was first grinded into a powder. Then, this may have been mixed with water and also with some thick or sticky substance such as animal fat or gum or resin from trees. Red colour was obtained from hematite (known as *geru* in India), green from a green variety of a stone called chalcedony and white might be from limestone. These colours have survived

5 **Chalcolithic Age** The term chalcolithic is a combination of two words Chalco and Lithic which means copper and stone or Copper age. It was the first metal age of India. In this period, copper and stone were highly used to make tools and weapons. The period of Chalcolithic age is between 2000 BC to 700 BC.

thousands of years of adverse weather conditions. It is believed that the colours have remained intact because of the chemical reaction of the oxide present on the surface of the rocks.

- The brushes were made of plant fibre.
- The artists made their paintings on the walls and ceilings of the rock shelters. Some of the paintings are found from the shelters where people lived while some others were found from places which did not have living spaces.
- Some of the most beautiful paintings are found very high up on rock shelters or close to the ceilings of rock shelters. The paintings were made at these areas might be for people to be able to notice them from a distance.

The paintings are from the remote past, but they do not lack pictorial quality. Despite various limitations such as acute working conditions, inadequate tools, materials, etc they show beautiful scenes of the environment in which the artists lived.

Storytelling in Paintings

The primitive artists had a great interest for storytelling. Their paintings, depict both men and animals engaged in the struggle for survival in a dramatic way. The practice of depicting storytelling in the painting is common among primitive people of today also. They engrave or paint on rocks as part of the rituals they perform at birth, death, at being young and at the time of marriage. One of the painting which depicts storytelling is based on the theme that some people were dancing while a group of people were hunting the animals that were difficult to find or kill.

Significance of Pre-historic Paintings

- The pre-historic paintings help to understand about early human beings, their lifestyle, their food habits, their daily activities and the way they thought.
- Pre-historic period remains are a great witness to the evolution of human civilisation, through the numerous rock weapons, tools, ceramics and bones. The rock paintings are the greatest wealth that the primitive human beings of this period left behind.

Examples of Pre-historic Paintings

- **Painting of Hunting Scene** In this scene, a group of people are shown hunting a bison. Some injured men are depicted lying scattered on the ground.
- **Painting of Dancing Scene** This painting can be found to the South of Cave no. 47. In this scene of wizard's dance from **Bhimbetka**, hand-linked figures in dancing mode are shown. It also recalls the dancing scene from the Lakhudiyar rock painting found in Uttarakhand.

Hunting Scene

In this scene, an animal is shown in the agony (pain) of death. In the centre, 14 figures of dancers are depicted dancing in three groups of eight, four and two and a person is depicted playing a big musical instrument. Other people are depicted in sitting position and watching the people dancing.

Dancing Scene or Wizard's Dance

EXAM PRACTICE

Multiple Choice Questions

1. Pre-historic time period is marked by
   (a) absence of fossil
   (b) absence of written records
   (c) absence of rock art
   (d) absence of tools

Ans. (b) absence of written records

2. What is the time period of Lower Palaeolithic age?
   (a) 1.5 million to 2 million years
   (b) 1.5 million to 3 million years
   (c) 1 million to 2 million years
   (d) 2 million to 4 million years

Ans. (a) 1.5 million to 2 million years

3. Who first discovered the rock paintings in India?
   (a) Archibold Carlleyle
   (b) Cockburn
   (c) Anderson
   (d) Mitra

Ans. (a) Archibold Carlleyle

4. Where are caves of Altamira situated?
   (a) Mexico
   (b) France
   (c) Indonesia
   (d) Spain

Ans. (d) Spain

5. In which of the following Indian state, the famous rock painting site of Lakhudiyar is situated?
   (a) Uttarakhand
   (b) Madhya Pradesh
   (c) Maharashtra
   (d) Himachal Pradesh

Ans. (a) Uttarakhand

6. What is the literal meaning of Lakhudiyar?
(a) Hand-linked dancing figure
(b) Hunting animals
(c) One lakh caves
(d) Mound of the dead

Ans. (c) One lakh caves

7. Bhimbetka, a famous rock painting site is located in which of the following Indian state ?
(a) Jharkhand
(b) Madhya Pradesh
(c) Haryana
(d) Kashmir

Ans. (b) Madhya Pradesh

8. Who discovered the caves of Bhimbetka?
(a) VS Wakankar
(b) BL Joshi
(c) Ghosh
(d) RP Singh

Ans. (a) VS Wakankar

9. During pre-historic times, the largest number of paintings belong to which period?
(a) Mesolithic (b) Neolithic
(c) Chalcolithic (d) Palaeolithic

Ans. (a) Mesolithic

10. During pre-historic times, brushes were made of
(a) plant fibres
(b) plastic
(c) silk
(d) None of the above

Ans. (a) plant fibres

11. Match the following.

List I (Stone)	List II (Colour)
(a) Hematite	1. Green
(b) Chalcedony	2. White
(c) Limestone	3. Red

Codes
(a) A-3, B-1, C-2 (b) A-2, B-1, C-3
(c) A-3, B-2, C-1 (d) A-2, B-3, C-1

Ans. (a)

12. Match the following.

List I (Pre-historic caves)	List II (State)
(a) Lakhudiyar	1. Karnataka
(b) Bhimbetka	2. Uttarakhand
(c) Piklihal	3. Madhya Pradesh

Codes
(a) A-3, B-1, C-2 (b) A-2, B-3, C-1
(c) A-3, B-2, C-1 (d) A-2, B-1, C-3

Ans. (b)

Assertion-Reason

Directions (Q. Nos. 13-14) There are two statements marked as Assertion (A) and Reason (R). Read the statement and answer the questions according to codes given below.
(a) Both A and R are true and R is the correct explanation of A
(b) Both A and R are true, but R is not the correct explanation of A
(c) A is true, but R is false
(d) A is false, but R is true

13. **Assertion** (A) Hunting scenes predominate Mesolithic paintings.
Reason (R) Pre-historic men only knew how to paint animals.

Ans. (c) A is true, but R is false

14. **Assertion** (A) The pre-historic men used variety of colours for cave painting i.e. red, green, white, etc.
Reason (R) They were able to extract these colours from natural stone like hematite, chalcedony, limestone.

Ans. (a) Both A and R are true and R is the correct explanation of A

Source Based Question

15. Read the source given below and answer the following questions.

Remnants of rock paintings have been found on the walls of the caves situated in several districts of Madhya Pradesh, Uttar Pradesh, Andhra Pradesh, Karnataka and Bihar. Some paintings have been reported from the Kumaon hills. The rock shelters of Lakhudiyar, bear these pre-historic paintings. Lakhudiyar literally means one lakh caves.

The paintings here can be divided into three categories i.e. man, animals and geometric patterns in white, black and red ochre.

Humans are represented in stick-like forms. A long snouted animal, a fox and a multiple legged lizard are the main animal motifs. Wavy lines, rectangle filled geometric designs and groups of dots can also be seen here.

(i) In which of the following rock painting sites, the painting of hand-linked dancing figures can be seen?

(a) Bhimbetka (b) Kupgallu
(c) Lakhudiyar (d) Piklihal

Ans. (c) Lakhudiyar

(ii) From which time period earliest paintings in India have been reported ?

(a) Mesolithic
(b) Neolithic
(c) Chalcolithic
(d) Upper Paleolithic

Ans. (d) Upper Paleolithic

(iii) The largest rock-shelter in India is located in

(a) Lakhudiyar
(b) Piklihal
(c) Bhimbetka
(d) Kupgallu

Ans. (c) Bhimbetka

(iv) The painting site of Kumaon hills is located in which of the following Indian site?

(a) Uttar Pradesh
(b) Andhra Pradesh
(c) Uttarakhand
(d) Madhya Pradesh

Ans. (c) Uttarakhand

(v) Lakhudiyar is situated on the bank of which river?

(a) Ganga (b) Tapti
(c) Suyal (d) Jhelum

Ans. (c) Suyal

True or False

1. Palaeolithic paintings have been found only in India.

Ans. False

2. In India, the earliest paintings have been reported from Chalcolithic times.

Ans. False

3. The granite rocks of Karnataka and Andhra Pradesh provided suitable canvases to the Neolithic man for his paintings.

Ans. True

4. The richest paintings are reported from the Vindhya ranges of Madhya Pradesh and their Kaimurean extensions into Uttar Pradesh.

Ans. True

5. Hunting scenes predominate in Mesolithic paintings.

Ans. True

Very Short Answer Type Questions

1. Define the old stone age.

Ans. The pre-historic period in the early development of human beings is known as old stone age. It is also referred as the Palaeolithic age. It was around 2.6 millions year ago and is characterised by the use of rudimentary stone tools.

2. Where do we find cave paintings in India? Analyse the kind of artefacts discovered from various parts of India.

Ans. Pre-historic rock or cave paintings have been found on the walls of caves situated in several districts of Madhya Pradesh, Uttar Pradesh, Andhra Pradesh, Karnataka and Bihar.

Some paintings have also been found from Kumaon hills in Uttarakhand. Rock weapons, tools, ceramics and bones are the artefacts that have been discovered from various parts of India. They provide a glimpse into the life of pre-historic people.

3. Throw light on the kind of living creatures depicted in Mesolithic rock paintings.

Ans. Mesolithic rock paintings are the finest example of pre-historic men's creativity. The various living creatures depicted in these paintings are bulls, elephants, sambhars, gazelles, sheep, goats, horses, stylised humans, tridents, etc.

4. Give examples of some major sites where pre-historic paintings have been found.

Ans. Pre-historic paintings have been found from various parts of India. For example, some major rock paintings have been found from Bhimbetka in Madhya Pradesh, Kupgallu in Telangana, Piklihal and Tekkalkota in Karnataka and Lakhudiyar in Uttarakhand.

5. According to your observation, how did the people of pre-historic times select themes for their paintings? *(NCERT)*

Ans. The people of pre-historic times selected themes for their paintings on various basis ranging from their daily routine activities to royal and sacred images such as hunting, food gathering, music, horse riding, honey collection, decoration of bodies and other household scenes.

6. In modern times, how have walls been used as a surface to make paintings, graphics, etc? *(NCERT)*

Ans. The various ways in which walls are used as surface for paintings, graphics, etc are

- For providing social message to people, when government promotes a particular message.
- For depicting various tribal arts.
- For mural paintings which are done directly on walls using water colours, acrylic paints, oil paints, etc.

Short Answer Type Questions

1. Comment on the status of rock paintings of Karnataka and Andhra Pradesh of pre-historic times.

Ans. For the rock paintings of Karnataka and Andhra Pradesh refer to text on pg. 10.

2. Describe the upper palaeolithic period of pre-historic paintings.

Ans. For description of upper palaeolithic period of pre-historic paintings, refer to text on pg. 11.

3. Evaluate the themes of painting found at major sites of rock art in India with reference to Lakhudiyar, Uttarakhand.

Ans. For themes of paintings in Lakhudiyar, Uttarakhand, refer to text on pg. 10 and 11.

4. Evaluate the themes of paintings found at major sites of rock art in India with reference to Bhimbetka, Madhya Pradesh.

Ans. The caves of Bhimbetka were discovered in 1957-58 by archaeologist VS Wakankar. Bhimbetka is located 45 kms South of Bhopal. It has about 800 rock shelters of which 500 rock shelters bear paintings.

The themes of paintings found here are of great diversity which range from boring events in daily life to sacred and royal images. These include hunting, dancing, music, horse and elephant riders, animal fighting, honey collection, decoration of bodies, etc.

The rock art has been classified into various groups on the basis of style, technique and superimposition. The drawings and paintings here can be classified into various phases i.e. Upper Palaeolithic, Mesolithic, Chalcolithic, etc.

5. What could have been the reasons for depicting more animal figures than human figures in cave paintings ? *(NCERT)*

Ans. Animal figures pre dominate in pre historic rock paintings. The reasons for depicting more animal figures then human figure could be

- These depictings could have been as the warning signs for the future generations about the dangers from animals and how to live with them.
- It could have been the guide for the hunting techniques and animals are suitable for the hunting.
- The depiction can also be seen as an informative guide on their lifestyle and how to deal with animals which was their major source of livelihood.

In conclusion, the pre-dominance of the image of animals show their significance in the lives of pre-historic men.

Long Answer Type Questions

1. Write an essay on the periodical classification of Bhimbetka paintings.

Ans. The rock art of Bhimbetka has been classified into various groups on the basis of style, technique and superimposition. The drawing and painting can be classified into seven different historical periods. Of these, Period I was Upper Palaeolithic, Period II was Mesolithic and Period III was Chalcolithic. For description of Upper Palaeolithic, Mesolithic and Chalcolithic periods, refer to text on pg. no. 11 and 12.

2. The Mesolithic phase of pre-historic paintings was the richest phase. How would you justify the statement?

Ans. The Mesolithic phase of paintings was the richest one because of diverse themes, various techniques and the painting equipments used by early pre-historic people. For its description, refer to text on pg. 11 and 12.

3. Mention about the material and methods used by earliest artists to make paintings?

Ans. For material and methods used by earliest artists to make paintings, refer to text on pg. no. 12 and 13.

CHAPTER 03

Arts of the Indus Valley

In this chapter

- Period and Location of Indus Valley Art
- Examples of Arts of Indus Valley Civilisation
- Fashion Trends of Indus Valley Civilisation

Period and Location of Indus Valley Art

The arts of the Indus Valley Civilisation emerged during the second half of the third millennium BCE (250 BCE). The artists of this period were very creative and imaginative. Their portrayal of human and animal figures was highly realistic in nature, as the bodily details included in them were unique. The modeling of animal figures was done in an extremely careful manner specifically, in the case of terracotta art.

The two major sites of the Indus Valley Civilisation, along the Indus river were the cities of **Harappa** in the North and **Mohenjodaro** in the South. They are the earliest examples of town planning in which houses, markets, storage facilities, offices, public baths, etc were arranged in a grid-like pattern.

There was also a highly developed drainage system. Harappa and Mohenjodaro are the sites situated in Pakistan, while the important sites excavated in India are Lothal, Rangpur and Dholavira in Gujarat, Rakhigarhi and Banawali in Haryana, Ropar in Punjab, Kalibangan in Rajasthan and Alamgirpur in Uttar Pradesh.

Examples of Arts of Indus Valley Civilisation

Many forms of art were found from various sites of Indus Valley Civilisation which include sculptures (statues), seals, pottery, jewellery, terracotta figures, etc.

Stone Statues of Indus Valley Civilisation

The stone statues of Harappa and Mohenjodaro are the excellent examples of three-dimensional statues. Two stone statues of male figures can be found in the sites of Indus Valley Civilisation. One is the statue of a male torso and other is the statue of a bearded man.

Examples of Stone Statues

Male Torso

This statue was made from red sandstone. It is a fine example of the earliest proto-historic work. The sculpture is completely nude and its arms and head are broken. There are three socket holes made on this torso where the head and arms can be attached. The shoulders are clear and the abdomen is slightly bulging.

Bearded Man

This statue was made from soapstone. The figure of the bearded man is interpreted as a priest. He is wrapped in a shawl which is coming under the right arm and covering his left shoulder. The shawl is intricately decorated with the **trefoil**[1] patterns. His right hand can also be seen in the statue. He is wearing an armlet on the right hand and the holes around the neck suggest that he is wearing a necklace.

His eyes are a little elongated, and half-closed as in meditative concentration. His nose is well formed and of medium size. His mouth is of average size with close-cut moustache and a short beard and whiskers. His ears resemble double shells with a hole in the middle. His hair is parted in the middle, and a plain woven fillet (a band or ribbon) is worn around the head.

Name : Male Torso
Dimension : 9.2×5.8×3 cm
Circa : 2500 BC
Collection : National Museum, New Delhi

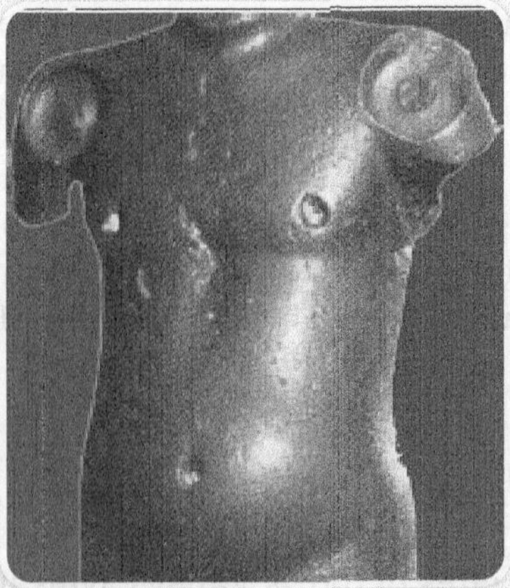

Name : Bust of a Bearded Priest

1 **Trefoil** An ornamental design of three rounded sections, like a clover leaf, which is used in designing of architecture and stones.

Bronze Casting of Indus Valley Civilisation

Bronze casting was popular at all the major centres of the Indus Valley Civilisation. The art of bronze-casting was practised on a wide scale by the Harappans. The figures of animal and human, made of bronze can be seen in the Indus Valley sites. One of the best example of human figure is the statue of the **Dancing Girl**.

Among animal figures, the statue of buffalo with uplifted head, back and large horns and the goat are best examples of artistic skills. The copper dog, bird of Lothal and the bronze statue of a bull from Kalibangan are similar in artistic features to the human figures of copper and bronze from Harappa and Mohenjodaro.

Method of Bronze Casting

The bronze statues were made using the **lost-wax technique** in which the wax figures were first covered with a coating of clay and allowed to dry. Then, the wax was heated and the molten wax was drained out through a tiny hole made in the clay cover. The molten metal was drained into the hollow mould (shape) of the object. Thus, after cooling down the metal takes the original shape of the object.

Once the metal cooled down, the clay cover was completely removed. Metal casting appears to be a continuous tradition as the late Harappan and **Chalcolithic**[2] sites like Daimabad in Maharashtra provide excellent examples of metal-cast sculptures.

Examples of Bronze Casting

Dancing Girl

This figure was made from copper. It is approximately four-inch-high. It was found in Mohenjodaro. Its exquisite casting depicts a girl whose long hair is tied in a bun. She is wearing bangles on her left arm and a bracelet and an amulet or bangle on her right arm.

A cowry shell necklace can be seen around her neck. Her right hand is on her hip and her left hand is made in a gesture of traditional Indian dance. The girl is standing in the dancing position.

She has large eyes and flat nose. This figure is full of expression and bodily strength and it conveys a lot of information.

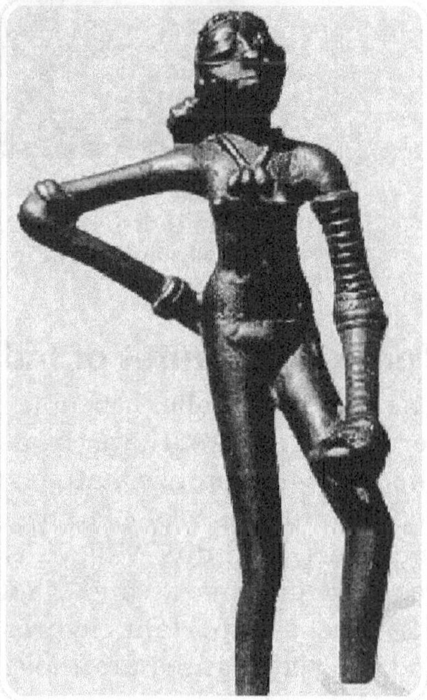

Name : Dancing Girl
Material : Bronze (Copper)
Dimension : 10.5×5×2.5cm
Circa : 2500 BC
Collection : National Museum, New Delhi

2 **Chalcolithic** The term Chalcolithic is a combination of two words. Chalco + lithic which means copper and stone or copper age. It is the first metal age of India. In this period, copper and stone was highly used in making tools and weapons. The period of Chalcolithic age is between 2000 BC to 700 BC.

Bull

This bronze figure of a bull was found from Mohenjodaro. The massiveness and the intense emotion of the bull is perfectly represented in this figure. The animal is shown standing with his head turned to the right and with a cord around the neck.

Name	: Bull	**Material**	: Bronze
Dimension	: 2.5×2.5×1.4 cm	**Circa**	: 2500 BC
Collection	: National Museum, New Delhi		

Terracotta Figures of Indus Valley Civilisation

The Indus Valley people also made terracotta figures. However, as compared to the stone and bronze statues, the terracotta representations of human form are imperfect in Indus Valley. They are more realistic in Gujarat and Kalibangan sites. The most important figures among the Indus valley figures are those representing the Mother Goddess.

Terracotta Figures

In terracotta, few figurines of bearded males with coiled hair are found. Their posture is rigidly upright. Their legs are slightly apart and their arms are parallel to the sides of the body. The repetition of this figure in exactly the same position suggested that he was a deity. A terracotta mask of a horned deity has also been found. Toy carts with wheels, whistles, rattles, birds and animals, gamesmen and discs were also made in terracotta.

Mother Goddess as an Example of Terracotta Figure

The Mother Goddess figures are usually imperfectly carved. They are standing female figures adorned with necklaces and wearing a loin cloth and a girdle (a belt worn around the waist). The fan-shaped head-dress with a cup-like projection on each side is a distinct decorative feature of the Mother Goddess figures of the Indus Valley. The figure has small rounded eyes and pointed nose which are imperfectly carved. The mouth is depicted by a slit (a long, narrow cut).

Name	:	Mother Goddess
Material	:	Terracotta
Dimension	:	22×8×5cm
Circa	:	2500 BC
Collection	:	National Museum, New Delhi

Seals of Indus Valley Civilisation

Archaeologists have discovered thousands of seals from Indus Valley, mostly made of steatite and occasionally, made of agate, chert, copper, faience and terracotta. They are decorated with beautiful figures of animals, such as unicorn bull, rhinoceros, tiger, elephant, bison, goat, buffalo, etc.

The realistic rendering of the animals in various moods is a remarkable feature of these seals. The purpose of producing seals was mainly commercial. It appears that the seals were also used as amulets. They were carried by their owners, perhaps as a modern-day identity cards. The standard Harappan seal was a square plaque of 2×2 square inches, made from steatite.

Every seal is engraved in a pictographic (a pictorial representation) script which is yet to be deciphered. Some seals have also been found in ivory. They all bear a great variety of motifs, most often of animals including those of the bull, with or without the hump, the elephant, tiger, goat and also monsters. Sometimes trees or human figures were also depicted. Figures and animals are carved in **intaglio**[3] on their surfaces.

Unicorn Seal

3 **Intaglio** A design sculpted into a material like stone/wood/ metal.

Square or rectangular copper tablets, with an animal or a human figure on one side and an inscription on the other, or an inscription on both sides have also been found. The figures and signs are carefully cut with a burin (a steel tool used for engraving). These copper tablets also appear as amulets. They have inscriptions associated with the animals portrayed on them.

Pashupati Seal as an Example of Seals

This seal is depicted with a figure in the centre and animals around. This seal is generally identified as the Pashupati Seal by some scholars whereas some identify it as the female deity. It depicts a human figure seated cross-legged.

Pashupati Seal

An elephant and a tiger are depicted to the right side of the seated figure, while rhinoceros and a buffalo are depicted on the left side. In addition to these animals, two antelopes are shown below the seat. Such seals belong to the period between 2500 and 1900 BCE and were found in considerable numbers in sites such as the ancient city of Mohenjodaro in the Indus Valley.

Pottery of Indus Valley Civilisation

A large number of pottery have been excavated from Indus Valley sites. They helps to understand the gradual evolution of various design motifs as employed in different shapes and styles.

Pottery

The Indus Valley pottery consist chiefly of very fine wheel-made wares of which very few were hand-made. Plain pottery is more common than painted ware in Indus Valley Civilisation. It is generally of red clay, with or without a fine red or grey slip. It includes knobbed ware, decorated with rows of knobs.

The black painted ware has a fine coating of red slip on which geometric and animal designs are decorated in glossy black paint. Pottery for household purposes is found in many shapes and sizes, which was used daily, but the straight and the angular shaped pottery were not used for daily activities of households. Pottery with graceful curves are in the majority. Miniature vessels, mostly less than half an inch in height are beautifully crafted for decoration purpose.

Types of Pottery

- **Polychrome Pottery** It is rare and mainly comprises small vases which were decorated with geometric patterns in red, black and green colours. White and yellow colours were rarely used for their decoration.
- **Incised Pottery** It is also rare and confined to the bases of the pans and the dishes which were used as offering. Incised decoration was always done inside the utensils.
- **Perforated Pottery** It includes a large hole at the bottom and small holes all over the wall or body. It was probably used for serving beverages.

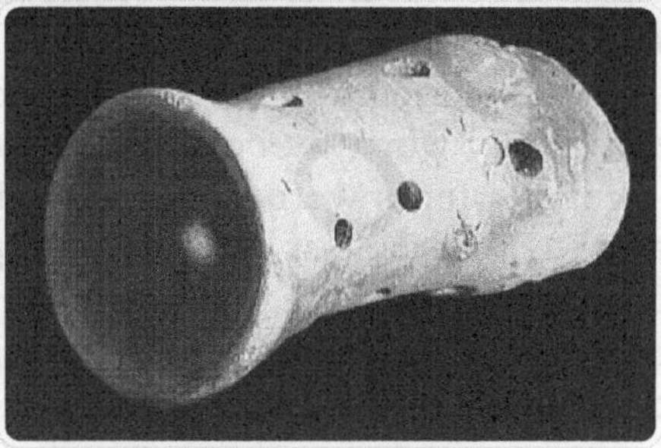

Perforated Pottery

Painted Earthen Jar

This jar was found in Mohenjodaro. It was made on a potter's wheel with clay. The shape was designed by the pressure of the crafty fingers of the potter. After baking the clay model, it was painted with black colour.

High polishing was done to give it a finishing touch. The motifs used are of vegetals (relating to plants) and geometric forms. Designs are simple, but they are abstract (conceptual).

Name : Painted Earthen Jar
Material : Clay
Collection : National Museum, New Delhi

Beads of Indus Valley Civilisation

The bead industry seems to have been well developed in Indus Valley Civilisation. This was evident from the factories discovered at Chanhudaro and Lothal.

Beads were made of carnelian, amethyst (a violet coloured stone), jasper, crystal, quartz, steatite, turquoise, lapis lazuli, etc. Metals like copper, bronze, gold, shell, faience and terracotta or burnt clay were used for manufacturing beads. The beads have different shapes like disc-shaped, cylindrical, spherical, barrel-shaped, and segmented. Some beads were made of two or more stones fixed together and some were made of stone with gold covers.

Some beads were decorated by incising or painting and some had designs carved onto them. Great technical skill has been displayed in the manufacture of these beads. The Harappan people made naturalistic models of animals, especially monkeys and squirrels. These models were used as pin-heads and beads.

Ornaments of Indus Valley Civilisation

The Harappan men and women decorated themselves with a large variety of ornaments. These ornaments were produced from different materials ranging from precious metals and gemstones to bone and baked clay. Necklaces, fillets, armlets and finger-rings were commonly worn by both sexes, while women wore girdles, earrings and anklets. Many jewellery items were found at Mohenjodaro and Lothal. These include necklaces of gold and semi-precious stones, copper bracelets and beads, gold earrings and head ornaments, faience pendants and buttons and beads of steatite and gemstones. All ornaments are well crafted. A **cemetery**[4] has been found at Farmana in Haryana where dead bodies were buried with ornaments.

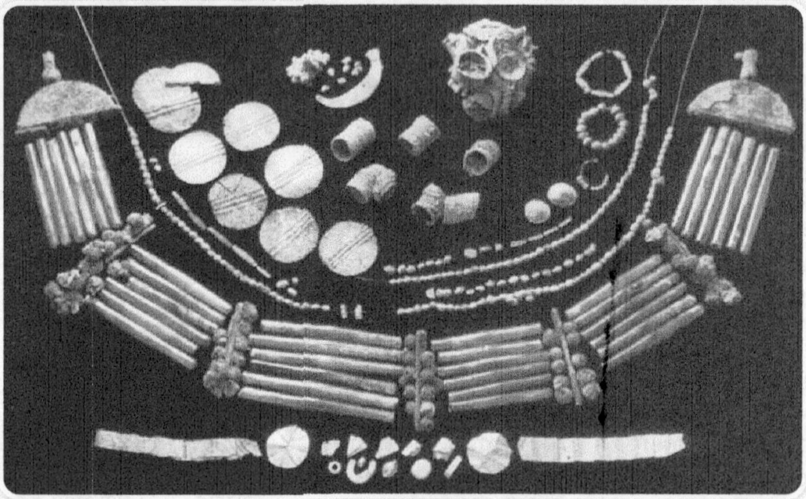

Beadwork and Jewellery Items

Spinning Activity in Indus Valley Civilisation

Spinning of cotton and wool was very common in Indus Valley. It is evident from the discovery of a large number of spindles (straight rod used for spinning) and spindle whorls (small pulley used to weight a spindle), found in the houses of the Indus Valley people. The whorls were made of the expensive faience as well as of the cheap pottery and shell.

Fashion Trends of Indus Valley Civilisation

The people of the Indus Valley were conscious of fashion. According to the archaeological finds, different hairstyles were in fashion in Indus Valley Civilisation and having a beard was popular among all the people of Indus Valley. Cinnabar was used as a cosmetic. Facepaint, lipstick and collyrium (eyeliner) were also known to them. The men and women of Indus Valley wore two separate pieces of attire, similar to the dhoti and shawl. The shawl covered their left shoulder passing below the right shoulder.

4 **Cemetery** A place where remains of dead people are buried.

EXAM PRACTICE

Multiple Choice Questions

1. Which of the following Harappa site is located in Gujarat?
   (a) Kalibangan (b) Rakhigarhi
   (c) Lothal (d) Ropar

Ans. (c) Lothal

2. The stone statues of Harappa and Mohenjodaro are the excellent examples of .... dimensional statues
   (a) one (b) four (c) two (d) three

Ans. (d) three

3. Which of the following material has been used in the making of the statue of Male Torso ?
   (a) Red limestone (b) Red sandstone
   (c) Red soapstone (d) Red chunarstone

Ans. (b) Red sandstone

4. Where is site of Farmana situated?
   (a) Haryana (b) Gujarat
   (c) Maharashtra (d) Punjab

Ans. (a) Haryana

5. Which of these metals was not used in Harappan Civilisation?
   (a) Gold (b) Copper
   (c) Bronze (d) Iron

Ans. (d) Iron

6. In which of the following museum the figure of the Male Torso can be seen?
   (a) National Museum, New Delhi
   (b) The Indian Museum
   (c) Metropolitan Museum of Art, New York
   (d) Kerala Folklore Museum

Ans. (a) National Museum, New Delhi

7. At which site do we find the famous artefact 'The Dancing Girl'?
   (a) Harappa (b) Dholavira
   (c) Mohenjodaro (d) Ropar

Ans. (c) Mohenjodaro

8. Archaeologists have discovered thousands of seals from Indus Valley, mostly made of steatite and other materials like agate copper, terracotta, etc. For which purpose seals were used?
   (a) Commercial
   (b) Artistic
   (c) Spiritual
   (d) Educational

Ans. (a) Commercial

9. Which of the following animals are not sculpted in Pashupati seals?
   (a) Rhinoceros (b) Elephant
   (c) Cow (d) Antelope

Ans. (c) Cow

10. At which place bead industry was well developed?
    (a) Lothal (b) Kalibangan
    (c) Rakhigarhi (d) Daimabad

Ans. (a) Lothal

11. What was Cinnabar used as?
    (a) Cosmetic (b) Drink
    (c) Food (d) None

Ans. (a) Cosmetic

12. Which of the following pottery were used for serving beverages in Indus Valley Civilisation?
    (a) Polychrome pottery
    (b) Incised pottery
    (c) Perforated pottery
    (d) Miniature pottery

Ans. (c) Perforated pottery

13. Which of the following materials were not used for making beads in Indus Valley Civilisation?
    (a) Faience
    (b) Platinum
    (c) Turquoise
    (d) Jasper

Ans. (b) Platinum

14. Match the following.

Sites	State (Place)
A. Farmana	1. Pakistan
B. Ropar	2. Haryana
C. Harappa	3. Punjab
D. Daimabad	4. Maharashtra

Codes

(a) A-2, B-3, C-1, D-4
(b) A-3, B-4, C-2, D-1
(c) A-4, B-2, C-3, D-1
(d) A-1, B-3, C-4, D-2

Ans. (a)

Assertion - Reason

Directions (Q. Nos. 15-18) There are two statements marked as Assertion (A) and Reason (R). Read the statements and answer the questions according to the codes given below.

(a) Both A and R are true and R is the correct explanation of A
(b) Both A and R are true, but R is not the correct explanation of A
(c) A is true, but R is false
(d) A is false, but R is true

15. **Assertion** (A) Large number of seals have been discovered from Indus Valley sites.

Reason (R) The discovery of seals shows that the people of Indus Valley were deeply spiritual in nature.

Ans. (c) A is true, but R is false

16. **Assertion** (A) At Indus Valley sites, the portrayal of human and animal figures was highly realistic in nature, as the bodily details included in them were unique.

Reason (R) The artists of Indus Valley were very creative and imaginative.

Ans. (a) Both A and R are true and R is the correct explanation of A

17. **Assertion** (A) Seals of Indus Valley Civilisation are the most distinctive artpieces of pre-historic times.

Reason (R) Seals were decorated with figures of tiger, cow, goat, eagle which makes it unique.

Ans. (c) A is true, but R is false

18. **Assertion** (A) Beads were used by people of Indus Valley Civilisation as jewelleries.

Reason (R) These beads were made from precious stones and metals which makes it attractive.

Ans. (a) Both A and R are true and R is the correct explanation of A

True or False

1. The arts of the Indus Valley Civilisation emerged during the second half of the third millennium BCE.

Ans. True

2. In bronze, only human figures are found.

Ans. False

3. The standard Harappan seal was a square plaque of 2×2 square inches, made from steatite.

Ans. True

4. Facepaint and lipstick were not known to Harappan people.

Ans. False

5. The Indus Valley people never made terracotta images.

Ans. False

Very Short Answer Type Questions

1. Would you agree that the people of the Indus Valley Civilisation were great art lovers? Give reasons for your answer. *(NCERT)*

Ans. The artists of Indus Valley Civilisation were great art lovers. This can be justified by their perfection in art. Their portrayal of human and animal figures was highly realistic in nature, as the bodily details included in them were unique.

Specifically, in the case of terracotta art, the modeling of animal figures was done in an extremely careful manner. The bronze and copper figures were also excellent.

2. Mention few Indus Valley sites excavated in India.

Ans. The important Indus Valley sites excavated in India are
- Lothal, Rangpur and Dholavira in Gujarat
- Rakhigarhi and Banawali in Haryana
- Ropar in Punjab
- Kalibangan in Rajasthan
- Alamgirpur in Uttar Pradesh

3. What do the art objects that have survived tell us about the daily life of the people of the Indus Valley Civilisation? *(NCERT)*

Ans. Art objects like bronze, terracotta sculpture, stone statues and seals give information about on the kind of society which existed in the Indus Valley. It also give information about spiritual beliefs of Indus Valley people, their commercial motives, etc. It also shows the kind of pottery wares they used, fashion ornaments like beads, jewellery, facepaint, etc.

4. What are the various forms of art found from the sites of Indus Valley Civilisation and when were it emerged?

Ans. The forms of art found from various sites of the Indus Valley Civilisation include sculptures, seals, pottery, jewellery, terracotta figures, etc.

The arts of the Indus Valley Civilisation emerged during the second half of the third millennium BCE.

5. Describe the bronze figure of bull found from Mohenjodaro.

Ans. In the bronze figure of a bull from Mohenjodaro the bull is shown standing with his head turned to the right and with a cord around the neck. The massiveness of the bull and its rage are beautifully expressed in the figure.

6. What was the purpose of producing seals?

Ans. The purpose of producing seals was mainly commercial. It appears that the seals were used as amulets. They were carried by their owners, perhaps as modern-day identity cards.

7. What were Harappan seals made of?

Ans. Harappan seals were mostly made of steatite and occasionally made of agate, chert, copper, faience and terracotta.

8. Define the incised and perforated pottery.

Ans. Incised pottery is confined to the bases of the pans and dishes which were used as offerings. Incising is technique for decorating pottery that involves cutting linear designs. Incised decoration was always done inside the utensils.

Perforated pottery includes a large hole at the bottom and small holes all over the wall or body of a utensil. It was probably used for serving beverages.

9. Comment on the spinning culture of Indus Valley Civilisation.

Ans. Spinning of cotton and wool was very common in Indus Valley. It is evident from the discovery of a large number of spindles (straight spike used for spinning) and spindle whorls (small pulley used to weigh a spindle), found in the houses of the Indus Valley people.

The whorls were made of the expensive faience as well as of the cheap pottery and shell.

Short Answer Type Questions

1. Terracotta art was prevalent in Indus Valley Civilisation. Justify this statement by taking examples of the figurines of the Bearded Males found in Terracotta and Mother Goddess.

Ans. For the description of the figurines of Bearded Males and Mother Goddess, refer to text on pg. 22 and 23.

2. Write an elaborative essay on the terracotta figures of Indus Valley Civilisation.

Ans. For description of terracotta figures of Indus Valley Civilisation, refer to text on pg. no. 22.

3. Describe the Pashupati seal.

Or

In this seal, a female deity is portrayed in the centre along with different animals.

(a) Identify this seal of Indus Valley Civilisation.

(b) Appreciate the beauty of this respective seal.

Ans. Pashupati seal is the most remarkable seal of Indus Valley Civilisation. For its description, refer to text on pg. 24.

4. Throw light on the types of pottery with their features in the Indus Valley Civilisation.

Ans. For the types of pottery in the Indus Valley Civilisation, refer to text on pg. 25.

5. Write a short note on the fashion trends of Indus Valley Civilisation.

Ans. For description of fashion trends of Indus Valley Civilisation, refer to text on pg. 26.

Long Answer Type Questions

1. Throw light on the bronze casting used in the Indus Valley Civilisation and the artefacts discovered in bronze and copper.

Ans. For bronze casting used in the Indus Valley Civilisation and the artefacts discovered in bronze and copper, refer to text on pg. 21.

2. Evaluate the beauty and aesthetics of

(a) The Pashupati seal

(b) Painted earthen jar

(c) Male torso

Ans. (a) For the beauty and aesthetics of the Pashupati Seal, refer to text on pg. 24.

(b) For the beauty and aesthetics of painted Earthen Jar, refer to text on pg. 25.

(c) For the beauty and aesthetics of Male Torso, refer to text on pg. 20.

3. The Harappan men and women decorated themselves with a large variety of ornaments. In this regard, throw light on the kind of ornaments they wore and the bead industry.

Ans. For the kind of ornaments, the Harappan, men and women wore, refer to text on pg. 26.

4. What kind of similarities and differences do you find between present-day terracotta and the Indus Valley terracotta? *(NCERT)*

Ans. The similarity between present-day terracotta and the Indus Valley terracotta is that terracotta still has a religious tradition as it was in Indus Valley. The terracotta deities can be found in all the Hindu households.

The differences found between present-day terracotta and the Indus Valley terracotta are

- The Indus Valley people were not aware of use of terracotta beyond art and craft as compared to the people now-a-days who use terracotta in different ways.
- The Indus Valley people only used terracotta art for making idols of local gods and goddesses.
- In present time, the product made of terracotta is not as vital as that of the Indus one.
- In Indus Valley Civilisation, the figures of human were imperfect as compared to the figures made in the present times.
- In present times, terracotta is usually made from a fairly coarse, porous type of clay which is first shaped and then fired until it get hard.
- On the other hand, in the Indus Valley Civilisation, terracotta was left in the heat of the Sun to get hard. Later, it was baked in primitive ovens created in the ashes of open fires and ultimately, it was fired in special ovens known as kilns.

CHAPTER 04

Arts of the Mauryan Period

In this chapter

- Mauryan Empire and its Religious Practices
- Appreciation of the Sculptures of Mauryan Period

The 6th century BCE marks the beginning of new religious and social movements in the Gangetic Valley. Buddhism and Jainism emerged as a new religious movements. They were part of the ***shraman* tradition**[1]. Both religions became popular as they opposed the *varna* and *jati* system of the Hindu religion.

Mauryan Empire and its Religious Practices

By the 4th century BCE, the Mauryas established their power in India and by the 3rd century BCE, a large part of India was under Mauryan control. Magadha emerged as a powerful kingdom and exerted its control over the other regions. **Ashoka** emerged as the most powerful king of the Mauryan dynasty. He patronised the Buddhist *shraman* tradition in the 3rd century BCE.

During this period, religious practices had many dimensions. They were not confined to just one particular mode of worship so, multiple forms of worship existed.

Worship of *Yakshas* and mother-Goddesses were prevalent during this period. However, Buddhism became the most popular social and religious movement. *Yaksha* worship was very popular before and after the advent of Buddhism. Gradually, it was assimilated in Buddhism and Jainism.

1 **Shraman Tradition** It was the tradition that gave rise to Jainism, Buddhism and Yoga. This tradition was also responsible for the related concepts of *samsara* (cycle of birth and death) and *moksha* (liberation from life cycle.)

Architecture During Mauryan Period

In Mauryan period, stone pillars, rock-cut caves and monumental figure sculptures were carved at several places, apart from ***stupas***[2] and ***viharas***[3] that became a part of Buddhist tradition.

Pillars

The tradition of constructing pillars is very old. The erection of pillars was prevalent in the **Achamenian**[4] empire as well. However, the Mauryan pillars are different from the Achamenian pillars. The Mauryan pillars are rock-cut pillars, whereas the Achamenian pillars are constructed in pieces by a mason (a builder and worker in stone).

Stone pillars were erected by Ashoka. They have been found in the North Indian part of the Mauryan empire with inscriptions engraved on them. The top portion of the pillar was carved with capital figures like the bull, the lion, the elephant, etc. All the capital figures are shown strong and are carved standing on a square or circular **abacus**[5].

Abacuses are decorated with stylised lotuses. Some of the existing pillars with capital figures were found at Basarah-Bakhira, Lauriya-Nandangarh and Rampurva in Bihar and Sankisa and Sarnath in Uttar Pradesh.

Rock-Cut Architecture

An example of rock-cut architecture of Mauryan period is the rock-cut cave carved at Barabar hills near Gaya in Bihar, known as the **Lomus Rishi cave**. This cave was donated by Ashoka for the **Ajivika**[6] sect.

The front of the cave is decorated with the semi-circular *chaitya* arch as the entrance. The elephant sculpture is carved in high relief on the *chaitya* arch that shows considerable movement. The interior hall of this cave is rectangular

Elephant, Dhauli

---

2 **Stupa** It is a mound-like or hemispherical structure containing relics that is used as a place of meditation.

3 **Vihara** It is an early type of Buddhist monastery consisting of an open court surrounded by open compartments.

4 **Achamenian** It was the famous dynasty in Persia which was ruled by CyrusI to Darius III (553-330 BC).

5 **Abacus** A square wooden block.

6 **Ajivika** An ascetic sect that emerged in India and lasted until 14th century.

with a circular chamber at the back. The entrance is located on the side wall of the hall. Another example of rock-cut architecture is monumental figure of rock-cut elephant at Dhauli (Odisha). It has been modelled in round shape with linear rhythm.

Sculptures

The finest example of Mauryan sculptural tradition is the Mauryan pillar capital found at Sarnath popularly known as **Lion Capital**. The Lion Capital had been discovered more than a hundred years ago at Sarnath, Varanasi. It is generally referred to as **Sarnath Lion Capital**. It shows considerable mastery in the sculptural techniques.

The huge standing image of a ***Yakshini*** holding a *chauri* (flywhisk) from Didargunj near modern Patna is another example of the sculptural tradition of the Mauryan Period. ***Yaksha*** worship was very popular and it became part of figure representation in Buddhist and Jaina religious tradition.

The monumental images and large statues of *Yaksha* and *Yakshinis* are found in different parts of India like Patna, Vidisha and Mathura. These images are mostly in standing position and have polished surface. Brahmanical Gods were also carved in the sculptural representations.

The ***Jataka***[7] stories also became an important part for sculptural tradition. Mainly, **synoptic narrative**[8], continuous narrative and episodic narrative are used in the pictorial tradition. The *Jataka* stories that are frequently depicted are Chhadanta *Jataka*, Vidurpundita *Jataka*, Ruru *Jataka*, Sibi *Jataka*, Vessantra *Jataka* and Shama *Jataka*.

Stupas

During Mauryan period, *stupas* and *viharas* were constructed on a large scale due to the popularity of Buddhism and Jainism.

The *stupas* were constructed over the relics of the Buddha at

- Rajagraha, Vaishali, Vethadipa and Pava in Bihar.
- Kapilavastu, Allakappa and Ramagrama in Nepal.
- Kushinagar and Pippalvina in Uttar Pradesh.
- Avanti and Gandhara which are outside the Gangetic valley.

The great Stupa at Sanchi was built during the time of Ashoka. It was built with bricks and later it was covered with stone and many new additions were made.

---

7 **Jataka** It refers to the stories of previous births of Gautama Buddha.

8 **Synoptic Narrative** It is a art of telling story either as a moment in an ongoing story or as a sequence of events unfolding over time.

Structure of the Stupa

The *stupa* consists of a cylindrical drum and a circular *anda* and with a harmika and chhatra on the top. Harmika is a square fence like enclosure symbolising heaven on top of the dome of a stupa. Chhatra is an auspicious symbol in Hinduism, Jainism and Buddhism. It is in the form of a stone disks which typically decorates the axis at the apex of a Buddhist stupa. This basic structure remained consistent throughout with minor variations and changes in shape and size.

An example of the structure of *stupa* in the 3rd century BCE is *stupa* at Bairat in Rajasthan. In 2nd century BCE, *stupas* were built with certain additions like enclosing of the **circumambulatory path**[9] with railings and sculptural decoration. Apart from this gateways were added.

Depiction on Stupas

During the early phase of Buddhism, Buddha is depicted symbolically through footprints, *stupas,* lotus throne, *chakra,* etc. This indicates simple worship or paying respect. Sometimes, this also depicts **historisisation**[10] of life events.

Gradually, narrative became a part of the Buddhist tradition. Events from the life of Buddha i.e. the *Jataka* stories were depicted on the railings and ***torans***[11] of the *stupas.*

The main events associated with Buddha's life which were frequently depicted were events related to the birth, renunciation, enlightenment, dhammachakrapravartana and *mahaparinibbana* (liberation from the cycle of birth).

Donations and Patronage during Mauryan Period

- From the 2nd century BCE onwards, there are inscriptional evidences mentioning donors and their profession. Mostly, the patronage was collective and there are few examples of royal patronage. The patrons include lay devotees, *gahapatis* (big land owner) and kings. Donations by the guilds are also mentioned at several sites.
- Traders also recorded their donation along with their place of origin. Artisans' categories like stone carvers, goldsmiths, stone-polishers, carpenters, etc are also mentioned in the inscriptions. However, only few inscriptions mention the names of artisans such as Kanha at Pitalkhora caves and his disciple Balaka at Kondane caves in Maharashtra.

---

9 **Circumambulatory Path** It is the sacred path around a temple or a shrine on which the devotees move around.

10 **Historisisation** It refers to the process of presenting an event as a product of history which involves showing differences between past and present.

11 **Torans** It is a free standing ornamental or arched gateway for ceremonial purposes seen in the Hindu, Buddhist and Jain architecture of the Indian subcontinent, South-East Asia and some parts of East Asia.

Appreciation of the Sculptures of Mauryan Period

Lion Capital, Sarnath

Lion Capital was built by Ashoka in rememberance of the first sermon or *dhammachakrapravartana* by the Buddha. This sculpture was made by polished sandstone, through the technique of carving. The Lion Capital or pillar originally consisted of five component parts which are

(i) The shaft which is now broken in many parts.
(ii) A lotus bell base.
(iii) A drum on the bell base with four animals proceeding clockwise.
(iv) The figures of four majestic enthroned lions.
(v) The crowning element, *Dhammachakra* which is a large wheel. However, this wheel is lying in a broken condition and is displayed in the site museum at Sarnath. The capital without the crowning wheel and the lotus base has been adopted as the **National Emblem** of Independent India.

Name : Lion Capital, Sarnath
Medium : Polished Sandstone
Period : 3rd century BCE
Collection : Sarnath Museum, Uttar Pradesh

The Lion Capital is now has been kept in the archaeological museum at **Sarnath**. The capital has four lions firmly seated back to back on a circular stone abacus. The lion figures of the capital are very impressive and massive. The sculpture is monumental (huge). The facial features of the lions are strong depicting muscularity.

The inversed lines of the lips and its subsequent effect of projection at the end of the lips show the sculptor's observation for naturalistic depiction. The lions appear as if they have held their breath. The lines of the hairs of the lion are sharp and follow the traditions that were in practice during that time.

Their curly manes (hairs on the neck) are depicted by extending mass. The weight of the body of each lion is firmly shown by the stretched muscles of the feet. The surface of the sculpture is heavily polished which is the distinctive feature of sculptures of the Mauryan Period.

The abacus has the depiction of a *chakra* (wheel) having twenty-four spokes in all the four directions. The figures of a bull, a horse, an elephant and a lion are carved between every *chakra*. The design of the *chakra* in Lion Capital is significant as it represents the Buddhist symbol of *Dhammachakra*.

Despite having limited space between each chakra, these animal figures display considerable command over the depiction of movement in a limited space. The circular abacus is supported by an inverted lotus capital. Each petal of the lotus is sculpted according to its density. The lower portion has neatly carved curved planes.

Chauri Bearer from Didargunj (*Yakshini*)

This is a tall, well proportioned and free standing sculpture. This sculpture was made by using the polished sandstone, through the techique of carving. It is in round shape. The sculpture of *Yakshini* is holding a *chauri* (flywhisk) in her right hand whereas the left hand is broken. The **flywhisk**[12] is shown with incised lines continued on the back of the sculpture.

The face of the *Yakshini* has round, fleshy cheeks. The neck is relatively small in proportion and the eyes, nose and lips are sharp.

She is wearing a necklace made of beads that are round in shape and hanging to the belly. The tightening of garment around the belly creates the effect of a bulging belly.

The lower garment has been rendered with great care. Every fold of the garment on the legs is shown by boldlines that are hanging to the legs which also creates a transparent effect. The middle band of the garment falls till the feet. The feet of the *Yakshini* are decorated with thick bell-ornaments. The sculpture stands firmly on its legs. Heaviness is depicted in the torso of the sculpture by heavy breasts.

The hair of *Yakshini* is tied in a knot at the back. The back of the sculpture is depicted bare. Drapery at the back, covers both the legs. The curves in the body of *Yakshini* is clearly depicted in the sculpture and the round body of the figure is perfectly carved by sculptor.

Name : Chauri Bearer from Didargunj (Yakshini)
Medium : Polished Sandstone
Period : 3rd Century BCE
Collection : Patna Museum, Bihar

12 **Flywhisk** It is a device used for brushing away flies. It is made of horsehair and is also used to keep cool in hot and humid climate.

EXAM PRACTICE

Multiple Choice Questions

1. Buddhism and Jainism were part of which tradition?
(a) *Shraman* (b) Sufism
(c) Taoism (d) Christianity

Ans. (a) *Shraman*

2. By the 3rd century BCE, which empire was controlling large part of India?
(a) Palas (b) Mauryan
(c) Rashtrakutas (d) Guptas

Ans. (b) Mauryan

3. Lauriya Nandangarh is famous for its intricately designed pillars. The pillars of this site are decorated with the figurines of capital figures. In which of the following state of India, is this famous site located?
(a) Bihar (b) Haryana
(c) Punjab (d) Jharkhand

Ans. (a) Bihar

4. Sankisa, a place where pillar with capital figures of animals are founded, belongs to which of the following states of India?
(a) Madhya Pradesh (b) Rajasthan
(c) Uttar Pradesh (d) Bihar

Ans. (c) Uttar Pradesh

5. Where are Barabar hills located?
(a) Maharashtra (b) Karnataka
(c) Bihar (d) Jharkhand

Ans. (c) Bihar

6. The Mauryan capital found at Sarnath is popularly known as
(a) Elephant Capital
(b) Lion Capital
(c) Bull Capital
(d) None of the above

Ans. (b) Lion Capital

7. Largest number of stupas, chaityas and viharas belong to which religion?
(a) Jainism (b) Buddhism
(c) Hinduism (d) Sikhism

Ans. (b) Buddhism

8. In which of the following region of Indian sub-continent, is the famous site 'Ramagrama' located?
(a) Gujarat (b) Nepal
(c) Haryana (d) Madhya Pradesh

Ans. (b) Nepal

9. *Mahaparinibbana* was highly depicted on the sculptures of Sanchi. According to Buddhist traditions, what is the literal meaning of *mahaparinibbana?*
(a) First sermon by the Buddha
(b) Liberation from the cycle of birth
(c) Birth of Buddha
(d) Enlightenment

Ans. (b) Liberation from the cycle of birth

10. In which of the following Territory of India, Kondane cave can be found ?
(a) India (b) Maharashtra
(c) Myanmar (d) Bhutan

Ans. (b) Maharashtra

11. Match the following.

List I	List II
A. Vethadipa	1. Uttar Pradesh
B. Allakappa	2. Bihar
C. Pippalvina	3. Nepal
D. Rampurva	4. Bihar

Codes
(a) A-3, B-2, C-1, D-1
(b) A-3, B-4, C-1, D-2
(c) A-1, B-3, C-3, D-2
(d) A-2, B-3, C-1, D-4

Ans. (d)

12. Match the following.

List I	List II
A. Jataka	1. First sermon of Buddhism
B. Torans	2. An ascetic sect
C. Dhammachakra	3. Stories of previous births of Buddha
D. Ajivika	4. Arched gateways

Codes
(a) A-4, B-3, C-2, D-1
(b) A-2, B-1, C-4, D-3
(c) A-4, B-2, C-1, D-3
(d) A-3, B-4, C-1, D-2

Ans. (d)

Assertion-Reason

Directions (Q. Nos. 13-14) In the following questions, there are two statements marked as Assertion (A) and Reason (R). Read the statements and answer the questions according to the codes given below.

(a) Both A and R are true and R is the correct explanation of A
(b) Both A and R are true, but R is not the correct explanation of A
(c) A is true, but R is false
(d) A is false, but R is true

13. **Assertion** (A) The Mauryan pillars are different from the Achamenian pillars.

Reason (R) The Mauryan pillars are rock-cut pillars thus, displaying the carver's skills, whereas the Achamenian pillars are constructed in pieces by a mason.

Ans. (a) Both A and R are true and R is the correct explanation of A

14. **Assertion** (A) During the early phase of Buddhism, Buddha is depicted symbolically through footprints, *stupas*, lotus throne, *chakra*, etc.

Reason (R) The *Jataka* stories also became equally important for sculptural decorations.

Ans. (b) Both A and R are true, but R is not the correct explanation of A

Source Based Question

15. Read the source given below and answer the following questions.

The capital has four lions firmly seated back to back on a circular abacus. The lion figures of the capital are very impressive and massive. The image is monumental. The facial musculature of the lions is strong. The way lips of the lions are carved throws light on the naturalistic depiction. The lions appear as if they have held their breath. The lines of the mane are sharp and follow the conventions that were in practice during that time. The surface of the sculpture is heavily polished which is typical of the Mauryan Period. Their curly manes have visible volume. The weight of the body of each lion is firmly shown by the stretched muscles of the feet. The abacus has the depiction of a *chakra* (wheel) having twenty-four spokes in all the four directions. The figures of a bull, a horse, an elephant and a lion in vigorous movement, between every *chakra* is finely carved.

(i) Which of the following sculptures has been adopted by Indian Government as their National Emblem?
(a) Lion Capital (b) Seated Buddha
(c) Chauri Bearer (d) Edicts of Ashoka

Ans. (a) Lion Capital

(ii) The sculpture is built by which of the following great rulers of ancient India?
(a) Chandragupta (b) Skandagupta
(c) Brihadratha (d) Ashoka

Ans. (d) Ashoka

(iii) The sculpture is established in the region of ....
(a) Kushinagar (b) Kapilvastu
(c) Sarnath (d) Sanchi

Ans. (c) Sarnath

(iv) This sculpture belongs to which of the following period?
(a) 3rd AD (b) 4th AD
(c) 6th AD (d) 2nd AD

Ans. (a) 3rd AD

(v) In which of the following museum, this sculpture has been kept?
(a) National Museum, New Delhi
(b) Sarnath Museum, Uttar Pradesh
(c) Patna Museum, Bihar
(d) Archaeological Survey of India

Ans. (b) Sarnath Museum, Uttar Pradesh

True or False

1. *Stupa*, *vihara* and *chaitya* are part of Buddhist and Jaina monastic complexes, but the largest number belongs to the Jain religion.

Ans. False

2. The rock-cut cave carved at Barabar hills near Gaya in Bihar is known as the Lomus Rishi cave.

Ans. True

3. The Lomus Rishi cave was donated by Ashoka for the Buddhist sect.

Ans. False

4. Many *stupas* were constructed which shows the popularity of Hinduism.

Ans. False

5. *Yaksha* worship was very popular before and after the advent of Buddhism and it was assimilated in Buddhism and Jainism.

Ans. True

Very Short Answer Type Questions

1. Evaluate the meaning of the term *Shraman*.

Ans. *Shraman* was a tradition in ancient India which was brought by the ascetics who renounced worldly life to search for the truth about life and universe. The *Shramans* rejected the authority of Brahmanas and opposed the ritualistic orthodox religious ideas.

2. What was made/carved as part of the earliest Buddhist tradition?

Ans. Construction of *stupas* and *viharas* as part of monastic establishments became part of the earliest Buddhist tradition. However, in this period, apart from *stupas* and *viharas*, stone pillars, rock-cut caves and monumental figure sculptures were carved at several places.

3. State any one characteristic of the pillars established by Ashoka.

Ans. Stone pillars erected by Ashoka have been found in the North Indian part of the Mauryan empire with inscriptions engraved on them. The top portion of the pillar was carved with capital figures like the bull, the lion, the elephant, etc.

4. What are the *Jatakas*? How do the *Jatakas* relate to Buddhism? Find out. *(NCERT)*

Ans. *The Jataka* tales are a voluminous body of literature native to India concerning the previous births of Gautama Buddha. They are related to Buddhism as they tell about the previous lives of the Buddha, in both human and animal form.

5. Write the name of the places, where relics of Buddha can be found?

Ans. The relics of Buddha are found at Rajagraha, Vaishali, Vethadipa and Pava in Bihar, Kapilavastu, Allakappa and Ramagrama in Nepal, Kushinagar and Pippalvina in Uttar Pradesh and Avanti and Gandhara which are outside the Gangetic valley.

6. Write a brief note on the structure of *stupas*.

Ans. The *stupa* consists of a cylindrical drum and a circular *anda* and with a *harmika* and *chhatra* on the top. This basic structure remained consistent throughout with minor variations and changes in shape and size. An example of the structure of *stupa* in the 3rd century BCE is *stupa* at Bairat in Rajasthan.

7. What are the five component parts of Lion Capital?

Ans. The five component parts of Lion Capital are

(i) The shaft which is now broken in many parts.
(ii) A lotus bell base.
(iii) A drum on the bell base with four animals proceeding clockwise.
(iv) The figures of four majestic addorsed lions.
(v) The crowning element, *Dharamchakra* (a large wheel).

Short Answer Type Questions

1. Do you think that the art of making sculptures in India began during the Mauryan period? *(NCERT)*

Ans. Yes, it can be considered that the art of making sculptures in India began during Mauryan period as the art of sculptures began in Indus valley period, but reached its zenith in Mauryan period. The Mauryan period saw the highest quality art of the times.

Due to increasing prosperity and economy, the state could concentrate on artistic elements too and hence, the Mauryan art of sculptures is the best one till the times. It was started in Magadhan times and thus, the gradual evolution was achieved till Mauryan times. The figurines of *Yakshas* and *Yakshinis*, capital figures of bull, lion and elephant that have been found are realistic in nature, having three dimensional volumes.

The sculptures carved on the caves are extremely delicate and intricate. The equally beautiful figures are made in Indus Valley times and they included the dancing girl, the priest, the mother-goddesses figurines. This showed that the carving started in Indus Valley and then reached its best during Mauryan times.

2. What was the significance of the *stupa* and how did *stupa* architecture develop? *(NCERT)*

Ans. Significance of *stupas* was

- It increased the popularity of the king across state.
- *Stupa* was developed as a religious place.
- *Stupas* were important to spread the philosophy of Buddhism.
- *Stupas* provide historical evidence in the form of inscriptions. The narratives or stories depicted on *stupas* are source of historical information on the life in these times.

3. Evaluate the themes that were depicted on the *stupas* of Mauryan period.

Ans. For the themes that were depicted on the *stupas* of Mauryan period, refer to text on pg. 34.

4. Which were the four events in the life of the Buddha which have been depicted in different forms of Buddhist art? What did these events symbolise? *(NCERT)*

Ans. The main events associated with the Buddha's life which were frequently depicted were events related to the birth, renunciation, enlightenment, *dhammachakrapravartana* and *mahaparinibbana* (death).

The events can be symbolised as

- **Birth** It generally depicts the birth of Gautama Buddha.
- **Renunciation** It depicts the departure of Buddha from all worldly pleasures.
- **Enlightenment** It is the attainment of enlightenment near Bodhgaya. It has mostly been represented by a Peepal tree.
- **Dhammachakrapravartana** It is the depiction of first sermon of Buddha at Sarnath.
- **Mahaparinibbana (death)** This has been well represented at the Ajanta caves.

5. Write a short note on the donations and patronage during the Mauryan period.

Ans. For description on the donations and patronage during the Mauryan period, refer to text on pg. 34.

Long Answer Type Questions

1. The tradition of constructing pillars is very old. Justify this statement by giving a brief explanation.

Ans. It is true that the tradition of constructing pillars is very old as the erection of pillars was prevalent from the period of the Achamenian Empire. However, the Mauryan pillars are different from the Achamenian pillars. The Mauryan pillars are rock-cut pillars, whereas the Achamenian pillars are constructed in pieces by a mason.

Stone pillars were erected by Ashoka of Mauryan Empire. They have been found in the North Indian part of the Mauryan empire with inscriptions engraved on them. The top portion of the pillar was carved with capital figures like the bull, the lion, the elephant, etc. All the capital figures are robust and carved standing on a square or circular abacus. Abacuses are decorated with stylised lotuses.

Some of the existing pillars with capital figures were found at

- Basarah-Bakhira in Bihar
- Lauriya-Nandangarh in Bihar
- Rampurva in Bihar
- Sankisa in Uttar Pradesh
- Sarnath in Uttar Pradesh

2. The Lion Capital at Sarnath is an exquisite example of Mauryan sculpture. How would you justify this statement? Throw light on the features of Lion Capital at Sarnath.

Ans. The Lion Capital at Sarnath is an exquisite example of Mauryan sculpture due to its features. For description of its features, refer to text on pg. 35 and 36.

3. Didargunj *Yakshini* is a good example of Mauryan sculptural tradition. What are its main features?

Ans. For the features of Didargunj *Yakshini*, refer to text on pg. 36.

CHAPTER 05

Introduction to Art During Post-Mauryan Period

In this chapter

- *Sculptures of Post-Mauryan Period*
- *Appreciation of Sculptures of Post-Mauryan Period*

From the 2nd century BCE onwards or the post-Mauryan period, various rulers established their control over the vast Mauryan Empire. These were

- The Shungas, Kanvas, Kushanas and Guptas in the North and parts of Central India.
- The Satvahanas, Ikshavakus, Abhiras, Vakataks in Southern and Western India.

The period of the 2nd century BCE also marked the rise of the main Brahmanical sects such as the Vaishnavas and the Shaivas. There are numerous sites that belong to the 2nd century BCE in India.

Sculptures of Post-Mauryan Period

Some of the important examples of the finest sculptures of post-Mauryan period are found at Vidisha, Bharhut (Madhya Pradesh), Bodhgaya (Bihar), Jaggayyapeta (Andhra Pradesh), Mathura (Uttar Pradesh), Khandagiri-Udaigiri (Odisha), Bhaja near Pune and Pavani near Nagpur (Maharashtra).

Sculptures at Bharhut

Bharhut sculptures are early Indian sculptures of Shunga period (mid-2nd century BCE). These sculptures are tall like the images of *Yaksha* and *Yakshini* in the Mauryan period. The modeling of sculptural volume in these sculptures is in low relief. Linearity is maintained in these sculptures and images are attached to the sculptures. In the **relief**[1], **panels**[2] depicting narratives and illusion of three-dimensionality is shown in inclined position. Clarity in the narrative has been increased by selecting main events.

1 **Relief** It is a sculptural technique in which the sculpted elements remain attached to a solid background of the same material.

2 **Panel** It is a rigid support or surface on which the painting is made.

At Bharhut, narrative panels are shown with fewer characters. However, gradually other characters also started appearing in the picture space. Sometimes more than one event at one geographical place is shown together in the picture space while sometimes, only a single main event is depicted in the picture space.

Some of the sculptures found at Bharhut are displayed in Indian Museum, Kolkata.

Narratives and Jataka Stories in Bharhut Sculptures

Narrative reliefs at Bharhut show how artisans used the pictorial language very effectively to communicate stories. In one such narrative, showing **Queen Mayadevi's** (mother of Siddhartha Gautam) **dream**, a descending elephant is shown. The queen is resting on the bed. An elephant is sculpted above the queen which can be seen moving towards the womb of the Queen Mayadevi.

The depiction of a *Jataka* story is very simple. Jataka stories are narrated by gathering the events according to the geographical location of the story. For example, the depiction of **Ruru *Jataka*** where the Bodhisattva deer is rescuing a man on his back. The other event in the same picture frame depicts the King standing with his army and about to shoot an arrow at the deer.

The man who was rescued by the deer is also shown along with the king pointing a finger at the deer. According to the story, the man promised the deer after his rescue that he would not tell his identity to anybody. But when the king makes an announcement of reward for telling the identity of the deer, he turns greedy. He broke the promise and took the king to the same jungle where he had seen the deer. Such *Jataka* stories became part of *stupa* decoration.

Jataka Panel, Bharhut

Queen Maya's dream, Bharhut

Development in the Method of Carving

- Initially, the folded hands of the figures in narratives as well as single figures are shown flat holding the chest. Later in some cases, the hands are shown with the natural depiction against the chest. This shows the understanding of the artists of the method of carving who were working at a collective level.
- Initially, dressing the stone surfaces was difficult. The human body and other forms were sculpted, but due to shallow carving of the picture surface, depiction of hands and feet was not possible. Thus, folded hands are depicted and the position of the feet was not appropriate and there is general stiffness in the body and arms. However, such depiction was modified by making images with deep carvings, strong volume and a very naturalistic representation of human and animal bodies.

Sculptures at Sanchi

Sanchi is located about 50 km from Bhopal. It is the capital of Madhya Pradesh and a world heritage site. The figures at Sanchi, despite being small in dimension, show considerable mastery of sculpting. Their **physiognomic**[3] treatment of the body shows both depth and dimension which are very naturalistic.

There are three main *stupas* at Sanchi along with other relatively small *stupas*.

(i) Stupa-1 It is presumed to have the relics of the Buddha.

(ii) Stupa-2 It has the relics of ten less famous ***arhats***[4] belonging to three different generations. Their names are found on the relic casket.

(iii) Stupa-3 It has the relics of Sariputta and Mahamougalayana.

Stupa-1 at Sanchi

The Stupa-1 at Sanchi was expanded during the later rule of Shunga with stone slabs that were almost twice its original size. It is the oldest stupa. It is known for the carvings on its gateways.

Stupa-1 at Sanchi has upper as well as lower *pradakshinapatha* or **circumambulatory path**[5]. It has four beautifully decorated *toranas* (gateways) depicting various events from the life of the Buddha and the *Jatakas*. The four gateways are decorated greatly with sculptures.

The *pradakshinapatha* around the *stupa* is enclosed with the *vedika* (low wall). There is also the upper *pradakshinapatha* which is unique feature of this site. The Ashokan Lion-Capital pillar with an inscription is found on the Southern side of the *stupa*. The historical narratives such as the seige of Kushinara, Buddha's visit to Kapilavastu, visit of Ashoka to the Ramgrama Stupa are carved on the stupa with great details.

---

3 **Physiognomic** It is the practice of assessing a person's character or personality from their outer appearance especially the face.

4 **Arhat** In Buddhism, an *arhat* is the one who has gained insight into the true nature of existence and has achieved *nirvana* (a state of enlightenment).

5 **Circumambulatory Path** It is the passage for encircling around the temple's *garbhagriha* on which worshipers move in a clockwise direction.

Features of Sculptures of Stupa-1

- Figure compositions are highly sculpted that filled up the entire space.
- The depiction of the posture in figures is naturalistic and there is no hardness in the body.
- Heads of the figures are fairly depicted in the picture space.
- Stiffness in the shape gets reduced and images are shown in motion.
- Narration in the sulptures gets detailed and carving techniques appear more advanced than Bharhut.
- Symbols continue to be used in representing the Buddha. The Buddha has been represented through symbols like the empty throne, feet, chhatra, stupa, etc.
- At Sanchi Stupa-1, narratives get more elaborated however, the depiction of the dream episode as in narrative relief of Bharhut, remains very simple. It shows the resting image of the queen and the elephant at the top.

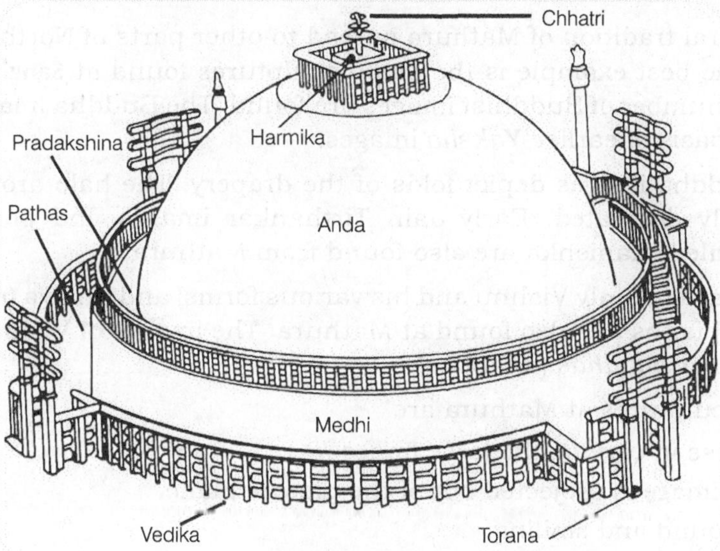

Plan of Stupa-I, Sanchi

Stupa-2 at Sanchi

The carving of images on the *vedica* of Stupa-2 are earlier than those on Stupa-1. There are guardian images on pillars and the *shalbhanjika* (i.e. *lady* holding the branch of a tree) sculptures are remarkable as they are made in large sizes. The rigidity of the earlier sculptures of Stupa-2 is no more there.

Each *torana* of this *stupa* consists of two vertical pillars and three horizontal bars on the top. Each horizontal bar is decorated with different sculptural themes on the front as well as at the back. The images of *shalbhanjikas* are supporting the extensions of the lowermost horizontal bar from below.

Sculptures of Mathura, Sarnath and Gandhara Schools

After 1st century CE, Mathura in Northern India, Sarnath and Gandhara (now in Pakistan) emerged as important centres of art production. Earlier the Buddha was represented by abstract symbols, but in Mathura and Gandhara school he was represented by human figures.

Sculptures of Mathura

Mathura was a great centre for making sculptures in smaller size and the figures of the sculpture are made more muscular and thick. A large number of images dating back to the Kushana period is from Mathura.

Mathura sculptures from Kushana period are made in smaller sizes and the figures of the sculpture are made more muscular and more thick. A distinct way of sculpting practised at Mathura makes the images found here different from those at other centres in the country.

The local sculptural tradition of Mathura spread to other parts of Northern India due to its popularity. The best example is the *stupa* sculptures found at **Sanghol** in Punjab. In Mathura, a large number of Buddhist images are found. The Buddha image at Mathura is modelled on the basis of earlier *Yaksha* images.

The Mathura Buddha images depict folds of the drapery. The halo around the head of Buddha is greatly decorated. Early Jain Tirthankar images and portraits of kings, specially the headless Kanishka are also found from Mathura.

Images of Vaishnava (mainly Vishnu and his various forms) and Shaiva (mainly the *lingas* and *mukhalingas*) faiths are also found at Mathura. The images of Vishnu and Shiva are represented by their *ayudhas* (weapons).

The features of sculptures at Mathura are

- There is boldness in carving the large images.
- The size of the image is projected out of the picture plane.
- The faces are round and smiling.
- The heaviness in the sculptural volume is reduced to relaxed body posture.
- The garments of the body are clearly visible and they cover the left shoulder.
- Images of the Buddha, *Yakshas*, *Yakshinis*, Shaivite and Vaishnavite deities and portrait statues are beautifully sculpted.

In the 2nd century CE, images in Mathura get sensual. Their importance increases and they become abundant. The trend continues in the 4th century CE, but in the late 4th century CE, the massiveness and hugeness is reduced. The body becomes more tightened and the volume of the drapery (cloth) also gets reduced. In the 5th and 6th centuries CE, the drapery is integrated into the sculptural mass. Transparent quality in the robes of the Buddha images is evident.

Sculptures of Sarnath

The Buddha images that belong to Gupta period are finest examples of sculptures of Sarnath. The aim of the sculptors in ancient India had always been to represent the Buddha as a great human being who achieved *nibbana*.
Sarnath Buddha images show considerable softness in the depiction of the surface and volume. They have plain transparent drapery covering both shoulder. The halo around the head has very little ornamentation.

There are many other Buddha images in the standing position from Sarnath having features like transparent drapery and fine gesture. They were carved separately and placed around the Dharmarajika Stupa as the memorial *stupas*.

These images are now preserved in the Sarnath Museum. They are either single or with the attendant figures of Bodhisattvas, Padmapani and Vajrapani.

Sculptures of Gandhara

The finest examples of sculptures of Gandhara belong to Kushana period. The sculptural tradition in Gandhara was the combination of **Bactria**[6], **Parthia**[7] and the local Gandhara tradition.

The Gandhara images have physiognomic features of the Greco-Roman tradition. However, they display a very distinct way of treating physiognomic details that are not completely Greco-Roman.

A large number of images have been found in the Gandhara region. They consist of narratives related to the life of the Buddha, narrations from the *Jataka* stories and Buddha and Bodhisattva images.

Name : Bodhisattva, Gandhara
Period : 5th–6th Century CE

6 **Bactria** It was the province of the Persian empire located in modern Afghanistan, Uzbekistan and Tazikistan.

7 **Parthia** It is a historical region located in the North-Eastern part of Iran. This region was a major political and cultural power in ancient Iran from 247 BC to 224 AD.

Appreciation of Sculptures of Post-Mauryan Period

Seated Buddha, Katra Mound, Mathura

This sculpture of the Buddha from the Katra mound belongs to the 3rd century CE. This red spotted sandstone sculpture was made by the technique of carving. It represents the Buddha with two Bodhisattva attendants. The Buddha is seated in *padmasana* (cross-folded legs). The right hand is in the ***abhayamudra***[8] which is raised a little above the shoulder level.

The left hand is placed on the left thigh. The *ushanisha* i.e. hair knot, is shown with a vertically raised projection. The shoulders are broad. One of the shoulders of the Buddha is covered by *Sanghati* (garment). It also covers the left hand of the Buddha. A thin piece of cloth is worn over the left shoulder leaving the right shoulder uncovered.

The Buddha is seated on a lion throne. The attendant figures are identified as the images of the Padmapani and Vajrapani Bodhisattvas as one holds a lotus and the other holds a *vajra* (thunderbolt). They are wearing crowns and are on either side of the Buddha.

Name : Seated Buddha from Katra Mound, Mathura
Medium : Red-spotted Sandstone
Period : 3rd Century AD (Kushana Period)
Collection : Government Museum, Mathura

The halo around the head of the Buddha is very large. It is decorated with simple geometric motifs. There are two flying figures placed diagonally above the halo. They bear a lot of movement in the picture space. The curves of the body are perfectly carved in the sculpture. The upright posture of the Buddha image has a distinctive visual aesthetic. The face is round with fleshy cheeks. The bulge of the belly is sculpted with muscularity.

This sculpture is representative and is important for the understanding of the development of the Buddha image in the subsequent periods.

8 **Abhayamudra** It is a sacred hand gesture which is used during yoga and meditation practice.

Jain Tirthankara

This sculpture belong to the Gupta period and made in Mathura style. This stone sculpture was made by the technique of carving.

In this sculpture, Jain Tirthankara Vardhaman Mahavira (24th Tirthankara) is depicted in sitting position of *padmasana.* His both hands are kept upon each other.

The figure of Mahavira is represented nude. The hair locks are rounded but other features like nose, eyes, eyebrows and ears are depicted by curved lines.

This sculpture depict Mahavira as calm concentrating his mind in *dhyana mudra* (half closed eyes) to attain enlightenment.

The halo around the head of Mahavira has been engraved with some geometric shapes and floral motifs. The torso of the sculpture has been shown with great clarity.

Name : Jain Tirthankara
Medium : Stone
Period : 5th century AD (Gupta Period)
Collection : State Museum, Lucknow, Uttar Pradesh

EXAM PRACTICE

Multiple Choice Questions

1. Which of the following dynasty doesn't belong to Northern-Central India?
   (a) Kanvas (b) Kushanas
   (c) Abhiras (d) Guptas

Ans. (c) Abhiras

2. Vaishnavism and Shaivism, which is the famous religious cult of India belongs to which of the following religious sects?
   (a) Jainism (b) Brahmanism
   (c) Buddhism (d) Ajivika

Ans. (b) Brahmanism

3. Bhaja caves, which are famous for the sculptures of post-Mauryan period is located in which of the following Indian state?
   (a) Odisha (b) Maharashtra
   (c) Andhra Pradesh (d) Tamil Nadu

Ans. (b) Maharashtra

4. Who was the mother of Gautama Buddha?
   (a) Mayadevi (b) Gautami
   (c) Radhika (d) Yashoda

Ans. (a) Mayadevi

5. .... is a process of providing a proper shape, size and smooth finish to the rough surfaced broken stone.
(a) Dressing (b) Chiseling
(c) Weathering (d) Sculpting

Ans. (a) Dressing

6. Which of the following part of Sanchi stupa has the relics of Buddha?
(a) Stupa-3 (b) Stupa-2
(c) Stupa-1 (d) None of these

Ans. (c) Stupa-1

7. The world famous Sanchi stupa which contains the relics of Gautama Buddha is located in which of the following Indian state?
(a) Gujarat (b) Madhya Pradesh
(c) Haryana (d) Uttar Pradesh

Ans. (b) Madhya Pradesh

8. In which of the following schools, Buddha was represented in the human forms?
(a) Barhut (b) Taxila
(c) Sanchi (d) Mathura

Ans. (d) Mathura

9. Where is Dharmarajika stupa situated?
(a) Madhya Pradesh
(b) Uttar Pradesh
(c) Telangana
(d) Andhra Pradesh

Ans. (b) Uttar Pradesh

10. Match the following.

List I (Caves)	List II (Location)
A. Khandagiri-Udaigiri	1. Andhra Pradesh
B. Bhaja	2. Odisha
C. Jaggayyapeta	3. Pune
D. Bagh	4. Madhya Pradesh

Codes
(a) A-2, B-3, C-1, D-4
(b) A-2, B-4, C-3, D-1
(c) A-3, B-2, C-1, D-4
(d) A-3, B-1, C-2, D-4

Ans. (a)

11. Match the following.

List I	List II
A. Seated Buddha (Katra Mound)	1. Bharhut
B. Jataka Panel	2. State Museum, Lucknow
C. Jain Tirthankara	3. Government Museum, Mathura

Codes
(a) A-1, B-3, C-2 (b) A-3, B-2, C-1
(c) A-3, B-1, C-2 (d) A-2, B-3, C-1

Ans. (c)

Assertion-Reason

Directions (Q. Nos. 12-15) There are two statements marked as Assertion (A) and Reason (R). Read the statement and answer the questions according to codes given below.

(a) Both A and R are true and R is the correct explanation of A
(b) Both A and R are true, but R is not the correct explanation of A
(c) A is true, but R is false
(d) A is false, but R is true

12. **Assertion** (A) In the sculptures of Bharhut, narrative panels are shown with fewer characters.
Reason (R) Sometimes more than one event at one geographical place is shown together in the picture space while sometimes, only a single main event is depicted in the picture space.

Ans. (a) Both A and R are true and R is the correct explanation of A

13. **Assertion** (A) *Jataka* stories became the part of stupa decoration.
Reason (R) *Jataka* stories were depicted on Jain stupas as these stories were highly inspired from the previous incarnations of 24th Tirthankara of Jainism i.e. Mahavira.

Ans. (c) A is true, but R is false

14. **Assertion** (A) The figures at Sanchi, were made in small sizes and show the considerable mastery of sculpting.

Reason (R) The physiognomic of the body shows both depth and dimension which are very naturalistic.

Ans. (A) Both A and R are true and R is the correct explanation of A

15. **Assertion** (A) Mathura was a great centre for making sculptures during the early historic period.

Reason (R) Mathura was the capital of Kushanas who were the vivid followers of Shaivism and Vaishnavism.

Ans. (c) A is true, but R is false

Source Based Questions

16. Read the source given below and answer the following questions.

From the 1st century CE onwards, Gandhara, Mathura in Northern India and Vengi in Andhra Pradesh emerged as important centres of art production. Buddha in the symbolic form got a human form in Mathura and Gandhara. The sculptural tradition in Gandhara had the mix of Bactria, Parthia and the local Gandhara tradition.

The local sculptural tradition at Mathura became so strong that the tradition spread to other parts of Northern India. The best example is the *stupa* sculptures found at Sanghol in Punjab. The Buddha image at Mathura is modelled on the lines of earlier *Yaksha* images. In Gandhara it has Hellenistic (Greek) features.

(i) Where do we find the portrait of headless Kanishka?

(a) Sarnath
(b) Mathura
(c) Vengi
(d) Amaravati

Ans. (b) Mathura

(ii) In Mathura, images of Vishnu and Shiva are represented by their

(a) face (b) weapons
(c) hand gestures (d) None of these

Ans. (b) weapons

(iii) Bactria was an ancient region in

(a) India (b) Pakistan
(c) Central Asia (d) Bangladesh

Ans. (c) Central Asia

(iv) Parthian empire, an ancient dynasty, belongs to which region?

(a) Central Asia (b) Rome
(c) Iraq (d) Iran

Ans. (d) Iran

(v) The Kindgom of Bactria belongs to which of the following region?

(a) Persia (b) Greek
(c) Iran (d) Egypt

Ans. (a) Persia

17. Read the source given below and answer the following questions.

The left hand is placed on the left thigh. The *ushanisha* i.e. hair knot, is shown with a vertically raised projection. The shoulders are broad. One of the shoulders of the Buddha is covered by *Sanghati* (garment). It also covers the left hand of the Buddha. A thin piece of cloth is worn over the left shoulder leaving the right shoulder uncovered.

The Buddha is seated on a lion throne. The attendant figures are identified as the images of the Padmapani and Vajrapani Bodhisattvas as one holds a lotus and the other holds a *vajra* (thunderbolt). They are wearing crowns and are on either side of the Buddha.

(i) Which sculpture has been discussed above?

(a) Seated Buddha
(b) Buddha head
(c) Relics of Buddha
(d) Jain Tirthankara

Ans. (a) Seated Buddha

(ii) Which of the following dynasties is responsible for the construction of this sculpture?
(a) Ganga
(b) Rashtrakuta
(c) Chola
(d) Kushana

Ans. (d) Kushana

(iii) This sculpture was made in the period of
(a) 6th Century AD
(b) 12th Century AD
(c) 5th Century AD
(d) 3rd Century AD

Ans. (d) 3rd Century AD

(iv) This art piece belongs to which of the following schools of sculpture?
(a) Gandhar
(b) Sarnath
(c) Mathura
(d) Taxila

Ans. (c) Mathura

(v) Which material has been used in the making of this sculpture?
(a) Grey basalt rock
(b) White sandstone
(c) Red-spotted sandstone
(d) Makrana marbles

Ans. (c) Red-spotted sandstone

True or False

1. The Satvahanas, Ikshavakus, Abhiras, Vakataks ruled over Northern and Central India.

Ans. False

2. Bharhut sculptures are tall like the images of *Yaksha* and *Yakshini* in the Mauryan period.

Ans. True

3. Udaigiri-Khandagiri caves are scattered and have inscriptions of Kharavela Jain kings.

Ans. True

4. Rock-cut caves are found only in Maharashtra.

Ans. False

Very Short Answer Type Questions

1. How many kingdoms gained prominience after 2nd century BCE?

Ans. From the 2nd century BCE onwards, various rulers established their control over the vast Mauryan Empire and became prominent. These were

- The Shungas, Kanvas, Kushanas and Guptas in the North and parts of Central India.
- The Satvahanas, Ikshavakus, Abhiras, Vakataks in Southern and Western India.

2. What are *Jatakas*? Give any one example of *Jatakas* that are depicted on the Jataka panel of Bharhut in brief.

Ans. The *Jatakas* are an important part of Buddhist art and literature. They describe the previous existences or births of the Buddha (the enlightened one) when he appeared as Bodhisattvas (beings who are yet to attain enlightenment or *moksha*), in both human and non-human forms.

The *Jataka* that is depicted on the *Jataka panel of Bharhut is Ruru Jataka* where the Bodhisattva deer is rescuing a man on his back. The other event in the same picture frame depicts the King standing with his army and about to shoot an arrow at the deer.

3. Write a brief note on the three sub-types of Sanchi Stupa.

Ans. The three sub-types of Sanchi Stupa are

(i) **Stupa-1** It is presumed to have the relics of the Buddha.

(ii) **Stupa-2** It has the relics of ten less famous *arhats* belonging to three different generations. Their names are found on the relic casket.

(iii) **Stupa 3** It has the relics of Sariputta and Mahamougalayana.

4. What is the basic structure of Stupa-1 at Sanchi?

Ans. Stupa-1 at Sanchi has upper as well as lower *pradakshinapatha* or circumambulatory path.

It has four beautifully decorated *toranas* (gateways) depicting various events from the life of the Buddha and the *Jatakas*.

5. Mention any three distinctive characteristics of the sculptures of Stupa-1.

Ans. Three distinctive characteristics of the sculptures of Stupa-1 are

(i) Figure compositions are highly sculpted that filled up the entire space.

(ii) The depiction of the posture in figures is naturalistic and there is no hardness in the body.

(iii) Heads of the figures are fairly depicted in the picture space.

6. What were the important centres of art production in India after 1st century CE?

Ans. After 1st century CE, Gandhara (now in Pakistan), Sarnath and Mathura in Northern India emerged as important centres of art production. Buddha in the symbolic form got a human form in Mathura and Gandhara.

The sculptural tradition in Gandhara had the mix of Bactria, Parthia and the local Gandhara tradition.

7. What kind of sculptural images and portraits do we find from Mathura?

Ans. Early Jain Tirthankar images and portraits of kings, specially the headless Kanishka are found from Mathura. Images of Vaishnava (mainly Vishnu and his various forms) and Shaiva (mainly the *lingas* and *mukhalingas*) faiths are also found at Mathura. Buddhist images are also found in large numbers in Mathura.

8. State any four salient features of the sculptures of Mathura.

Ans. The features of sculptures at Mathura are

(i) There is boldness in carving the large images.

(ii) The size of the image is projected out of the picture plane.

(iii) The heaviness in the sculptural volume is reduced to relaxed body posture.

(iv) The faces are round and smiling.

Short Answer Type Questions

1. Briefly describe the features of Bharhut sculptures.

Ans. For the features of Bharhut sculptures, refer to text on pg. 42 and 43.

2. What is depicted on Ruru *Jataka*?

Ans. For description about the depiction on Ruru *Jataka*, refer to text on pg. 43.

3. Sanchi Stupa-1 is an example of excellent ancient sculptural work. Throw light on its features.

Or

Describe the physical and aesthetic features of Sanchi Stupa-1. *(NCERT)*

Ans. Sanchi Stupa-1 is considered the excellent sculptural work because of its features. For its description, refer to text on pg. 45.

4. Throw light on the evolution of images in Mathura in and after 2nd century CE.

Ans. The evolution of images in Mathura in and after 2nd century CE is discussed below

- In the 2nd century CE, images in Mathura get sensual. Their importance increases and they become abundant. The trend continues in the 4th century CE.
- In the late 4th century CE, the massiveness and hugeness is reduced. The body becomes more tightened and the volume of the drapery (cloth) also gets reduced.
- In the 5th and 6th centuries CE, the drapery is integrated into the sculptural mass. Transparent quality in the robes of the Buddha images is evident.

5. Analyse the stylistic trends of the sculptures in North India during the 5th and 6th centuries. *(NCERT)*

Ans. The stylistic trends in North India are divided into three school i.e. Mathura School, Sarnath and Gandhara School.

In Mathura, large number of Buddhist images are found. The Buddha image at Mathura is modelled on the basis of earlier *Yaksha* images. The Mathura Buddha images to depict folds of the drapery. The halo around the head of Buddha is profusely decorated.

The sculptural tradition in Gandhara was the combination of Bactria, Parthia and the local Gandhara tradition. The Gandhara images have physiognomic features of the Greco-Roman tradition. However, they display a very distinct way of treating physiognomic details that are not completely Greco-Roman.

They consist of narratives related to the life of the Buddha, narrations from the *Jataka* stories, Buddha and Bodhisattva images.

Sarnath School sculptures are intricately carved, especially Buddha's halo. There is no necked-ness in the sculptures. Drapery is shown transparently in the sculptures.

Long Answer Type Questions

1. Write an essay on any sculpture of the Kushana period which you like or dislike. Justify your choice by giving the proper explanation on the methods, material and distinctive features which could support your answer.

Ans. I like the sculpture of Seated Buddha from Katra Mound, Mathura that belong to Kushana period, due to its features. For the description of this sculpture, refer to text on pg. 48.

2. Appreciate the sculpture of Jain Tirthankara on the grounds of its method, material and visual aesthetics.

Ans. For the appreciation of the sculpture of Jain Tirthankara on the grounds of its method, material and visual aesthetics, refer to text on pg. 49.

CHAPTER 06

Introduction to Ajanta Caves

In this chapter
- *Ajanta Caves*
- *Paintings and Sculptures at Ajanta Caves*

Ajanta Caves

Location and Period

In Western India, many Buddhist caves dating back to the 2nd century BCE onwards have been excavated. One of the most famous cave site among them is Ajanta, which is located in Aurangabad, Maharashtra. Ajanta is the only surviving example of painting of the 1st century BCE and the 5th century CE.

Number of Caves at Ajanta

Ajanta has twenty-nine caves. It has four ***chaitya***[1] caves that belong to the earlier phase i.e. the 2nd and the 1st century BCE (Cave Nos. 10 and 9) and the later phase i.e. the 5th century CE (Cave Nos. 19 and 26). Rest of the caves are *viharas-chaitya* caves. The *chaityas* and ***viharas***[2] are decorated with sculptures and paintings.

Characteristics of Caves at Ajanta

- The caves at Ajanta as well as in Western Deccan in general have no precise chronology because of the lack of knowledge about dated inscriptions.
- Cave Nos. 10, 9, 12 and 13 belong to the early phase. Cave Nos. 11, 15 and 6 (both the upper and lower compartment) and Cave No. 7 belong to the period before 5th century CE. The rest of the caves belong to late 5th century CE to early 6th century CE.

1 **Chaitya** It is a place where devotees gather to worship.

2 **Viharas** It is a place of residence of Buddhist monk.

- The *chaitya* Cave Nos. 19 and 26 have detailed carvings. Their front is decorated with Buddha and **Bodhisattva**[3] images. They are of the **apsidal-vault-roof**[4] variety.
- Cave No. 26 is very big and the entire interior hall is carved with a variety of Buddha images.The biggest image is that of **Mahaparinibbana**[5] image.
- The *vihara-chaitya* caves at Ajanta consist of a pillared veranda, a pillared hall and cells along the walls. The back wall has the main Buddha shrines which are grand in size.
- Some of the *vihara* caves are unfinished such as Cave Nos. 5, 14, 23 24, 28 and 29.

Ajanta Caves

Patrons at Ajanta

The important patrons at Ajanta were

- Varahadeva (patron of Cave No. 16), the Prime Minister of the Vakataka king, Harishena.
- Upendragupta (patron of Cave Nos. 17–20), the local king of the region and feudatory of the Vakataka king, Harishena.
- Buddhabhadra (patron of Cave No. 26).
- Mathuradasa (patron of Cave No. 4).

3 **Bodhisattva** In Buddhism, Bodhisattva refers to the previous births of Gautama Buddha.

4 **Apsidal-vault-roof** It means roof in the form of an arch representing a large semi-circular space.

5 **Mahaparinibbana** It refers to the ultimate state of *Nirvana* (everlasting, highest peace and happiness) entered by an awakened being at the moment of physical death.

Paintings and Sculptures at Ajanta Caves

Many paintings have survived in Ajanta Cave Nos. 1, 2, 16 and 17. Paintings at Ajanta have many attributes and variations. Some of these attributes are

- Outward projections (bulge) are used in the Ajanta paintings of the 5th century CE.
- The lines are very rhythmic and clearly defined. The body colour of the figures get merged with the outer line and create a volume (massive) effect.

Sculptural Panel in the Veranda of Cave No. 2, Ajanta

- The figures are heavy like the sculptures of Western India.

First Phase of Paintings at Ajanta Caves

The first phase of painting can be studied from the paintings of Cave Nos. 9 and 10 that belong to 1st century BCE.

The features of these paintings are

- The figures in the paintings of these caves are broad with heavy proportion and they are arranged in the picture space in a linear way. Arrangement of the figures in horizontal manner in the cave paintings were the most convenient choice of artisans.
- The paintings in these caves shows limited use of colours with sharp lines.
- Figures in these caves are painted with **naturalism**[6] and there is no over stylisation.
- Events are grouped together according to geographical location. The outward architectural slabs are used to indicate different geographical regions.
- The figures were highly influenced by the figures of the Sanchi sculptures. This indicates the development in that **lithic**[7] and painting traditions simultaneously.
- The frontal knot of the headgear (cap) of the figures follows the same pattern as that of the sculptures. However, there are also some different patterns of headgear.

Second Phase of Paintings at Ajanta Caves

The second phase of paintings can be studied from the images of Buddha painted on the walls and pillars of Cave Nos. 9 and 10. These Buddha figures are different from the figures painted in the 5th century CE.

6 **Naturalism** Naturalism in art refers to the depiction of realistic objects in a natural setting. In this, artist pays attention to very accurate and precise details and portrays things in exact form.

7 **Lithic** It is essentially any artefact made of stone and it is the most common type of artefact archaeologists find at pre-historic archaeological site.

Cave excavation and painting were simultaneous processes and dating of the paintings follows the date of the cave excavations.

Third Phase of Paintings at Ajanta Caves

The third phase of the development in the cave paintings of Ajanta can be seen in the paintings of Cave Nos. 16, 17, 1 and 2. The pictures have been painted in typological variations in almost all the caves, but only very few have survived.

In paintings, various skin colours are used such as brown, yellowish brown, greenish, yellow ochre, etc. which represent a multi-coloured population.

The features of paintings of Cave Nos. 16 and 17 are

- They have precise and elegant quality and they do not carry the heavy volume of the sculptures in the caves. Movements in the figures are very rhythmic.
- Thick dark lines of brown colour are used in outlining of figures. These lines are very dark and bold that they highlights figural compositions.

Painting of the Buddha, Yashodhra and Rahul, Cave No. 17, Ajanta

The features of paintings of Cave Nos. 1 and 2 are

- They are very neat and naturalistic and well integrated with the sculptures in the caves.
- Architectural setting is simple and the arrangement of figures in these paintings is delineated in the circular form to create three-dimensionality and special effects.
- The figures depict half-closed elongated eyes.
- Naturalistic postures, facial features are used in the paintings of these caves.
- Different guilds of artisans have worked on the paintings of these caves which can be inferred from their typological and stylistic variations.

Subject Matter or Theme of Ajanta Paintings

The themes of Ajanta paintings are the events from the life of the Buddha, the *Jatakas* and the **Avadanas**[8]. Some paintings such as *Simhala Avadana, Mahajanaka Jataka* and *Vidhurpundita Jataka* cover the entire wall of the cave.

8 **Avadanas** A Buddhist religious book which gives the detail about the person's worthy deeds in his previous life.

The *Chaddanta Jataka* has been painted in the Cave No. 10 with many details and events grouped according to their geographical locations. The events that happened in the jungle and the events that happened in the palace are separated by their locations. The painting of *Chaddanta Jataka* in Cave No. 10 are highly influenced from Pali texts, whereas the one painted in Cave No. 17 is very different. In one of the paintings, *Chaddanta* (the other incarnation of Bodhisattva) is shown removing his own tusk and giving it to the hunter, Sonuttar.

Painted ceiling, Cave No. 10, Ajanta

The other themes are the famous paintings of Padmapani and Vajrapani. The images of Padmapani and Vajrapani are very common in Ajanta, but the best preserved paintings are in Cave No. 1. Cave No. 1 also has many interesting paintings of Buddhist themes such as *Mahajanak Jataka, Umang Jataka*, etc. The *Mahajanak Jataka* is painted on the entire wall side and is the biggest narrative painting.

Some figures in Cave No. 2 have themes related to the **Vengi sculptures**[9]. The influence of the **Vidarbha sculptures**[10] is also observed in the delineation of some sculptures.

Technique of Ajanta Paintings

The painting techniques at Ajanta were similar to **European fresco techniques**[11]. The main colours used were red ochre, yellow ochre, brown ochre, lamp black, white and lapis lazuli which were imported from Northern India, Central Asia and Persia. The green colour was made by mixing lapis lazuli with Indian yellow ochre.

In the paintings, all the figures were painted in bright and multi-colours. All the ceilings, walls and plasters are covered with overlapping figures, which were beautifully made by the artists with strong and contrasting colours.

9 **Vengi Sculptures** The sculptures belonging to the Krishna and Godavari delta region of Tamil Nadu. These sculptures belongs to the post-Mauryan period and were highly influenced from Amravati School of Art.

10 **Vidarbha Sculptures** The sculptures belonging to Vidarbha region of Maharashtra. These sculptures of Vidarbha belongs to the post-Mauryan period.

11 **European Fresco Techniques** It is a method of painting with water colour on freshly applied plaster, usually on wall surfaces. The walls are painted with the grinded dry-powder colours which are mixed with pure water. When the colour dries and set with the plaster it becomes the permanent colour of the wall.

EXAM PRACTICE

Multiple Choice Questions

1. How many caves are there at Ajanta?
(a) 54 (b) 29 (c) 32 (d) 40

Ans. (b) 29

2. Which among the following is considered as a place for worship of Buddhist monks?
(a) *Chaitya* (b) *Vihara*
(c) *Stupa* (d) *Jataka*

Ans. (a) *Chaitya*

3. .... are a place of residence of Buddhist monk.
(a) Chaitya (b) Stupa
(c) Tomb (d) Viharas

Ans. (d) Viharas

4. Which *chaitya* caves are elaborately carved and decorated with Buddha and Bodhisattva images?
(a) Cave Nos. 19 and 26
(b) Cave Nos. 2 and11
(c) Cave Nos. 15 and 27
(d) Cave Nos. 8 and 10

Ans. (a) Cave Nos. 19 and 26

5. This cave have been decorated with intricately designed *Mahaparinibbana* images of Buddhist tradition. It is one of the most significant cave of India. Which of the following cave has been discussed above?
(a) Cave No. 12
(b) Cave No. 25
(c) Cave No. 26
(d) Cave No. 6

Ans. (c) Cave No. 26

6. Which of the following is patron of Cave No. 16 and also the Prime Minister of Vakataka king, Harishena?
(a) Varahadeva (b) Upendragupta
(c) Buddhabhadra (d) Mathuradasa

Ans. (a) Varahadeva

7. In one of the events, the Bodhisattva, *Chaddanta*, is shown removing his own tusk and giving it to the hunter.
(a) Sonuttar (b) Mara Vijaya
(c) Harishena (d) Upendragupta

Ans. (a) Sonuttar

8. The famous paintings of Vajrapani and Padmapani are located in which of the following caves of Ajanta?
(a) Cave No. 2 (b) Cave No. 3
(c) Cave No. 4 (d) Cave No. 1

Ans. (d) Cave No. 1

9. Match the following.

List-I	List-II
A. Cave No. 4	1. Upendragupta
B. Cave No. 16	2. Mathuradas
C. Cave No. 17	3. Varahadeva
D. Cave No. 26	4. Buddhabhadra

Codes
(a) A-1, B-2, C-3, D-4
(b) A-2, B-4, C-3, D-1
(c) A-3, B-2, C-1, D-4
(d) A-2, B-3, C-1, D-4

Ans. (d)

10. Match the following.

List-I	List-II
A. *Chaddanta Jataka*	1. Ajanta Cave No. 19
B. *Chaitya Cave*	2. Ajanta Cave No. 2
C. *Vengi Sculptures*	3. Ajanta Cave No. 10
D. Painting of Buddha, Yashodhra and Rahul	4. Ajanta Cave No. 17

Codes
(a) A-3, B-1, C-2, D-4
(b) A-2, B-3, C-4, D-1
(c) A-4, B-2, C-1, D-2
(d) A-3, B-2, C-1, D-4

Ans. (a)

Assertion-Reason

Directions (Q. Nos. 11-12) There are two statements marked as Assertion (A) and Reason (R). Read the statement and answer the questions according to codes given below.

(a) Both A and R are true and R is the correct explanation of A
(b) Both A and R are true, but R is not the correct explanation of A
(c) A is true, but R is false
(d) A is false, but R is true

11. **Assertion** (A) The mural paintings of Ajanta are very renowned and known for their artistic illustration.

Reason (R) The paintings have large typological variate, clear lines, rhythmic movements and merging designs. Paintings are multicolour, with lot of emotions and facial expressions, make them realistic.

Ans. (a) Both A and R are true and R is the correct explanation of A

12. **Assertion** (A) The second phase of paintings can be studied from walls and pillars of Cave Nos. 10 and 9. In this phase, Buddha figures are different from the figures painted in the 5th century CE.

Reason (R) Paintings of Cave Nos. 16 and 17 have precise and elegant quality and they do not carry the heavy volume of the sculptures in the caves.

Ans. (c) A is true, but R is false

Source Based Question

13. Read the source given below and answer the following questions.

The *Chaddanta Jataka* has been painted in the Cave No. 10 with many details and events grouped according to their geographical locations. The events that happened in the jungle and the events that happened in the palace are separated by their locations.

The painting of *Chaddanta Jataka* in Cave No. 10 are highly influenced from Pali texts, whereas the one painted in Cave No. 17 is very different. In one of the paintings, *Chaddanta* (the other incarnation of Bodhisattva) is shown removing his own tusk and giving it to the hunter, Sonuttar.

(i) Which of the following themes are depicted on Ajanta paintings?
(a) *Simhala Avadana*
(b) *Mahajanaka Jataka*
(c) *Vidhurpundita Jataka*
(d) All of the above

Ans. (d) All of the above

(ii) Which of the following images are common in Ajanta caves?
(a) Padmapani
(b) Vajrapani
(c) Vishnu
(d) Both (a) and (b)

Ans. (d) Both (a) and (b)

(iii) Which of the following are the main colours used in the painting of Ajanta Caves?
(a) Yellow ochre
(b) Lamp black
(c) Red ochre
(d) All of the above

Ans. (d) All of the above

(iv) The painting of Cave No. 2 of Ajanta are influenced by
(a) Vengi sculptures
(b) Buddha sculptures
(c) Avadanas
(d) None of the above

Ans. (a) Vengi sculptures

(v) The paintings of Ajanta Caves are preserved by
(a) National Gallery of Modern Arts
(b) Kala Bhavan
(c) Archaeological Survey of India
(d) National Museum

Ans. (c) Archaeological Survey of India

True or False

1. The most famous cave site Ajanta is located in Karnataka state.

Ans. False

2. Cave No. 26 is very big and the entire interior hall is carved with a variety of Buddha images, the biggest one being the *Mahaparinibbana* image.

Ans. True

3. Avadanas refers to Buddhist religious books which give the detail about person's worthy deeds in his previous lives.

Ans. True

Very Short Answer Type Questions

1. Mention the location and period of Ajanta Caves.

Ans. The most famous cave site Ajanta is located in Aurangabad, Maharashtra. Ajanta has twenty-nine caves. It has four *chaitya* caves that belong to the earlier phase i.e. the 2nd and the 1st century BCE (Cave Nos. 10 and 9) and the later phase i.e. the 5th century CE (Cave Nos. 19 and 26).

2. Why are mural paintings of Ajanta renowned? *(NCERT)*

Ans. Ajanta paintings at Aurangabad are extremely renowned for its Buddhist paintings. The paintings have large typological variate, clear lines, rhythmic movements and merging designs. Paintings like Vajrapani, Avalokiteshvara and Apsara are famous. These paintings are multi-coloured with lot of emotions and facial expressions, that make them realistic.

3. Which cave of Ajanta depicts the *Mahaparinibbana* image? Also define *Mahaparinibbana.*

Ans. Cave No. 26 of Ajanta cave depicts the *Mahaparinibbana* image. The rest of the caves are *vihara-chaitya* caves.

Mahaparinibbana refers to the ultimate state of *Nirvana* (everlasting, highest peace and happiness) entered by an awakened being at the moment of physical death.

4. What are the distinctive characteristics of the cave paintings of Cave Nos. 1 and 2 of Ajanta?

Ans. The paintings of Cave Nos. 1 and 2 at Ajanta are very neat and naturalistic that integrates with the sculptures in the caves.

Architectural setting is simple and the arrangement of figures is delineated in the circular form to create three dimensionality and special effects.

5. Write a brief note on the central theme of the Ajanta paintings.

Ans. The central themes of the Ajanta paintings are the events from the life of the Buddha, the *Jatakas* and the *Avadanas*. Some paintings such as *Simhala Avadana*, *Mahajanaka Jataka* and *Vidhurpundita Jataka* cover the entire wall of the cave. The *Chaddanta Jataka* has been painted in the Cave No. 10 with many details and events grouped according to their geographical locations.

Short Answer Type Questions

1. What are the characteristics of Ajanta Caves?

Ans. For the characteristics of Ajanta Caves, refer to text on pg. 55 and 56.

2. What are the features of paintings at Ajanta?

Ans. The features of paintings at Ajanta Caves are

- Outward projections (bulge) are used in the Ajanta paintings of the 5th century CE.
- The lines are very rhythmic and clearly defined. Their body colour gets merged with the outer line and create a volume effect.

- The figures are heavy like the sculptures of Western India.
- In paintings of Cave Nos. 9 and 10, the figures are broad with heavy proportion. They are arranged in the picture space in a linear way. The paintings in these caves shows limited use of colours with sharp lines. Figures in these caves are painted with naturalism and there is no over stylisation.

3. What was the subject matter of paintings at Ajanta Caves?

Ans. For the subject matter of the paintings at Ajanta Caves, refer to text on pg. 58 and 59.

4. What do you like about the paintings of Ajanta caves?

Ans. The paintings of Ajanta are widely regarded as masterpieces of Buddhist religious art. The caves include paintings and rock-cut sculptures that are described as among the finest surviving examples of ancient Indian art, particularly expressive paintings that present feelings through gesture, pose and shape.

The features that I like in the paintings of Ajanta are

- These paintings contained the stories from Jatakas and the life of Buddha.
- Red ochre, yellow ochre, brown ochre, lamp black, white and lapis were the main colours used for the paintings. These were imported from Northern India, Central Asia and Persia. The use of these colours made the paintings beautiful.
- All the walls and plasters are covered by overlapping figures, which were made bright and contrasting colours by the artists and are full of life.
- The colours used in the paintings were made of plants and minerals and are vivid even after 1500 years.

Long Answer Type Question

1. Write an elaborate synopsis of the themes of Ajanta paintings.

Ans. The themes of Ajanta paintings are

- The themes of Ajanta paintings include the events from the life of the Buddha, the *Jatakas* and the Avadanas. Some paintings such as Simhala Avadana, Mahajanaka Jataka and Vidhurpundita Jataka cover the entire wall of the cave.
- Another theme is the Chaddanta *Jataka* which has been painted in the Cave No. 10 with many details and events grouped according to their geographical locations. The painting of Chaddanta *Jataka* in Cave No. 10 are highly influenced from Pali texts, whereas the one painted in Cave No. 17 is very different. In one of the paintings, Chaddanta (the other incarnation of Bodhisattva) is shown removing his own tusk and giving it to the hunter, Sonuttar.
- The other themes are the famous paintings of Padmapani and Vajrapani. The images of Padmapani and Vajrapani are very common in Ajanta, but the best preserved paintings are in Cave No. 1. Cave No. 1 also has many interesting paintings of Buddhist themes such as Mahajanak *Jataka*, Umang *Jataka*, etc. The *Mahajanak Jataka* is painted on the entire wall side and is the biggest narrative painting.
- Some figures in Cave No. 2 have themes related to the Vengi sculptures. The influence of the Vidarbha sculptures is also observed in the delineation of some sculptures.

2. Discuss about the phases of paintings at Ajanta Caves.

Ans. For description of the phases of paintings at Ajanta Caves, refer to text on pg. 57 and 58.

CHAPTER 07

Temple Architecture and Sculpture and the Nagara Style

In this chapter

- *Early Temples*
- *The Nagara or North Indian Style of Temple*
- *Appreciation of Temple Sculptures*

Most of the art and architectural remains that survived from ancient and medieval India are based on religious themes. Religious shrines were also made for many local cults in village and forest areas, but these shrines were destroyed as they were made from wood and clay instead of stones.

Early Temples

The early temples include Brahmanical temples and images of God which started getting constructed simultaneously, while the construction of stupas continued. Each temple had a principal image of a God. The shrines of the temple were of three kinds

(i) *Sandhara* type i.e. without ***pradikshinapatha***[1].

(ii) *Nirandhara* type i.e. with *pradikshinapatha.*

(iii) *Sarvatobhadra* type which can be accessed from all sides.

Some of the important temple sites of early period are Deogarh in Uttar Pradesh and Eran, Nachna-Kuthara and Udaygiri near Vidisha in Madhya Pradesh. These temples are simple structures consisting of a veranda, hall and a shrine at the rear.

1 **Pradikshinapatha** It is a clockwise encircling of sacred entities moving on a circular path around the temple, shrine or stupa.

Basic Form of the Hindu Temple

The basic form of Hindu temple comprises the following

- **Sanctum (*Garbhagriha*, literally means 'womb-house')** It was a small chamber with a single entrance. The size of *garbhagriha* increased gradually to a large chamber. It is made to place the main icon which is itself the focus of much ritual attention.
- **Mandapa** It is the entrance to the temple which may be a veranda or a gallery that include space for a large number of worshippers.
- ***Shikhara*** It is a mountain shaped cone located on the top of the temple. It has curved shape in North India and pyramid shape in South India. *Shikhar* is known as ***vimana*** in South India.
- ***Vahan*** It refers to the mount, seat or vehicle of the temple's main deity along with a standard pillar or *dhvaj* which is placed vertically before the sanctum.

Style of Hindu Temple

In India, major number of Hindu temples were made in three broad styles

(i) **Nagara *Style*** This style was prevalent in North India.

(ii) **Dravida *Style*** This style was prevalent in South India.

(iii) ***Vesara Style*** This was an independent style created through the combination of *Nagara* and *Dravida* style.

As temples grew more complex, more surfaces were created through additive geometry i.e. by adding more and more rythymically projecting, symmetrical walls and niches (places) without ignoring the fundamental plan of shrine.

Sculpture and Ornamentation on Temples

The temples of India are covered with elaborate sculpture and ornament that forms a fundamental part of its conception. The placement of an image in a temple is carefully planned. For example, river goddesses (Ganga and Yamuna) are usually found at the entrance of *garbhagriha* in a *Nagara* style. *Dvarapalas* (doorkeepers) are usually found on the gateways or *gopurams* of *Dravida* temples. *Mithunas* (erotic images), *navgrahas* (the nine auspicious planets) and *yakshas* are also placed at entrances to guard them.

Various forms or aspects of main divinity are to be found on the outer walls of sanctum. The deities of direction i.e. the *ashtadikpalas* are sculpted on the outer wall of *garbhagriha* or on the outer wall of temple. They are sculpted in such a way that they are facing all the eight key directions at a point of time. Subsidiary shrines around the main temple are dedicated to the family or incarnation of the main deity.

Various elements of ornamentation such as *gavaksha* (bulls eye), *vyala* (body of a lion with a head of beast), *kalpa-lata* (hanging plant of paradise), *amalaka* (Indian gooseberry), *kalasha* (pot), etc are used in distinct ways and places in a temple.

Iconography

Iconography refers to study of images of deities that falls within a branch of art history. It consists of identification of images based on certain symbols and mythologies associated with them.

The fundamental myth and meaning of deity may remain the same for centuries, but its specific usage at a spot is based on its local, social, political or geographical context. Every region and period produced its own distinct style of images with its regional variations in iconography.

The Nagara or North Indian Style of Temple

The style of temple architecture that became popular in Northern India is known as *Nagara*. In North India, it is common for an entire temple to be built on a stone platform with steps leading up to it.

It doesn't usually have elaborate boundary walls or gateways unlike the temples of South India. The earliest temple had just one tower of *shikhara*, while the later temples had several towers. The *garbhagriha* is always located directly under the tallest tower.

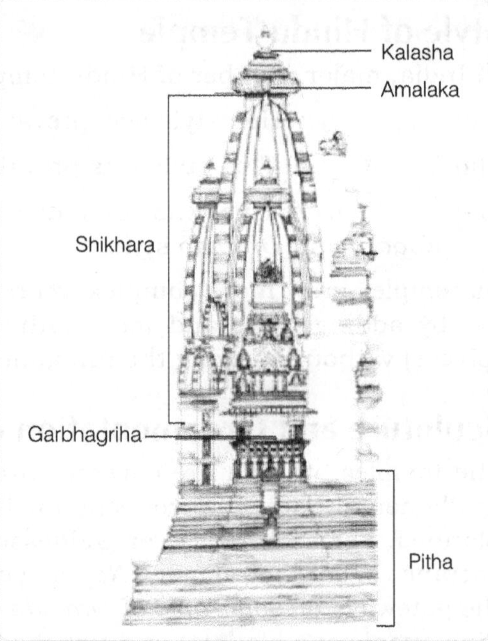

Nagara Temple

Sub-divisions of Nagara Style

There are many sub-divisions of *Nagara* temples depending on the shape of the *shikhara*. There are different names for the various parts of the temple in different parts of India. The sub-divisions are

Latina

It is the first major type of architectural form in the *Nagara* order. It is the simple *shikhara* which is in shape of square at the base and whose walls curve or slop inward to a point on top. It is also called the ***rekha-prasada*** type of *shikhara*.

Phamsana

It is the second major type of architectural form in the Nagara order *Phamsana* buildings tend to be broader and shorter than latina ones. Their roofs are composed of several slabs that gently rise to a single point over the centre of the building, unlike the latina ones which look like sharply rising tall towers. The roofs of *phamsana* do not curve inward, instead they slope upward on a straight incline.

In many North Indian temples, *phamsana* design is used for *mandapas*, while the main *garbhagriha* is placed in a latina building. Later on, the latina building grew complex and instead of appearing like a single tall tower, the temple began to support many smaller towers. These towers were clustered together like rising mountain peaks in which the tallest one was in the centre and was always above the *garbhagriha*.

Valabhi

It is the third main sub-type of *Nagara* building. These are rectangular buildings with a roof that rises into a vaulted chamber. The edge of this vaulted chamber is rounded like the bamboo or wooden wagons (vehicles) that have been pulled by bullocks in ancient times. They are usually called **wagon-vaulted buildings**.

This form of the temple is influenced by ancient building forms that were already in existence before 5th century CE. For example, the ground plan of many of the Buddhist rock-cut *chaitya* caves are shaped as long halls with curved back. The roof of this *chaitya* also looks like a wagon-vaulted roof from inside.

Temples of Nagara Style in Central India

In Central India, the ancient temples of Uttar Pradesh, Madhya Pradesh and Rajasthan has many similarities. The most visible similarity is that they are made of sandstone.

Some of the oldest surviving structural temples from the Gupta period are located in Madhya Pradesh. These are relatively simple looking shrines. Each shrines have four pillars that support a small *mandapa* which looks like a simple square porch-like extension before an equally small room that served as the *garbhagriha*.

Important Temples of Central India

Temples at Udaygiri and Sanchi

The temple of Udaygiri is situated on the border of Vidisha and it is a part of a larger Hindu complex of cave shrines. The temple of Sanchi is situated near the Sanchi Stupa and it is the first temple which have a flat roof. The features similar to that of these temples were being incorporated in the architecture of the temples of different religions i.e. Hindu and Buddhism.

Temple of Deogarh (Lalitpur District, Uttar Pradesh)

It was built in early 16th century CE. This temple was constructed after 100 years of construction of small temples of Sanchi and Udaygiri. The temple of Deogarh is the classic example of late Gupta period. The tall and curvilinear shaped *shikhara* of this temple also belongs to the early 16th century.

The temple is made in the *panchayatana* style of architecture where the main shrine is built on a rectangular base with four smaller subsidiary shrines at the four corners (making it a total number of five shrines). The presence of this curving latina or *rekha-prasada* type of *shikhara* also makes it clear that this is an early example of a classic *Nagara* style of temple.

This temple is West facing, which is less common as most temples are East or North facing. This temple has a grand doorway with standing sculptures of female figures that represent the Ganga on the left side and Yamuna on the right side. Earlier, this temple was mistakenly assumed as Dasavatara temple. It is because this temple depicts Vishnu in various forms and it was assumed that the four subsidiary shrines must also have included Vishnu's *avatars*. The temple has three main reliefs (pictures) of Vishnu on its walls i.e. ***Sheshnarayana***[2] on the South, ***Nara-narayana***[3] on the East and ***Gajendramoksha***[4] on the West.

Dashavtara Vishnu temple, Deogarh, fifth century CE

Sheshashayana Vishnu, Dashavatara temple, Deogarh

Lakshmana Temple of Khajuraho

It is dedicated to **Lord Vishnu** and was built in 954 CE by the Chandela king, **Yashovarman**. This temple is made in Nagara style and it is placed on a high platform accessed by stairs. The plan of this temple is of a *panchayana* type. This temple is constructed on a heavy base. It consists of an *ardhamandapa* (entrance porch or veranda), *mandapa* (porch), the maha *mandapa* (greater hall) and the *garbhagriha* with *vimana*.

The outerwalls of the *garbhagriha* and the outer and inner walls around the circumambulatory path are decorated with sculptures. The *shikhara* on the *garbhagriha* is tall. The interior halls are also greatly decorated. The entrance of the *garbhagriha* is sculpted with massive pillars and **lintels**[5] carved with small images as part of the door decoration.

There are four smaller temples in the corners which include images of Vishnu in three shrines and Surya in one shrine. All the towers or *shikharas* of the temple rise high and are upwarded in a curved pyramidal fashion.

---

2 ***Sheshnarayana*** It is the form of Vishnu where he is shown reclining on the *sheshanaga* called Ananta.

3 ***Nara-Narayan*** It shows the discussion between the human soul and the eternal divine.

4 ***Gajendramoksha*** It is the story of achieving moksha, symbolically communicated by Vishnu's suppression of an *asura* who had taken the form of an elephant.

5 **Lintels** It is a horizontal beam which is used as a finishing piece over a door or window.

These towers highlights the temples vertical height at the end of which a horizontal circular disc called *amalak* is placed at the top with a *kalash* or vase. The top-most elements which are *amalak* and *kalash* are found in all Nagara temples of this period. The temple also has huge balconies and verandahs and this feature made Lakshmana temple different from the temple of Deogarh.

Lakshmana Temple

The Kandariya Mahadeo Temple at Khajuraho

It is the symbol of temple architecture in Central India. This temple was built by **Vidhyadhara**, an eminent ruler of Chandela dynasty. In the architecture and sculpture of this temple, the features of Central Indian temples can be seen which belong to medieval India and appreciated all over the world.

Chausath Yogini Temple

This temple belong to 10th century. This temple is small in size and have squared shrines which were made from roughly hewn (chopped) granite blocks. These shrines were dedicated to devis or goddesses associated with the rise of *Tantric* workship after the 7th century. Several such temples were dedicated to the cult of the *yoginis* across Madhya Pradesh, Odisha and Tamil Nadu. These temples were built between the 7th and 10th centuries, but only few of them have survived.

Sculptures at Khajuraho's Temples

Khajuraho's temples are known for their extensive erotic sculpture. The erotic expression is given equal importance as human expression in the sculptures of Khajuraho. Many Hindu temples include *mithun* (embracing couple) sculptures and these sculptures are considered auspicious. These sculptures are usually placed at the entrance of temple or on an exterior wall. Sometimes, they may also be placed on the walls between the *mandapa* and the main shrine.

Khajuraho sculptures are highly stylised with typical features. These sculptures are in almost full relief. They are made by cutting the surrounding stone with sharp nose, prominent chins, long slanting eyes and eyebrows.

Temples of Nagara Style in Western India

The temples of North-Western part of India including Gujarat, Rajasthan and some parts of Western Madhya Pradesh are made with the stones of different colour and types. Sandstone is commonly used to build these temples, while a grey to black basalt is used in some of the 10th to 20th century temple sculptures. The most prominent material used in these temples is white marble which can be seen in some of the 10th to 12th century Jain temples in Mount Abu and 15th century temples at Ranakpur.

The most important art–historical sites in the Western Indian region is **Samlaji** in Gujarat. It shows how earlier artistic tradition of the region combined with post-Gupta style and gave rise to a distinct style of sculpture.

A large number of sculptures made of grey schist (grey metamorphic rock) have been found in this region which belong to the period between the 6th and 8th centuries CE. The information about the patron of this style is not known and the date of the sculpture is established on the basis of the style.

Sun Temple at Modhera

This temple belong to early 11th century and was built by Raja Bhimdev I of the Solanki dynasty in 1026 CE. In the temple, a massive rectangular stepped tank called the ***surya kund*** can be seen in front of the temple. The construction of sacred places such as temples near the water bodies like tank, river or pond is prevalent from the earliest times. They had become a part of many temples by the early 11th century.

Sun Temple, Modhera, Gujarat

The hundred square meter rectangular pond of Sun temple is the grandest temple tank of India. 108 miniature shrines are carved in between the steps inside the tank. There is a construction of huge ornamental (decorated) *arch-torana* that leads people to ***sabha mandapa***[6].

6 **Sabha mandapa** It is an assembly hall which is open from all sides.

The influence of woodcarving tradition of Gujarat is evident in the beautiful carving and sculpture work of this temple. But the walls of central small shrine did not have carvings and are left plain. As the temple faces the East, every year at the time of **equinoxes**[7], the Sun shines directly into this central shrine.

Temples of Nagara Style in Eastern India

Eastern Indian temples include the temples in the North-East, Bengal and Odisha. Each one of these areas have distinct types of temples. Terracotta was used as the main medium of construction for the temples. It was also used for moulding (shaping) **plaques**[8] which depicted Buddhist and Hindu deities in Bengal until the 7th century.

A large number of sculptures have been found in Assam and Bengal which shows the development of important regional schools in these regions.

Sculptures in Assam

The sculptures in Assam shows the influence of Gupta period. For example, an old 6th century sculpted door frame was found from DaParvatia near Tezpur and another sculptures were found from Rangagora Tea Estate near Tinsukia in Assam.

The post-Gupta period continued in the region till the 10th century. By the 12th to 14th century, a distinct regional style developed in Assam. The style that was discovered by the combination of **Tais**[9] influence and Pala style of Bengal led to the creation of **Ahom** style in and around Guwahati. The famous Kamakhya temple (a *Shakti Peeth*) dedicated to Goddess Kamakhya was built in 17th century in Ahom style.

Sculptures in Bengal

The style of the sculpture during the period between the 9th and 11th century in Bengal (including Bangladesh) and Bihar is known as the **Pala style**. This style was named after the ruling Pala dynasty of that time. On the other hand, the style of the sculptures during mid-11th to mid-13th century in Bengal is named after the Sena kings.

Temples in Bengal

Many of the temples from 9th to 12th century were located at Telkupi in Purulia district of Bengal. These temples were sub-merged when dams were built in the region. Several temples still survives in Purulia district which can be dated to this period.

The architectural styles of these temples showed the influence of *Nagara* sub-types that were prevalent in the rest of North India. The grey-black basalt and chlorite stone pillars and arched corners of these temples are heavily influenced by the earliest Bengal *sultanate* buildings at Gaur and Pandua.

---

7 **Equinoxes** It is the moment in which the Sun is exactly above the equator and day and night are of equal length.

8 **Plaques** A flat piece of stone or metal which contain the names and dates.

9 **Tais** Tais people refers to the population of descendents of speakers of a common Tai language.

The Palas are famous as patrons of many Buddhist monastic sites, but the temples from Bengal region are known to express the local **Vanga style**[10]. The 9th century Siddheshvara Mahadev Temple is a best example of the early Pala style.

This temple is situated in Barakar in Burdwan district. It shows a tall curving *shikhara* crowned by a large *amalaka*. The temple is quite similar to contemporaneous (modern) temples of Odisha. The size of the temple increases with the passing of centuries.

Many local **vernacular building**[11] traditions of Bengal also influenced the style of temples in that region. Most prominent of these styles was the shape of the curving or sloping side of the bamboo roof of a Bengali hut. This feature is known across North India as **Bangla roof**.

Temples in Bengal during Mughal Period

Mughal buildings also adopted the feature of Bangla roof. In the Mughal period and later, numbers of terracotta brick temples were built across Bengal and Bangladesh. These temples were built in a unique style. This style was the combination of local building style of bamboo huts and old architectural style of Pala dynasty. The arches and domes of these temples were inspired from Islamic architecture. These type of temples are found in and around Vishnupur, Bankura, Burdwan and Birbhum and mostly belong to 17th century.

Temples in Odisha

The main architectural features of Odisha temples are classified in three orders, i.e. ***rekhapida, pidhadeul*** and ***khakra***. Most of the main temple sites are located in ancient Kalinga (modern Puri district) including Bhubaneshwar or ancient Tribhuvaneswara, Puri and Konark.

The temples of Odisha constitute a distinct sub-style within the Nagara order. In Odisha, the shikhara are called ***deul***. The *deul* is vertical in shape and sharply curved inwards at its top. *Deuls* are preceeded as usual by *mandapas*. Mandapas are called *jagamohana* in Odisha.

The ground plan of the main temple is almost square in *shape*. Its superstructure is circular in shape to its upper reaches along the crowning *mastaka* (top most portion of the temple). This makes the top of the temple cylindrical in appearance in its length.

The compartments and corners of the temples are generally square. The exterior of the temples is beautifully carved and the interiors are generally plain. The temples of Odisha generally have boundary walls.

10 **Vanga style** This style of architecture was famous in Vanga kingdom. The Vanga kingdom is one of the greatest kingdom of Bengal region.

11 **Vernacular Building** It refers to the building that is built without any professional guidance.

Sun Temple of Konark, Odisha

The ruins of Sun temple is located in Konark on the shores of Bay of Bengal. This temple is built in stone around 1240 CE. The height of the *shikhara* of this temple is 70 m which fell in the 19th century.

The quadilateral shaped boundary of the temple contains the *jagmohana* or the dance-pavillion (*mandapa*) which has survived till now. However, this *mandapa* is no longer accessible. It is believed to be the largest enclosed space in Hindu architecture.

The Sun temple is set on a high base. The whole temple resembles a religious chariot. Its walls are covered with extensive (heavy) and detailed ornamental carving. These include 12 pairs of enormous wheels sculpted with spokes and hubs representing chariot wheels of Sun God.

The fourth wall had the doorway into the temple from where actual rays of Sun would enter the *garbhagriha*. This temple is also known as **Black Pagoda.** According to mythology, Sun rides a chariot driven by seven horses and this is sculpted in the entrance staircase of the temple.

A huge sculpture of *Surya* is carved out of green stone on the Southern wall of this temple. It is believed that there were three such sculpture which were carved out of different stone and were placed on the three temple walls with each facing different directions.

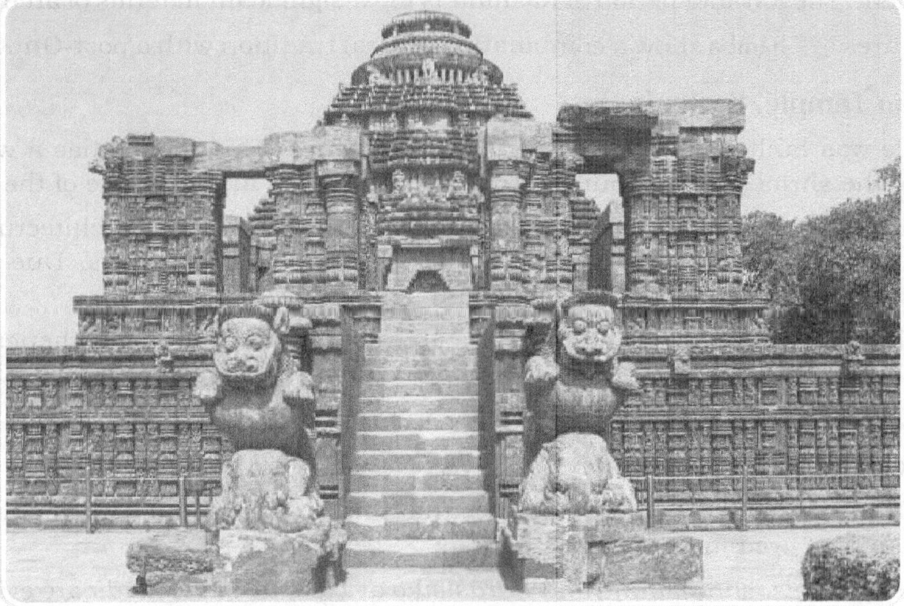

Sun Temple, Konark

Temples of Nagara Style in The Hills

A unique form of architecture developed in the hills of Kumaon, Garhwal (Uttarakhand), Himachal Pradesh and Kashmir.

The hills had their own tradition of wooden buildings with pitched roofs. At several places in the hills, main *garbhagriha* and *shikhara* are made in *rekha-prasada* or latina style. The *mandapa* is of an older form of wooden architecture. Sometimes the temples were made in a pagoda shape (the shape comprises of pyramidial tower or cone shaped structure).

In **Kumaon**, the temples at Jageshwar near Almora and Champavati near Pithorgarh are classic examples of *Nagara* architecture.

In **Kashmir** in the 5th century CE, the art and architectural styles were influenced by **Gandhara**. This was because Kashmir was located near the important sites of Gandhara such as Taxila, Peshawar and North-West frontier.

Architectural styles of Kashmir was also influenced by the Gupta and post-Gupta traditions that were brought from Sarnath, Mathura, Gujarat and Bengal. This influence occured due to travelling of Brahmin *pundits* and Buddhist monks to Kashmir, Garhwal, Kumaon and religious centres in the plains like Banaras, Nalanda Kanchipuram. As a result, both Hindu and Buddhist traditions spreaded to the hilly areas of Indian sub-continent. The Karkota period of Kashmir is most significant in terms of architecture.

The sculptures at **Chamba** show a combination of local tradition with a post-Gupta style.

Pandrethan Temple, Kashmir

This temple was built during the 8th and 9th centuries. This temple has a water tank attached to the shrine and it is built on a base constructed in the middle of the tank.

This is a Hindu temple and possibly dedicated to Lord Shiva. The architecture of this temple is made with old age Kashmiri tradition of wooden buildings. Due to snowy conditions in Kashmir, the roof is peaked and bents outwards.

This temple is fairly decorated and there are no traces of post-Gupta aesthetics of heavy carving. A row of elephants at the base and a decorated doorway are the only design on the shrine.

Laksna-Devi Mandir, Chamba

This temple bears an inscription that states that the temple was built during the reign of Meruvarman who lived in 7th century.

The images of *Mahisasuramardini* and *Narasimha* at *Laksna-Devi Mandir* are evidences of the post-Gupta tradition. Both the images show influence of metal sculpture tradition of Kashmir. The yellow colour of the images is possibly due to an alloy of zinc and copper which were popularly used to make images in Kashmir.

Appreciation of Temple Sculptures

Sculptures of Lakshmi Narayana, Kandariya Mahadev Temple

This sculpture was made by stone and using the technique of carving. In this sculpture, Hindu God Narayana and his wife Lakshmi have been carved on sandstone. They are decorated with different kinds of ornaments around the neck that are hanging on to the chest of both images. The idols are seen wearing loin clothes tied with belts and crowns on their heads.

In the sculpture, Lord Vishnu is closely embracing Lakshmi and placing his left hand on her waist in **'tribhanga'**[12] posture. Lakshmi's right hand can be seen on the shoulder of Vishnu.

In the sculpture, deities are shown in calm mood. Both the figures are sculpted in such a manner that it seems they are expressing their love to each other. This sculpture has been displayed in National Museum of New Delhi, but it belongs to Kandariya Mahadev Temple.

Name	:	Lakshmi Narayana, Kandariya Mahadev Temple
Medium	:	Stone
Period	:	10th century AD (Chandela Period)
Place	:	Khajuraho, Madhya Pradesh
Collection	:	National Museum, New Delhi

12 **Tribhanga** It is a standing body position used in the traditional Indian sculpture art and Indian classical dance forms like the Odissi. In this position, body bends in one direction at the knees, other at hips and shoulders.

Sculpture of Cymbal Player, Sun Temple

The sculptures of Cymbal Players were made by the stone, through the technique of carving. These sculptures are present in the complex of Sun temple. These are best example of rhythm in sculpture. The sculptures are placed outside the main shrine.

The sculptures are partially ruined, but the posture of the statue still looks very attractive and full of life. In the sculpture, the Cymbal Player is shown playing cymbals with both the hands.

The posture of her feet looks as if she is moving with rhythm of the music. Her jewellery was intricately designed and she is wearing head gear, earring, necklaces, bracelet, finger rings and anklets. Her dress is also shown swirling with her body movements and the upper portion of her body is shown naked.

Name : Cymbal Player, Sun Temple
Medium : Stone
Period : 13th century AD (Ganga Dynasty)
Place : Sun Temple, Konark, Odisha
Collection : Archaeological Survey of India

EXAM PRACTICE

Multiple Choice Questions

1. Which shrine of the temple had no *pradikshinapatha*?
   (a) *Sandhara* type (b) *Nirandhara* type
   (c) *Karundhara* type
   (d) *Sarvatobhadra* type

Ans. (a) *Sandhara* type

2. It is the entrance to the temple and may be a portico or colonnaded hall that incorporates space for a large number of devotees. Which form of Hindu temple is referred here?
   (a) *Vahan* (b) *Garbhagriha*
   (c) *Shikhara* (d) *Mandapa*

Ans. (d) *Mandapa*

3. The *vimana* type of *shikhara* was famous in which part of India?
   (a) Northern India (b) Southern India
   (c) Eastern India (d) Western India

Ans. (b) Southern India

4. Which river goddesses were prominent figure in sculptures of entrance of temples in *Nagara* style?
   (a) Yamuna (b) Godavari
   (c) Ganga (d) Both (a) and (c)

Ans. (d) Both (a) and (c)

5. The type of temple architecture that was prominent in North India was called as
   (a) *Dravida* style (b) *Nagara* style
   (c) Sub-Northern style (d) *Vesara* style

Ans. (b) *Nagara* style

6. There roofs are composed of several slabs that gently rise to a single point over the centre of the building. Which sub-type of architectural form has been described here?
   (a) *Phamsana* (b) *Vimana*
   (c) *Latina* (d) *Valabhi*

Ans. (a) *Phamsana*

7. The temples of Udaygiri and Sanchi belonged to which geographical section of *Nagara* style?
   (a) Western India
   (b) The hilly regions
   (c) Central India
   (d) Eastern regions

Ans. (c) Central India

8. Which of the following temple was made in *panchayatana* style of architecture?
   (a) Kandariya Mahadev temple
   (b) Sun temple
   (c) Udaygiri temple
   (d) Deogarh temple

Ans. (d) Deogarh temple

9. To which Hindu deity, the Lakshmana temple of Khajuraho is dedicated?
   (a) Lord Shiva (b) Lord Narsimha
   (c) Lord Bramha (d) Lord Vishnu

Ans. (d) Lord Vishnu

10. The Sun temple of Modhera was built by which royal dynasty?
    (a) Solanki (b) Rashtrakutas
    (c) Pala (d) Pratiharas

Ans. (a) Solanki

11. In which temple of Nagara style, the Sun can be clearly seen at the time of equinox?
    (a) Sun temple
    (b) Kandariya Mahadev temple
    (c) Udaygiri temple
    (d) Deogarh temple

Ans. (a) Sun temple

12. In which region of *Nagara* style, the terracotta is used as the main medium of construction and also for moulding plaques?
    (a) Northern region (b) Central region
    (c) Eastern region (d) South-East region

Ans. (c) Eastern region

13. The famous Kamakhya temple which is dedicated to Goddess Kamakhya was built in which style?
(a) *Vesara* style
(b) Gupta style
(c) Pala style
(d) Ahom style

Ans. (d) Ahom style

14. The sculpture of Lakshmi *Narayana* belonged to which of the following temple of *Nagara* style?
(a) Kandariya Mahadev temple
(b) Sun temple
(c) Kamakhya temple
(d) Dilwara temple

Ans. (a) Kandariya Mahadev temple

15. Match the following.

List I	List II
A. *Garbhagriha*	1. Temple entrance
B. *Mandapa*	2. Vehicle of deity
C. *Shikhara*	3. Womb house
D. *Vahan*	4. Cone shaped peak

Codes
(a) A-1, B-3, C-4, D-2
(b) A-4, B-1, C-2, D-3
(c) A-3, B-4, C-2, D-1
(d) A-3, B-1, C-4, D-2

Ans. (d)

16. Match the following.

List I	List II
A. Sun temple	1. Assam
B. Kandariya Mahadev temple	2. Bengal
C. Kamakhya temple	3. Odisha
D. Siddheshvara Mahadev temple	4. Khajuraho

Codes
(a) A-4, B-3, C-2, D-1
(b) A-3, B-4, C-1, D-2
(c) A-1, B-3, C-4, D-2
(d) A-2, B-4, C-3, A-1

Ans. (b)

Assertion-Reason

Directions (Q. Nos. 17-21) In the following questions, there are two statements marked as Assertion (A) and Reason (R). Read the statements and answer the questions according to the codes given below.

(a) Both A and R are true and R is the correct explanation of A
(b) Both A and R are true, but R is not the correct explanation of A
(c) A is true, but R is false
(d) A is false, but R is true

17. **Assertion** (A) The art pieces in the domestic dwelling of the people perished.
Reason (R) The domestic dwellings and the art pieces in them were made from material like wood and clay which became ruined over the time.

Ans. (a) Both A and R are true and R is the correct explanation of A

18. **Assertion** (A) River Goddesses like Ganga and Yamuna played vital role in temple architecture of *Nagara* style.
Reason (R) The temples of *Nagara* style were located on the bank of Ganga and Yamuna.

Ans. (c) A is true, but R is false

19. **Assertion** (A) Khajuraho temple are known for their extensive erotic sculpture.
Reason (R) The sculpture of Lakshmi Narayana shows extensive erotic moments and it was the best artpiece of Dravida style of temple sculpture.

Ans. (c) A is true, but R is false

20. **Assertion** (A) The Siddheshvara Mahadev temple is the best example of temples of early Solanki style.
Reason (R) The temple shows a tall curving *shikhara* crowned by large *amalaka*.

Ans. (d) A is false, but R is true

21. Assertion (A) The Karkota period of Kashmir is most significant in the terms of architecture.

Reason (R) The main *garbhagriha* or *shikhara* of temples of the hilly regions were made in *rekha-prasada* style.

Ans. (b) Both A and R are true, but R is not the correct explanation of A

Source Based Question

22. Read the source given below and answer the following questions.

In this sculpture, Lord Narayana is shown with four arms. He can be seen holding Shankha on one hand, Gada on the other hand. His third arm is shown on the shoulder of his wife Lakshmi and his fourth arm is broken in the sculpture. Narayana is shown wearing a jewelled crown with another dress on the body. In the sculpture both Lakshmi and Narayana are sitting in a Lalitasana on a slab of a huge stone. Brahma as well as Lord Shiva can also be seen on the right and left portion of this sculpture. In the sculpture male attendant can also be seen beside the figures of both the deities. Female attendants can also be seen behind the deities and devotees are sculpted on the front side.

(i) The above source is related to which sculpture?

(a) Cymbal Player
(b) Ravana shaking mount Kailasha
(c) Lakshmi Narayana
(d) Mother and Child

Ans. (c) Lakshmi Narayana

(ii) The sculpture belonged to which of the following temple?

(a) Temples of Elephanta
(b) Kandariya Mahadev temple
(c) Sun temple
(d) Ellora temples

Ans. (b) Kandariya Mahadev temple

(iii) The sculpture is made in which style of temple sculpture ?

(a) *Dravida* style (b) *Vesara* style
(c) *Nagara* style (d) Jain style

Ans. (c) *Nagara* style

(iv) The sculpture is made in which period?

(a) 6th century AD (b) 7th century AD
(c) 10th century AD
(d) 12th century AD

Ans. (c) 10th century AD

(v) In which of the following museum, the sculpture has been displayed?

(a) National Museum, New Delhi
(b) Safar Jung Museum, Hyderabad
(c) Indian Museum, Kolkata
(d) National Gallery of Art, New Delhi

Ans. (a) National Museum, New Delhi

True or False

1. The independent style created through the selective mixing of *Nagara* and *Dravida* style was called *Vesara* style.

Ans. True

2. The famous temples of Udaygiri and Sanchi perished over the time.

Ans. False

3. The Lakshmana temple of Khajuraho is dedicated to Lord Vishnu and was built in 954 CE by the Solanki king.

Ans. False

4. The temples of Chausath Yogini were built in Central India.

Ans. True

5. The Sun temple at Modhera dates back to early 12th century and was built by Raja Bhimdev I of Solanki dynasty in 1126 CE.

Ans. False

6. The Sun temple of Odisha contains 12 pairs of enormous wheels sculpted with spokes.

Ans. True

7. The sculpture of Cymbal Player belonged to Konark temple, Odisha.

Ans. True

Very Short Answer Type Questions

1. What are the different kinds of shrine in early temple architecture?

Ans. The shrines of the early temples were of three kinds

(i) **Sandhara Type** In this type, shrines are without *pradikshinapatha.*

(ii) ***Nirandhara* Type** In this type, shrines are with *pradikshinapatha.*

(iii) ***Sarvatobhadra* Type** In this type, shrines can be accessed from all sides.

2. With reference to Hindu temple architecture, explain the architectural style of *Garbhagriha* and *Mandapa.*

Ans. *Garbhagriha* literally means womb-house. It has a small chamber with a single entrance. It is generally made to place the main icon which is itself the focus of much ritual attention.

Mandapa is the entrance to the temple which may be a verandah or a gallery that include space for a large number of devotees.

3. What are the three broad styles in which the Hindu temples were built?

Ans. In India, major number of Hindu temples were made in three broad styles which are

(i) ***Nagara* Style** This style of temple architecture was prominent in North India.

(ii) ***Dravida* Style** This style of temple architecture was prominent in South India.

(iii) ***Vesara* Style** This independent style was created through the combination of *Nagara* and *Dravida* style.

4. Appreciate the beauty and visual aesthetics of *Nagara* style of temple architecture in brief.

Ans. In *Nagara* style of temple architecture, it is common for an entire temple to be built on a stone platform with steps leading up to it. This style doesn't usually have elaborate boundary walls or gateways. The earliest temples of *Nagara* style had only one *shikhara,* while the later temple had several. The *garbhagriha* is always located directly under tallest tower.

5. The temples of Deogarh are the classic example of later Gupta period. Justify this statement by giving a proper explanation in brief.

Ans. The temples of Deogarh is the classic example of later Gupta period. The temple is made in *panchayatana* style of architecture where the main shrine is built on a rectangular plinth with four smaller subsidiary shrines at the four corners.

6. Illustrate the architectural design of Lakshmana temple of Khajuraho.

Ans. The Lakshmana temple of Khajuraho is made in *Nagara* style and it is placed on a high platform accessed by stairs. The plan of this temple is of a *panchayana* type. This temple is constructed on a heavy base. It consists of an *ardhamandapa* (entrance porch or veranda), *mandapa* (porch), the maha *mandapa* (greater hall) and the *garbhagriha* with *vimana.*

7. Write distinctive features of Khajuraho's temple.

Ans. The distinctive features of Khajuraho's temples are their extensive erotic sculptures. Many Hindu temples of Khajuraho include *mithun* (embracing couple) sculptures and these sculptures are considered auspicious. These sculptures are usually placed at the entrance of temple or on an exterior wall.

8. Write the salient features of *Nagara* temples of Western India.

Ans. The salient features of *Nagara* temples of Western India are

- The temples of Western India were made with sandstone and grey to black basalt was used to make sculptures of Western Indian temple.
- The most attractive and famous material used in these temples was white marbles which can be seen in Jain temples of Mount Abu.

9. Appreciate the grandeur of *surya kund* of Sun temple at Modhera.

Ans. In the Sun temple, a massive rectangular stepped tank called the *surya kund* can be seen. The kund is made in hundred square meter rectangular pond and it is considered as grandest temple tank of India. 108 miniature shrines are carved between the steps inside the tank.

10. State the architectural features of Sun temple of Odisha.

Ans. The architectural features of Sun temple of Odisha are

- The Sun temple of Odisha is set on a high base. Its walls are covered with extensive and detailed ornamented carving.
- 12 pairs of enormous wheels are sculpted at the temple with spokes and hubs representing Chariot Wheel of Sun God.

11. Appreciate the visual aesthetics and beauty of the sculpture of Cymbal Player included in your course of study. Also mention its medium and place of origin.

Ans. The sculpture of Cymbal Players are the best example of rhythm in Indian sculpture. The sculptures are placed outside the main shrine. In the sculpture, the Cymbal Player can be seen playing the instrument with both hands. The posture of her feet looks as she is moving with rhythm of the music. The Cymbal Player is shown highly ornamented.

Short Answer Type Questions

1. The architectural style of Hindu temple comprises of four basic form of temple architecture. With context to this statement, explain the four basis form of Hindu temple.

Ans. For the basic form of Hindu temple, refer to text on pg. 65.

2. Write a short note on the Lakshmana temple of Khajuraho.

Ans. For description of Lakshmana temple of Khajuraho, refer to text on pg. 68 and 69.

3. The temples of Khajuraho are famous for their exceptional sculptures. Briefly evaluate the distinctive features of such sculptures.

Ans. Khajuraho's temples are known for their extensive erotic sculpture. The erotic expression is given equal importance as human experience in the sculptures of Khajuraho.

The features of these sculptures are

- Many Hindu temples include *mithun* (embracing couple) sculptures and these sculptures are considered auspicious. Usually, these sculptures are placed at the entrance of temple or on an exterior wall. Sometimes, they may also be placed on the walls between the *mandapa* and the main shrine.
- Khajuraho sculptures are highly stylised with typical features. These sculptures are made in full relief. They are made by cutting the surrounding stone with sharp nose prominent chins, long slanting eyes and eyebrows.

4. Write a brief synopsis on the architectural style of the temples of Bengal.

Ans. For the architectural styles of temples of Bengal, refer to text on pg. 71 and 72.

5. Briefly state the architectural style of Odisha with reference to the Sun temple.

Ans. For the architectural style of Odisha temples, refer to text on pg. 73.

6. What led to the spread of Hindu as well as Buddhist religion to the hilly areas of Kashmir, Kumaon, Garhwal and Himachal Pradesh? What were the consequences of such tradition expansion?

Ans. The spread of Buddhist and Hindu tradition occured due to travelling of Brahmin *pundits* and Buddhist monks to Kashmir, Garhwal, Kumaon and religious centres in the plains like Banaras, Nalanda and even as far South as Kanchipuram.

The consequence of such tradition expansion was that large number of Hindu temples and Buddhist monastries were constructed in Kashmir. For example, Pandrethan temple in Kashmir.

This temple was built during the 8th and 9th centuries. This temple has a water tank attached to the shrine and it is built on a base constructed in the middle of the tank. This is a Hindu temple and possibly dedicated to Lord Shiva. The architecture of this temple is made with old age Kashmiri tradition of wooden buildings. This temple is fairly decorated and there are no traces of post-Gupta aesthetics of heavy carving. A row of elephants at the base and a decorated doorway are the only design on the shrine.

7. Evaluate the architectural style of
(a) Pandrethan temple
(b) Laksna-Devi Mandir

Ans. (a) For architectural style of Pandrethan Temple, Kashmir, refer to text on pg. 74.
(b) For architectural style of Laksna-Devi Mandir, Chamba, refer to text on pg. 74.

Long Answer Type Questions

1. Write a detailed essay on iconography, ornamentation and sculptures of Indian temple.

Ans. For the iconography, ornamentation and sculptures of Indian temples, refer text on pg. no. 65 and 66.

2. In how many sub-divisions Nagara style of temple architecture is divided on the basis of shape of *shikhara*? Describe each category in a descriptive matter.

Ans. *Nagara* style of temple architecture has been divided into three sub-divisions on the basis of shape of *shikharas*. For description of these sub-divisions, refer text on pg. no. 66 and 67.

3. Appreciate the beauty and visual aesthetics of Lakshmi Narayana sculpture of Kandariya Mahadev temple. Also briefly evaluate the medium and the period of sculpture along with the distinct characteristics of the temple.

Ans. For appreciation of Lakshmi Narayana sculpture, refer to text on pg. 75.

4. "These are the best example of rythym in sculpture and some Cymbal Players are shown playing Cymbals with both the hands."
(a) Identify the sculpture.
(b) Define the method and material of the sculpture.
(c) Appreciate its visual aesthetics and beauty of the above mentioned sculpture.

Ans. (a) The sculpture is of Cymbal Player.
(b) This sculpture was made by using the technique of carving. Stone is used in this sculpture as a primary material.
(c) For appreciation of the sculpture of Cymbal Player, refer to text on pg. no. 76.

CHAPTER 08

The Dravida or South Indian Temple Style and Vesara Style

In this chapter

- Dravida or South Indian Temple Style
- Vesara Style of Temple

The *Dravida* style of temple architecture of South India was developed by the Pallavas who reigned in parts of Karnataka, Andhra Pradesh and Northern Tamil Nadu until the 9th century.

The *Vesara* style is a combination of *Nagara* and *Dravida* style of temple architecture. The term *Vesara* is believed to have been derived from the Sanskrit word *Vishra* meaning an area to take a long walk. Many historians agree that the *Vesara* style originated in the region which is today known as Karnataka.

Dravida or South Indian Temple Style

The *Dravida* style of temple architecture emerged in the Southern part of Indian sub-continent. The features of the temples of *Dravida* style are

- The *Dravida* or South Indian temples are surrounded within a compound wall. The front wall of such temples has an entrance gateway in its centre, which is known as **gopuram**.
- The shape of the main temple tower is known as *vimana* in Tamil Nadu. It is like a stepped pyramid that rises up geometrically as compared to the curving *shikhara* of *Nagara* style.

- In *Dravida* style, the word *'shikhara'* is used only for the crowning head element at the top of the temple which is usually shaped like a small *stupika* (octagonal roof). This is similar to *amalaka* and *kalasha* of North Indian temples. The style of multiple *shikharas* rising together as a cluster in North Indian temples was not popular in Dravida style.
- In this style, at the entrance to the temple's *garbhagriha*, the sculptures of fierce *dvarpalas* guarding the temple can be seen.
- In this style, it is common to have a large water reservoir or a temple tank enclosed within the complex of the temple.
- In this style, subsidiary shrines are either constructed within the main temple tower or located as separate small shrine beside the main temple.
- In this style, the main temple in which the *garbhagriha* is situated, has one of the most smallest tower. This is because, it is usually the oldest part of the temple.

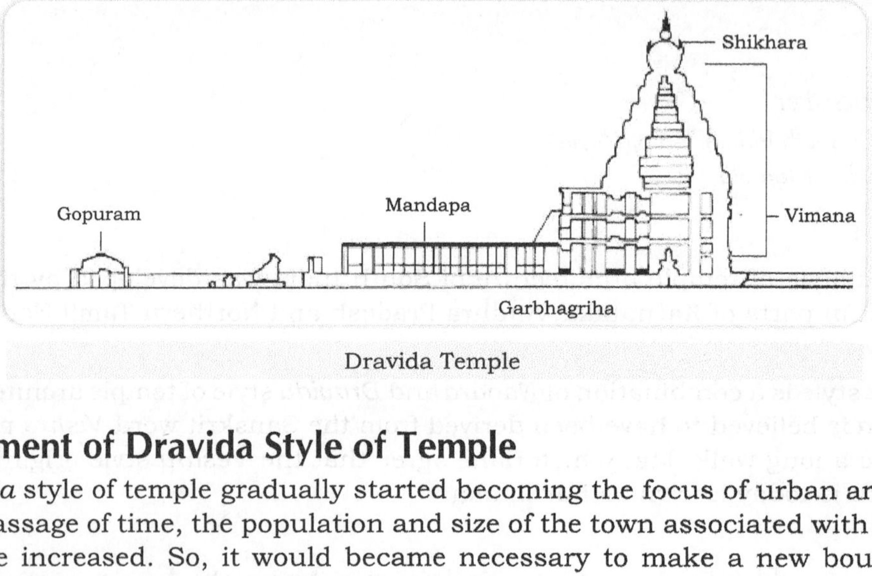

Dravida Temple

Development of Dravida Style of Temple

The *Dravida* style of temple gradually started becoming the focus of urban architecture. With the passage of time, the population and size of the town associated with the temple would have increased. So, it would became necessary to make a new boundary wall around the temple.

The new boundary wall was taller than the last one and its *gopurams* were higher. This development can be seen in **Srirangam temple** of Tiruchirapally. This temple has more than seven concentric (parallel) rectangular enclosure walls, each with *gopurams*. The outerwall is the newest, while the tower in the centre including the *garbhagriha* is the oldest.

During the 8th to 12th century, in the temple towns of Kanchipuram, Thanjavur (Tanjore), Madurai and Kumbkakonam of Tamil Nadu, the role of the temple was not only limited to religious matters. The temples in these towns became rich administrative centres and controlled vast areas of land.

Sub-divisions of Dravida Style

The *Dravida* styles are sub-divided on the basis of different shapes of *shikhara.* These are basically of five different shapes

(i) Square *shikhara* usually called *kuta* or *caturasra.*

(ii) Rectangular or *shala* or *ayatasra shikhara.*

(iii) Elliptical (egg shaped) *shikhara* usually called *gaja-prishta* (elephant backed or *vrittayata*). This shape has been derived from wagon-vaulted shapes of ***apsidal chaityas.***[1] These chaityas have a horse-shoe or 'U' shaped entrance which is usually called a *nasi.*

(iv) Circular or *vritta shikhara.*

(v) Octagonal or *ashtasra shikhara.*

The plan of the temple and the shape of the *vimana* were determined by the **iconographic**[2] nature of sacred deity, so it was appropriate to build a specific type of temple for specific type of icons. Several different shapes may be combined in specific periods and places to create a unique style.

South Indian Dynasty and its Contribution in Dravida Style

The Pallavas were one of the ancient South Indian dynasties that were active in the Andhra region from 2nd century CE onwards and later migrated to settle in Tamil Nadu.

The inscriptions of Pallavas from the 6th to 8th century shows their descriptive history. The powerful kings of Pallava dynasty played a great role in expansion of its empire. The boundaries of Pallava kingdom stretched to Odisha and their links with South-East Asia were also strong.

Pallavas were mostly Shaivite, but several Vaishnava shrines can also be seen of their reign. Pallavas were also highly influenced by the long Buddhist history of the Deccan.

The early buildings of Pallavas were generally assumed as rock-cut, while the later ones were structural. The early rock-cut buildings are generally attributed to the reign of Mahendravarman I, a contemporary of Chalukya king Pulakesin II of Karnataka.

Narsimhavarman I who is also known as ***Mamalla***, acceded the Pallava throne under 640 CE. He is famous for the expansion of the empire by revenging his father's defeat from Pulakesin II. *Mamalla* was also responsible for inaugurating most of the building works at Mahabalipuram which is renamed after him as **Mamallapuram**.

Mahabalipuram (Mamallapuram) is an important coastal town from the period of the Pallavas. It has several important rock-cut and free-standing structural temples mostly made in the 7th and 8th centuries.

1 **Apsidal *Chaitya*** A *chaitya* with a rounded arch at the end of the entrance and a high roof with a rounded profile.

2 **Iconographic** It refers to the science of identification, description, classification and interpretation of symbols, themes and subject matter in the visual art.

Examples of Temples of Dravida Style

The Shore Temple of Mahabalipuram

This temple was probably built in the reign of Narsimhavarman II who is also known as **Rajasimha**. He ruled from 700 to 728 CE. The temple faces the ocean from the East side.

The temple has three shrines. Among the three shrines, two were dedicated to Lord Shiva, one is facing East and the other is facing West. The third shrine is located at the centre of the temple and is dedicated to Vishnu who is shown as ***Anantashayana***[3].

The feature of three shrines is unusual, because temples generally have a single main shrine and not three areas of worship. This suggested that the three shrines were not constructed together and different shrines may have been constructed at different times under different patrons.

In the compound of the temple, there is an evidence of a water tank, an early example of a *gopuram* and several other images. The sculptures of the bull, **Nandi** (Shiva's vehicle or mount) are made on the temple walls. However, these sculptures along with carvings on the temple's lower walls are disfigured due to erosion by salt-water mixed air over the centuries.

Shore Temple, Mahabalipuram

3 ***Anantashayana*** *Anantashayi* Vishnu or also known as *Anantashayana* Vishnu means lord Narayana is sleeping on the serpent named Anant.

Shiva Temple of Thanjavur

The magnificient Shiva temple of Thanjavur also called the Rajarajeswara or Brahadeeshwarar is one of the largest and tallest Indian temple.

The temple was bigger in scale than anything and was built by the predecessors of Chola (Pallavas Chalukyas and Pandavas). It was completed in 1009 CE by Rajaraja Chola.

The pyramidal multi-storeyed *vimana* of this temple had a massive height of 70 metre (approx. 230 ft) and it is topped by a monolithic (formed from a single large block of stone) *shikhara* which is an octagonal dome shaped *stupika.*

In the temple, two large *gopurams* (gateway towers) can be seen. These include elaborate sculptural designs which was made along with the temple.

Huge Nandi figures are decorated at the corners of the *shikhara* and the *kalasha* on the top is about 3 metres and 8 centimetres in height.

The *vimana* of the temple is decorated with hundreds of stucco (cemented) figures. It is also possible that some of these figures might have been added during the Maratha period and did not always belong to the Chola period.

The main deity of the temple is Lord Shiva, who is shown as a huge ***lingam***[4] set in a two-storeyed sanctum (*garbhagriha*). The walls surrounding the *garbhagriha* have extended mythological narratives which are depicted through painted murals and sculptures.

Shiva Temple of Thanjavur

4 ***Lingam*** It is also known as *linga*. It is a religious object that symbolises the God Shiva and is worshipped as an emblem of power.

Appreciation of Dravida Temple Sculptures

Sculpture of Descent of Ganga, Mamallapuram, Tamil Nadu

Name : Descent of Ganga
Period : 7th century AD (Pallava Period)
Collection : Archaeological Survey of India.
Medium : Granite Rock
Place : Mahabalipuram (Mamallapuram) Tamil Nadu

Appreciation This is one of the largest and oldest sculptural of the world. This sculpture was made by granite rock, by using method of ***relief***[5] sculpture. It is nearly thirty metres long and fifteen metres high. There is a natural space in the rock which has been cleverly used by its sculptors as a channel for water to flow down. This water collects in a massive tank in front of the sculpted wall.

A temple has been depicted in the sculpture. Ascetics and worshippers are shown sitting in the temple. Above the temple, there is a bearded figure standing in penance on one leg and arms raised above his head. He has been identified by some as Bhagirath and by others as Arjuna. Arjuna's *penance* was to obtain the *pashupata* weapon from Shiva, whereas Bhagirath prayed to have Ganga brought to Earth.

Besides this, a figure of Shiva is shown standing whose one hand is shown as he is giving a boon or in the position of varada mudra. The small *gana* or dwarf who stands below this may be a personification of the powerful *pashupata* weapon.

All the figures are shown with a slender and linear quality in an animated state of movement. Apart from humans and flying celestials, several naturalistically birds and animals are also carved.

In the sculpture, figures of well-modelled and huge elephants are shown. A pair of deer is shown under the shrine. A figure of cat has been shown standing on his one leg, with his hands raised, imitating Bhagirath or Arjuna.

The cat represents as a symbol of Arjuna or Bhagiratha. Bhagiratha or Arjuna is surrounded by rats, which are unable to disturb him from his penance. Probably, this is a

5 ***Relief*** It is a sculptural technique of which the sculpted elements remain attached to a solid background of the same material.

metaphor used by the artist to show the strength of Arjuna's or Bhagirath's penance, who is standing still, undisturbed by his surroundings.

Scholars have interpreted the story depicted on this sculptural panel differently. Some scholars believe that it is the story of the descent of the Ganga from heaven to Earth.

On the other hand, others scholars believe that the main story is of Kiratarjuniya or Arjuna's penance, a poetic work by Bharvi which is known to have been popular in the Pallava court.

Some other scholars have interpreted the reason behind the sculptures to show that the whole sculpture was created to be a *prashasti,* or something to praise the Pallava king.

Sculpture of Trimurti

Name	:	Trimurti
Medium	:	Stone
Period	:	9th century AD
Place	:	Elephanta, Maharashtra
Collection	:	Archaeological Survey of India

This sculpture was made by using the rock-cut technique. This stone sculpture depicts the three headed images of Shiva. This is also called **Sadashiva** (God Mahadeva), **Maheshwara** (the Almighty) or **Maheshmurti** (Lord Shiva). It is placed at the back of the Elephanta cave facing in North-South direction. It is 20ft high.

The right side image of the Shiva has a young looking face with sensuous lips, that depicts youthfulness and vigor. It depicts feminine form of Shiva (Uma). There is rosebud like object in his hand which signifies creativity and life.

The face on the left side is of a bearded young man. It signifies the Rudra-Shiva or *Bhairav.* This face represents the destroyer.

The central face in the sculpture represents the supreme image of Shiva, the preserver.

All the three figures have same dimension which gives it a perfect balance and graceful symmetry. The composition of the sculpture is unique. The sculptor is successfull in depicting three expressions of Shiva i.e. his sensitive side, his furious side and his delightfulness in a single sculpture.

Vesara Style of Temple

After mid-7th century CE, a hybridised (mix) style become popular which is known as *Vesara* in some ancient texts. Many different styles of temple architecture that were influenced by both North and South Indian temples, were used in regions like Karnataka. Some scholars consider the buildings in this region as being distinctly either *Nagara* or

Dravida, while some scholars termed this distinct style as *Vesara.* This style was majorly prevalent in the **Deccan**.

Chalukyas and Rashtrakutas in the Deccan

Most of the part of Deccan was ruled by the early Western Chalukyas till the mid-8th century when they were dethroned by Rashtrakutas. Early Chalukyan rulers focused on construction of rock-cut temples, while the Rashtrakutas focused on structural temples.

The sculptures of the Rashtrakuta period at Ellora are very beautiful. The figures of the sculptures were made in large size. The figures were carved beautifully and showcases the grandeur and skills of the craftsmen. The greatest achievement of Rashtrakutas in architecture is the Kailashnath temple at Ellora which is a culmination of a long tradition in rock-cut architecture in India. The Rashtrakuta king 'Krishna I' built the Kailashnath temple.

Kailashnath Temple

It is a complete *Dravida* building with Nandi shrine. The temple is wholly dedicated to Lord Shiva. It has a *gopuram*-like gateway which is surrounded by cloisters (walkways). The temple has subsidiary shrines, staircases and an imposing tower (*vimana*) with a height of 30 m. All these architectural features are carved out of rock. The Kailashnath temple was carved out from the one portion of monolithic hill.

Kailashnath Temple

Hoysalas in the Deccan

The Hoysalas belong to Karnataka who grew to prominence in South India and became the most important patrons centred at Mysore.

The remains of around 100 Hoysala temples have been found at Southern Deccan, but only three temples had significant importance. These are temples at Belur, Halebid and Somnathpuram. The most important characteristics of these temples were that they grow extremely complex with so many pointed angles emerging from the straight forward square temple.

The plan of these temples looks like a star and is thus known as **stellate-plan**[6]. These three temples were made out of soapstone which is a relatively soft stone and due to this, artists were able to carve their sculptures intricately. This can be seen particularly in the jewellery of the Gods sculpted on temple walls.

Hoysala temples are sometimes called hybrid as their unique style was the combination of *Dravida* and *Nagara* styles. They are easily distinguishable from other medieval temples by their highly original star-like ground plans and a large number of decorative carvings.

Hoysaleshvara Temple at Halebid

The Hoysaleshvara temple (Lord of the Hoysalas) at Halebid in Karnataka was built by the Hoysala king in 1150 CE. It was built by using dark **schist**[7] stone.

Halebid Temple

The Halebid temple is dedicated to Lord Shiva as Nataraja. It has a double building with a large hall for the *mandapa* to facilitate music and dance. A nandi pavillion (canopy) is located in the front of each building.

The tower of the temple fell long ago and the temple's appearance can only be ascertained from their detailed remains flanking (bordering) the entrances.

The central square shape cuttings that are made from angular projections, creates the star effect in the monument. The walls are decorated greatly with the carvings of animal and deities. The carvings are made intricately, for example, the bottom most frieze (mural) features the continuous procession of hundred of elephants with their **mahaouts**[8]. Each elephant is carved in different pose.

Nataraja, Halebid

6 **Stellate-plan** The architectural style in which the shrines are designed in the form of a star.

7 **Schist** A type of rock formed by layers of different minerals, that breaks naturally into thin flat pieces.

8 **Mahaout** A person who works with, rides and tends an elephant.

Important Sites of Vesara Style Temples

In the Southern part of the Deccan i.e. in the region of Karnataka, some of the most experimental (unique) hybrid styles of *Vesara* architecture are found.

Site of Aihole

Ravan Pahadi cave at Aihole is an example of early rock-cut cave by Chalukyas. It is known for its distinctive sculptural style. One of the most important sculptures at this site is of Nataraja. This sculpture is surrounded by huge depiction of *saptamatrikas* (group of seven mother Goddesses).

Among the seven Goddesses, three are located at Shiva's left and four to his right. The figures in the sculpture has slim bodies, long oval faces decorated with extremely tall cylindrical crowns.

The figures are wearing short *dhotis* marked by fine incised striations (patterns) which indicates the pleating of the *dhotis*. The sculptures are distinctively different from contemporary (modern) Western Deccan or Vakataka styles seen at places such as Paunar and Ramtek in Maharashtra.

The architectural style of **Durga temple** of Aihole is unique. The temple is made in the earlier style of an apsidal shrine which is similar to the architectural style of Buddhist *chaitya* halls. The temple is surrounded by a veranda and has a *shikhara* which is similar to the *shikharas* of *Nagara* temples.

The **Lad Khan temple** of Aihole in Karnataka was inspired by wooden roofed-temples of the hills, but it is constructed out of stone.

Durga Temple Aihole

Site of Pattadakal

The most elaborate of all Chalukyan temples at Pattadakal is **Virupaksha temple**. The hybridisation (mixing) of several architectural styles was the hallmark of Chalukyan buildings. Virupaksha temple was made in the reign of Vikramaditya II (733-44 CE) by his chief queen Loka Mahadevi.

Another important temple from this site is **Papnath temple**, which is dedicated to Lord Shiva. This temple is one of the best example of early *Dravida* tradition. Other Eastern Chalukyan temples such as temple of Mahakuta (which is located at five kilometers from Badami) and Swarg Bramha temple of Alampur, shows the greater combination of Northern style of architecture of Odisha and Rajasthan.

Virupaksha temple,Pattadakal

Vijayanagara and its Architectural Style

The state of Vijayanagara (city of victory) was founded in 1336 CE. The state attracted a number of international travellers such as the Italian Nicolo di Conti, the Portuguese Domingo Paes, Fernao Nuniz, Duarte Barbosa and the Afghan Abd al-Razzaq. They have left vivid accounts of the city. A number of Sanskrit and Telugu works have recorded the vibrant literary tradition of this kingdom.

The architectural style of Vijayanagar was the combination of old *Dravida* style and Islamic styles demonstrated by the neighbouring sultanates. This combination of styles can also be seen in the sculptures of Vijayanagara.

The sculptures of Vijayanagara were fundamentally derived from Chola's sculptures and occasionally shows the presence of foreigner's influence. The extensive ruins of Vijayanagara empire of 15th and early 16th century shows its immense wealth and cultural fusion. These remains were very significant for tracing the history of Vijayanagara empire.

EXAM PRACTICE

Multiple Choice Questions

1. The shape of the main temple tower known as .... in Tamil Nadu is like a stepped pyramid that rises up geometrically rather than the curving *shikhara* of *Nagara* style.

   (a) *garbhagriha* (b) *gopuram*
   (c) *vimana* (d) *stupika*

Ans. (c) *vimana*

2. The Srirangam temple of South India which was made in the *Dravida* style was located in?

   (a) Tiruchirapally (b) Tanjore
   (c) Madurai (d) Badami

Ans. (a) Tiruchirapally

3. The square shaped *shikhara* was called *caturasra.* What was the name given to rectangular shaped *shikhara*?

   (a) *Kuta* (b) *Ashtasra*
   (c) *Nasi* (d) *Ayatasra*

Ans. (d) *Ayatasra*

4. The city of Mamallapuram was renamed after which great ruler of Southern India?

   (a) Pulakesin II
   (b) Narsimhavarman II
   (c) Narsimhavarman I
   (d) Mahendravarman I

Ans. (c) Narsimhavarman I

5. The Shore temple at Mahabalipuram was built in the reign of

   (a) Rajasimha
   (b) Pulakesin II
   (c) Narsimhavarman I
   (d) Mahendravarman II

Ans. (a) Rajasimha

6. Who is the main deity of the Rajarajeswara temple?

   (a) Durga (b) Vishnu
   (c) Bramha (d) Shiva

Ans. (d) Shiva

7. The Rajarajeswara temple was completed in .... by Rajaraja a Chola ruler and it is considered as the tallest and largest temple of India. In which year did the temple completed?

   (a) 1092 (b) 954 (c) 1009 (d) 1093

Ans. (c) 1009

8. The sculpture of Sun, Moon, water and other celestial body is depicted in which of the following sculptures of *Dravida* style?

   (a) Descent of Ganga
   (b) Trimurti
   (c) Sun temple
   (d) None of the above

Ans. (a) Descent of Ganga

9. The right side image of the Shiva in the sculpture of Trimurti signifies the Shiva as

   (a) destroyer (b) creator
   (c) warrior (d) preserver

Ans. (b) creator

10. The Kailashnath temple at Ellora was built in the reign of which renowned kingdom?

    (a) Rashtrakutas (b) Cholas
    (c) Chera (d) Pandyas

Ans. (a) Rashtrakutas

11. Who established the Western Chalukya kingdom around Badami in 543?

    (a) Mamalla
    (b) Pulakesin I
    (c) Mahendravarman I
    (d) Narsimhavarman II

Ans. (b) Pulakesin I

12. The plan of three famous temples of Belur, Halebid and Somnathpur has a close proximity to the shape of

    (a) Sun (b) Earth
    (c) celestial body (d) star

Ans. (d) star

13. The Halebid temple of *Vesara* style shows the Shiva in the form of
(a) *Ardhanareeshwar*
(b) *Rudra*
(c) *Kala-Bhairav*
(d) *Nataraja*

Ans. (d) *Nataraja*

14. The famous temples, Durga temple and Lad Khan temple were located in which famous site of South India?
(a) Badami (b) Alampur
(c) Aihole (d) Ellora

Ans. (c) Aihole

15. The Papnath temple which was dedicated to Lord Shiva was made in which style of temple architecture?
(a) *Dravida*
(b) *Vesara*
(c) *Nagara*
(d) None of the above

Ans. (a) *Dravida*

16. The Afghan traveller 'Abd al-Razzaq' visited which state of South Indian kingdom?
(a) Aihole (b) Badami
(c) Vijayanagara (d) Madurai

Ans. (c) Vijayanagara

17. Match the following.

List I	List II
A. Shore temple	1. Rajarajeswara
B. Brahadeeshwarar temple	2. Loka Mahadevi
C. Virupaksha temple	3. Narsimhavarman II
D. Descent of Ganga	4. Mahendravarman

Codes
(a) A-3, B-1, C-2, D-4
(b) A-4, B-2, C-1, D-3
(c) A-3, B-4, C-1, D-2
(d) A-3, B-2, C-4, D-1

Ans. (a)

18. Match the following.

List I	List II
A. Srirangam temple	1. Mahabalipuram
B. Shore temple	2. Thanjavur
C. Shiva temple	3. Aihole
D. Ravan Pahadi	4. Tiruchirapally

Codes
(a) A-1, B-3, C-4, D-2
(b) A-4, B-1, C-2, D-3
(c) A-2, B-4, C-3, D-1
(d) A-3, B-4, C-2, D-1

Ans. (b)

Assertion - Reason

Directions (Q. Nos. 19-23) There are two statements marked as Assertion (A) and Reason (R). Read the statements and answer the questions according to codes given below.
(a) Both A and R are true and R is the correct explanation of A
(b) Both A and R are true, but R is not the correct explanation of A
(c) A is true, but R is false
(d) A is false, but R is true

19. Assertion (A) New boundary wall has been constructed lately around the temples of Dravida style.
Reason (R) With the passage of time, the population and size of town associated with temple would have increased.

Ans. (a) Both A and R are true and R is the correct explanation of A

20. Assertion (A) The powerful kings of Pallava dynasty played a great role in development of *Dravida* temple.
Reason (R) The rulers of Pallava dynasty built the Lad Khan temple and Durga temple which shows distinctive architectural style of Pallavas.

Ans. (c) A is true, but R is false

21. **Assertion** (A) *Vesara* style was the hybrid style of *Nagara* as well as *Dravida* style.

Reason (R) The rock-cut temples of Ellora shows distinctiveness of *Vesara*.

Ans. (b) Both A and R are true, but R is not the correct explanation of A

22. **Assertion** (A) The Durga temple of Badami was made in a unique style.

Reason (R) It is made in earlier style of an apsidal shrine which is similar to Buddhist *chaitya* halls.

Ans. (d) A is false, but R is true

23. **Assertion** (A) The sculpture of Descent of Ganga shows the continuous style of narration.

Reason (R) In the sculpture, multiple stories from a series of events are portrayed on the same sculpture, allowing the viewers to observe different part of the narrative together and gather a rich experience from multiple scenes from a series of events.

Ans. (a) Both A and R are true and R is the correct explanation of A

Source Based Question

24. Read the source given below and answer the following questions.

The temple has three shrines. Among the three shrines, two were dedicated to Lord Shiva, one is facing East and the other is facing West. The third shrine is located at the centre of the temple and is dedicated to Vishnu who is shown as *Anantashayana*. The feature of three shrine is unusual, because temples generally have a single main shrine and not three areas of worship. This suggested that the three shrines were not constructed together and different shrines may have been constructed at different times under different patrons. In the compound of the temple, there is an evidence of a water tank, an early example of Gopuram and several other images. The sculptures of the bull, Nandi which were made on the temple wall. However, these sculpture along with carvings on the temple's lower walls have suffered severe disfiguration due to erosion by salt water mixed air over the centuries.

(i) The above source is related to which temple?
(a) Lad Khan temple
(b) Shore temple
(c) Shiva temple
(d) Virupaksha temple

Ans. (b) Shore temple

(ii) The temple in the passage was built in the reign of
(a) Narsimhavarman I
(b) Narsimhavarman II
(c) Mahendravarman I
(d) Rajarajeswara

Ans. (b) Narsimhavarman II

(iii) On which South Indian site is this temple located?
(a) Aihole
(b) Badami
(c) Madurai
(d) Mahabalipuram

Ans. (d) Mahabalipuram

(iv) The ruler who built this temple was also known as
(a) Pulakesin (b) Rajaraja
(c) Rajasimha (d) Mamalla

Ans. (c) Rajasimha

(v) Nandi was the .... of Shiva.
(a) worshipper (b) vehicle
(c) servant (d) friend

Ans. (b) vehicle

True or False

1. The Srirangam temple of Tiruchirapally has seven parallel rectangular enclosure walls each with their own *gopurams*.

Ans. True

2. In *Dravida* style of temple architecture, the images of *mithunas* and river Goddesses were carved.

Ans. False

3. The octagonal shaped *shikhara* were known as *ashtasra*.

Ans. True

4. The Kailashnath temple was built under the supervision of the rulers of Rashtrakuta dynasty.

Ans. True

5. The early Chalukyan rulers were focused on construction of rock-cut temples, while the later Chalukyan rulers were engaged in building mud-based temples.

Ans. False

6. The Swarg Bramha temple of Badami shows greater assimilation of Northern styles from Odisha and Rajasthan.

Ans. False

7. In the sculpture of Trimurti, Goddess Lakshmi along with her husband Vishnu is shown.

Ans. False

Very Short Answer Type Questions

1. Write any one difference between the architectural style of *Dravida* and *Nagara*.

Ans. A difference between the architectural style of *Dravida* and *Nagara* is that at the entrance to the North Indian temples's (*Nagara*) *garbhagriha*, the images of *mithunas*, river Goddesses such as Ganga and Yamuna can be seen, whereas in South Indian temples (*Dravida*), one can see the sculptures of ferocious *dvarpalas* guarding the temple.

2. Write any one similarity between the architectural style of *Dravida* and *Nagara*.

Ans. A similarity in architectural style of *Dravida* and *Nagara* is that in both the styles, a large water reservoir or a temple tank enclosed within the complex of the temple can be seen.

3. What circumstances led to the formation of boundary walls around the temples of South India?

Ans. The increased population and size of the town associated with the temple led to the formation of boundary walls around the temple. The new boundary wall was made taller than the earlier boundary wall.

4. *Dravida* style was divided on the basis of its shape of *shikharas*. Write a precise note describing the various shikharas of *Dravida* temples.

Ans. The *Dravida* style is sub-divided on the basis of different shapes of *shikharas*. These are basically of five different shapes

(i) Square *shikhara* usually called *kuta* or *caturasra*.

(ii) Rectangular or *shala* or *ayatasra shikhara*.

(iii) Elliptical (egg shaped) *shikhara* usually called *gaja-prishta* (elephant backed or *vrittayata*).

(iv) Circular or *vritta* shaped *shikhara*.

(v) Octagonal or *ashtasra shikhara*

5. As per historians, the Shore temple of Mahabalipuram is famous for its unusual features. Describe such features in brief.

Ans. The Shore temple of Mahabalipuram has three shrines. Among the three shrines, two are dedicated to Lord Shiva and the other shrine located at the centre of the temple is dedicated to Vishnu. The feature of three shrines is unusual because temples generally have a single main shrine and not three areas of worship.

6. Describe any two features of the sculpture of Descent of Ganga on the basis of narration.

Ans. Features of the sculpture of Descent of Ganga are

(i) The rock-cut relief is depicted as a continuous narrative where multiple stories from a series of events are portrayed on the same canvas.

(ii) The sculpture allows the viewers to observe different parts of the narrative together and gather a rich experience from multiple scenes from a series of events.

7. Appreciate the grandeur and visual aesthetics of Kailashnath temple of Ellora.

Ans. The Kailashnath temple is a complete *Dravida* building with a Nandi shrine. The temple is wholly dedicated to Lord Shiva. It has a *gopuram* like- gateway which is surrounded by walkways. The temple has subsidiary shrines, staircases and an imposing tower (*vimana*) with the height of 30 meters.

8. Evaluate the architectural style of the temple of Halebid in brief.

Ans. The Halebid temple which is dedicated to Lord Shiva as Nataraja has a double building with a large hall for the *mandapa* to facilitate music and dance. A nandi pavillion precedes each building. The tower of the temple fell long ago and the temple's appearance can now only be ascertained from their detailed remains which are bordering the entrances.

9. Write down the salient features of sculpture of Nataraja.

Ans. The features of sculpture of Nataraja are

- The sculpture of Nataraja is surrounded by huge depiction of *saptamatrikas* (group of seven Goddesses).
- The figures are characterised by graceful, slim bodies and long oval faces which were crowned with extremely tall cylindrical crowns and shown to wear short *dhotis* marked by fine incised patterns indicating pleating.

Short Answer Type Questions

1. Write a short note on the development of *Dravida* style of temple.

Ans. For description on the development of *Dravida* style of temple, refer to text on pg. 84.

2. Evaluate the significant role of Pallava dynasty in the development of temple architecture.

Ans. The Pallavas were one of the ancient South Indian dynasties that were active in the Andhra region from 2nd century CE onwards and later migrated to settle in Tamil Nadu. The inscriptions of Pallavas from the 6th to 8th century shows their descriptive history. The powerful kings of Pallava dynasty played a great role in expansion of its empire. The boundaries of Pallava kingdom stretched to Odisha and their links with South- East Asia were also strong.

The role of Pallavas in the development of temple architecture was

- Pallavas were mostly Shaivite, but several Vaishnava shrines can also be seen of their reign. Pallavas were also highly influenced by the long Buddhist history of the Deccan. The early buildings of Pallavas were generally assumed as rock-cut, while the later ones were structural.
- The early rock-cut buildings are generally attributed to the reign of Mahendravarman I, a contemporary of Chalukya king Pulakesin II of Karnataka.
- Narsimhavarman I who is also known as Mamalla, acceded the Pallava throne under 640 CE. He was responsible for inaugurating most of the building works at Mahabalipuram which is renamed after him as *Mamallapuram*.

3. Appreciate the sculpture of 'Trimurti' on the basis of its medium, size and visual aesthetics.

Ans. For the appreciation of the sculpture of Trimurti, refer to text on pg. 89.

4. Comment on the role of Rashtrakutas in the architectural development of the temples of Deccan area along with one example.

Ans. For the role of Rashtrakutas in the architectural development of the temples of Deccan area, refer to text on pg. 90.

5. Evaluate the architectural style of Ravan Pahadi Cave of Aihole.

Ans. For the architectural style of Ravan Pahadi Cave at Aihole, refer to text on pg. 92.

6. Discuss about the state of Vijayanagara and its architectural style.

Ans. For description of the state of Vijayanagara and its architectural style, refer to text on pg. 93.

Long Answer Type Questions

1. Write the distinctive features of *Dravida* style of temple architecture and sculpture.

Ans. For the features of Dravida style of temple architecture and sculpture, refer to text on pg. 83 and 84.

2. Elaborate the architectural style of
(a) Shore temple of Mahabalipuram
(b) Shiva temple of Thanjavur

Ans. (a) For architectural style of Shore temple of Mahabalipuram, refer to text on pg. 86.
(b) For architectural style of Shiva temple of Thanjavur, refer to text on pg. 87.

3. In which sculpture, the sculptor has shown Bhagirath or Arjuna doing penance and a large number of holy dieties as audience. Identify the sculpture and write an essay on its method, material and appreciation.

Ans. The sculpture is Descent of Ganga. For method, material and appreciation of this sculpture, refer to text on pg. no. 88 and 89.

4. Write a detailed note on any sculpture of *Dravida* style of your choice included in your course of study.

Ans. For description of Trimurti as a sculpture of *Dravida* style, refer to text on pg. no. 89.

CHAPTER 09

The Buddhist and Jain Architectural Developments

In this chapter
- *Buddhist Architectural Style*
- *Jain Architectural Style*

The period of 5th to 14th centuries was the period when Buddhist and Jain style of architecture developed along with Hindu style of architecture and all these styles were equally vibrant. Buddhist, Hindu and Jain monuments can be found at the site of Ellora, Badami, Khajuraho and Kannauj.

Buddhist Architectural Style

Some important sites of Buddhist architectural style are Bodhgaya, Nalanda, Sirpur, Odisha and Nagapattinam.

Bodhgaya

This is a pilgrimage site where Siddhartha achieved enlightenment and became Gautama Buddha. The ***Bodhi*** tree of Bodhgaya is of immense importance and the Mahabodhi Temple of Bodhgaya is an important reminder of the intricate brickwork of that time.

The first shrine located at the base of the *Bodhi* tree, is believed to have been constructed by King Ashoka. The *vedika* (a place for a sacred ceremony) around it is believed to be built in post-Mauryan period in about 100 BCE.

Many of the sculptures in Mahabodhi temple are made in the 8th century in the reign of Pala rulers. However, the actual Mahabodhi temple was reconstructed in colonial period replacing the old 7th century design. The design of the temple is unusual. It is neither *Dravida* or *Nagara*. It is narrow like a *Nagara* temple, but it rises without curve like a *Dravida* style of temple.

Nalanda

The University of Nalanda is a *mahavihara* as it is a complex of several monasteries (a place where monks live together) of various sizes. The most part of this site is buried under contemporary civilisation due to which only a small part of it has been excavated and it make further excavations impossible.

Most of the information about Nalanda is based on the records of **Xuan Zang** which states that the foundation of a monastery was laid by **Kumargupta I** in the 5th century CE. This tradition was carried forward by the later rulers who built up a university here.

There is evidence that all three Buddhist doctrines i.e. **Theravada**[1], many **Mahayana**[2] and **Vajrayana**[3], were taught here. Many monks visited Nalanda and its neighbouring sites of Bodhgaya and Kurkihar from China, Tibet and Central Asia in the North and Sri Lanka, Thailand, Burma and various other countries from South-Eastern parts of Asia.

Monks and pilgrims who visited Nalanda would take back small sculptures and illustrated manuscripts from here to their own countries. Buddhist monasteries like Nalanda, were rich centres of art production that had a decisive impact on the arts of all Buddhist countries in Asia.

Nalanda University

1 **Theravada** It is the world's oldest surviving Buddhist school. It literally means, ' Teaching of the Elders' or 'the Ancient Teaching'.

2 **Mahayana** It is a term for a broad group of Buddhist traditions, text, philosophies and practices. Mahayana Buddhism developed in India (Ist century BCE onwards) and it is considered one of the two main existing branches of Buddhism.

3 **Vajrayana** It is form of Buddhism probably originated from the Mahayana tradition. It is based on a complex philosophical and ritual system meant to provide a path towards enlightenment.

Sculptures of Nalanda

The sculptural artpieces of Nalanda were made from stucco, stone and bronze and were highly influenced by the Buddhist Gupta art of Sarnath.

By the 9th century, Nalanda school of sculpture was formed as a result of the combination of Sarnath Gupta tradition, local Bihar tradition and the tradition of Central India. This school was characterised by its distinctive facial features, body forms and depiction of clothing and jewelleries.

The characteristic features of Nalanda art includes high quality works by artists and accurately executed sculptures which have an unique appearance with little shading. Sculptures are not flat in relief, but are depicted in three-dimensional forms. The back slabs of the sculptures are detailed and the ornament are designed beautifully.

Large number of Nalanda bronze sculptures or images of 7th-8th century to 12th century has been found. These bronze images are more in number than the metal images discovered from all the sites of Eastern India. These bronze images of Nalanda constitutes a large number of Pala Period metal sculptures. The bronze images of Nalanda were initially inspired from Sarnath and Mathura Gupta traditions.

Depiction on Nalanda Sculptures

The Nalanda sculptures initially represent Buddhist deities of the Mahayana **pantheon**[4] such as standing Buddhas, Bodhisattvas such as Manjusri Kumara, Avalokiteshvara seated on a lotus and Naga- Nagarjuna.

During the late 11th and 12th centuries, when Nalanda emerged as an important *tantric* (use of *mantras*, meditation, *yoga* and ritual) centre, the sculptures started representing Vajrayana deities such as Vajrasharada (a form of Saraswati), Khasarpana, Avalokiteshvara, etc.

Depictions of crowned Buddhas came to be represented only after the 10th century. Various Brahmanical images have also been found at Nalanda. Many of these are still worshipped in small temples and villages around the site.

Other Sites

- **Sirpur** This site is located in Chhattisgarh and include the shrines of Buddhism and Hindu religion. It is considered as an early-Odisha style site and belongs to the period between 550 and 800 CE. The iconographic and stylistic elements of Buddhist sculptures in Sirpur are similar to the styles of Nalanda.
- **Odisha** Major Buddhist monasteries were developed in later period in Odisha of which Lalitagiri, Vajragiri and Ratnagiri are the most famous.

4 **Pantheon** The gods worshipped by a particular nation or people.

- **Nagapattinam** The port-town of Nagapattinam was a major Buddhist centre before the Chola period. The main reason behind this was its trade with Sri Lanka where a large number of Buddhists live. Bronze and stone sculptures in Chola style have been found at Nagapattinam that belonged to 10th century.

Jain Architectural Style

Jains were ardent temple builders like the Hindus and their sacred shrines and pilgrimage spots can be found in whole Indian region except the hilly areas. Important places where Jain pilgrimage or architectural sites are located are

- **Bihar** The oldest Jain pilgrimage sites are found in Bihar. Many of these sites are famous for early Buddhist shrines.
- **Deccan** In the Deccan, some of the most architecturally important Jain sites can be found in Ellora and Aihole. In Central India, Deogarh, Khajuraho, Chanderi and Gwalior have some excellent examples of Jain temples.
- **Karnataka** It has a rich heritage of Jain shrines. The famous statue of **Gomateshwara** (the granite statue of Lord Bahubali) is located at Sravana Belagola of Karnataka. This statue was commissioned by Camundaraya who was the General-in- Chief and Prime Minister of Ganga kings of Mysore. The statue has a height of 18 m or 57ft. This statue is the world's tallest monolithic (huge rock statue) free-standing structure.

Lord Bahubali, Gomateshwara, Karnataka

- **Mount Abu** At Mount Abu, the Jain temples were constructed by Vimal Shah. These are famous for their simple exterior in contrast with the excellent marble interiors. Their rich sculptural decoration with deep undercutting creates a shoe lace like structure appearance. Mount Abu temple is famous for its unique patterns on every ceiling and the graceful decorated figures along the domed ceilings.
- **Gujarat** In Gujarat, the jain pilgrimage site Shatrunjay hills near Palitana in Kathiawar, has large number of temples that are grouped together.

Appreciation of Jain Sculpture of Mother and Child

This sculpture was made on the ceiling of the Vimal Shah temple in Mount Abu. This sculpture was made by the white marble, through the technique of carving. This temple is decorated with many sculptures that depict the daily life of the Jain Tirthankaras.

The idols of Jain religion and geometric patterns are engraved on each part of the temple. This temple is dedicated to the first Tirthankara Adinath who is also known as **Vimal Shah**.

The sculpture of Mother and Child depict a mother deity of Jainism, Ambika and her child. The mother is sitting in slightly bent posture on a lion and her child can be seen on her lap who is supported by her left arm. Another child is standing beside her left leg.

The mother is holding a bunch of three mangoes in her right hand. She is looking very calm and affectionate. She is decorated with a crown and jewels like necklaces, armlets, anklets and girldles (waist bands).

The ornaments and garments are in linear form with appropriate curves. This sculpture clearly depicts motherhood and love between the mother and the child.

Name : Mother and Child, Vimal Shah Temple
Period : 13th century AD (Solanki Dynasty)
Place : Dilwara, Mount Abu, Rajasthan
Medium : White marble
Collection : Archaeological Survey of India

EXAM PRACTICE

Multiple Choice Questions

1. In which of the following site, one can find the monuments of Buddhist, Jain and Hindu style of architecture?
   (a) Ellora (b) Ajanta
   (c) Nalanda (d) Bagh caves

Ans. (a) Ellora

2. Gautama Buddha who was a great religious leader and founder of the Buddhism was born in Lumbini and later died and attained enlightenment at ....
   (a) Nalanda (b) Nagapattinam
   (c) Bodhgaya (d) Sarnath

Ans. (c) Bodhgaya

3. The first shrine which is located at the Bodhgaya was constructed by
   (a) King Kumargupta (b) King Narsimha
   (c) King Chandragupta (d) King Ashoka

Ans. (d) King Ashoka

4. The world famous Nalanda University was a significant centre of learning. Who among the following rulers laid the foundation stone of this University?
   (a) Skandgupta (b) Kumargupta
   (c) Xuan – zang (d) Fa-hien

Ans. (b) Kumargupta

5. The Buddhist sect that got the mention in the sculpture of Nalanda is
   (a) Mahayana (b) Hinayana
   (c) Vajrayana (d) All of these

Ans. (a) Mahayana

6. The Ratnagiri site which contained the sculpture of Buddhist traditions belonged to which of the following Indian state
   (a) Gujarat (b) Chhattisgarh
   (c) Odisha (d) Bengal

Ans. (c) Odisha

7. In which of the following Indian states, the oldest Jain pilgrimage centres are to be found?
   (a) Uttar Pradesh
   (b) Bihar
   (c) Rajasthan
   (d) Gujarat

Ans. (b) Bihar

8. The world tallest statue of Buddha was built by
   (a) Camundaraya
   (b) Kumargupta
   (c) Skandgupta
   (d) Fa-hien

Ans. (a) Camundaraya

9. The sculpture of Mother and Child has been made in the temple which is dedicatd to Adinath. What was the other name of Adinath?
   (a) Virjan Shah
   (b) Kumargupta
   (c) Vimal Shah
   (d) Rishabh Gupta

Ans. (c) Vimal Shah

10. Match the following.

List I (Place)	List II (Significance)
A. Bodhgaya	1. Bahubali statue
B. Nalanda	2. Dilwara temple
C. Sravana Belgola	3. Siddharth attained enlightenment
D. Mt Abu	4. Vajrayana depicted figures

Codes
(a) A-3, B-1, C-4, D-2
(b) A-3, B-4, C-1, D-2
(c) A-2, B-4, C-1, D-3
(d) A-4, B-1, C-2, D-3

Ans. (b)

Assertion-Reason

Directions (Q. Nos. 11-13) In the following questions, there are two statements marked as Assertion (A) and Reason (R). Read the statements and answer the questions according to the codes given below.

(a) Both A and R are true and R is the correct explanation of A
(b) Both A and R are true, but R is not the correct explanation of A
(c) A is true, but R is false
(d) A is false, but R is true

11. **Assertion** (A) The design of the Mahabodhi style was based on the nagara style of the architecture.

Reason (R) The narrow design of the temple has been inspired from nagara style of architecture.

Ans. (d) A is false, but R is true

12. **Assertion** (A) The Buddhist monk came from Central Asia, China, Tibet, Burma, Thailand, Sri lanka to Nalanda University.

Reason (R) The Buddhist monks visited Nalanda to worship in the shrines of Nalanda.

Ans. (c) A is true, but R is false

13. **Assertion** (A) In the site of Nalanda , one can find the *traces* of tantric worship.

Reason (R) The remains of Vajrayana deities such as Vajrasharada, Khasarpana, Avolokiteshwara, etc is remarkable.

Ans. (a) Both A and R are true and R is the correct explanation of A

Source Based Question

14. Read the source given below and answer the following questions.

This is a sculptural panel installed in the ceiling corner of Vimal Vasahi Temple. This temple is dedicated to the first Tirthankara, Adinath, who is also known as Vimal Shah. In this sculpture, the sculptor has shown Ambika, a mother deity of Jainism, and a child to show her motherhood. She can be seen holding a bunch of three mangoes in her right hand and a baby in her lap with arm support of left hand. Another child can also be seen standing beside her. The mother is mounted on a lion and a tree with ripe mangoes can be seen alongside. The sculptor has intricately carved and showed the motherhood as well as loveliness between child and mother. The mother posture is slightly bent. The expressions of the face and rest of the body is full of motherly woman.

(i) The above source is related to which of the following sculptures?
(a) Trimurti
(b) Ravana lifting mount Kailash
(c) Mother and Child
(d) Descent of Ganga

Ans. (c) Mother and Child

(ii) Which of the following architectural styles can be noticed in the sculpture?
(a) Buddhist style
(b) Islamic style
(c) Hindu style
(d) Jain style

Ans. (d) Jain style

(iii) Which of the following materials is used for the construction of the sculpture?
(a) White marble
(b) Brown sandstone
(c) Grey black basalt
(d) Red sandstone

Ans. (a) White marble

(iv) The sculpture was made in the period of
(a) 12th century AD
(b) 16th century AD
(c) 11th century AD
(d) 13th century AD

Ans. (d) 13th century AD

(v) This sculpture is made in the temple which was dedicated to

(a) Adiyogi (b) Adinath
(c) Adityanath (d) Adideva

Ans. (b) Adinath

True or False

1. Bodhgaya is a pilgrimage site where Gautama Buddha attained *moksha.*

Ans. False

2. The monastic university of Nalanda is a *mahavihara* as it is a complex of several monasteries of various sizes.

Ans. True

3. In Nalanda, three Buddhist doctrines i.e. Theraveda, Hinayana and Vajrayana were taught.

Ans. False

4. The iconography of Sirpur sculptures were highly influenced from sculptures of Nalanda.

Ans. True

5. The port town of Nagapattinam was a major Jain pilgrimage centre.

Ans. False

6. The height of Lord Bahubali statue is 18 m high which makes it one of the tallest statue of Gautama Buddha.

Ans. True

7. The Jain temples of Mount Abu were constructed under the supervision of Kumargupta.

Ans. False

Very Short Answer Questions

1. Write a brief note on the Buddhist pilgrimage centre of Bodhgaya?

Ans. Bodhgaya is a pilgrimage site where Siddhartha achieved enlightenment and became Gautama Buddha. The Bodhi tree of Bodhgaya is of immense importance and the Mahabodhi Temple of Bodhgaya is an important reminder of the intricate brickwork of ancient time.

2. Comment on the architectural style of Mahabodhi temple.

Ans. The sculptures in Mahabodhi temple are made in the 8th century in the reign of Pala rulers. The design of the temple is unusual. It is neither *Dravida* or *Nagara.* It is narrow like a *Nagara* temple, but it rises without curve like a *Dravida* one.

3. Write any one distinctive feature of the sculptures of Nalanda.

Ans. The characteristic features of the artpieces of Nalanda includes high quality works by artists and accurately executed sculptures which have an unique apperances with little shading. Sculptures are also usually not flat in relief, but are depicted in three-dimensional forms. The back slabs of the sculptures are detailed and the ornaments are designed intricately.

4. Mention some of the most important pilgrimage centres of Jains.

Ans. Some of the most important Jain pilgrimage or architectural sites are Bihar, Deccan and Karnataka. In the oldest Jain pilgrimage sites are found. In the Deccan, some of the most architecturally important Jain sites can be found in Ellora and Aihole. Karnataka has a rich heritage of Jain shrines. The famous statue of Gomateshwara (the granite statue of Lord Bahubali) is located at Sravana Belagola of Karnataka.

5. Appreciate the architectural style of Jain temple of Mount Abu which was constructed by Vimal Shah .

Ans. The Jain temple at Mount Abu is famous for its simple exterior in contrast with excellent marble interiors. Their rich sculptural decoration with deep undercutting creates a shoe lace like appearances. The temple is famous for its unique patterns on every ceiling and the graceful decorated figures along the domed ceilings.

Short Answer Type Questions

1. Write a note on the most significant Buddhist site Bodhgaya.

Ans. For description of Buddhist site Bodhgaya, refer to text on pg. 100.

2. Briefly elaborate the subjects which were depicted on the sculptures of Nalanda.

Ans. For the subject which were depicted on the sculptures of Nalanda, refer to text on pg. 102.

3. Write a precise note on
   (a) Sirpur
   (b) Odisha
   (c) Nagapattinam

Ans. For description of Sirpur, Odisha and Nagapattinam, refer to text on pg. 102 and 103.

4. Evaluate the important sites of Jain pilgrimage centre.

Ans. For description of the important sites of Jain pilgrimage centre, refer to text on pg. 103.

Long Answer Type Questions

1. Write a detailed explanation of the architectural developments of Buddhism in Nalanda.

Ans. Refer to text on pg. 101 and 102.

2. Appreciate the sculpture of Jain architectural style which is included in your course of study.

Ans. For the appreciation of Mother and Child as the sculpture of Jain architectural style, refer to text on pg. 104.

3. Trace the development in Buddhist art. *(NCERT)*

Ans. The Buddhist art developed in the following ways

- Early Buddhist art did not show Buddha in human form and invented new symbols to elucidate different events related to Buddha's life. Early Buddhist art used symbols like lotus and bull, horse, *Bodhi* tree, wheel and *stupa* to depict Buddha's life. Stupas play a great role in Buddhist art, as they contain Buddha/ Boddhisattva relics or artefacts.
- During Mauryan period, Mauryan king Ashoka made many stone pillars with Buddhist symbols on it.
- With the advent of Mahayana Buddhism, Buddha is started to be depict in human form and three style for sculpture came into existence.
- In Gandhara Buddhist art, which was the combination of Indian, Greek and Persian style, Buddha is depicted as Greek god. On the other hand, in Mathura Buddhist art, Buddha is depicted as Indian god.
- During Gupta period, standing statues of Buddha were started to be carved using red sandstone.
- New ways of depicting Buddha have been developed in different parts of the world such as Nepal, Sri Lanka, South-East Asia and China.
- Buddhist art is not only limited to sculptures, it led to the development of *chaitya* and *viharas.*
- Buddhist art is also depicted in *Jatakas* which included paintings that illustrates Buddha's life.

CHAPTER

10

Indian Bronze Sculpture

In this chapter

- *Introduction to Indian Bronze Sculpture*
  - *Method of Bronze Casting (Solid and Hollow)*
  - *Examples of Bronze Images in India*
  - *Development of Indian Bronze Sculptures in South India*

Indian sculptors had mastered the bronze medium and the casting, just like they had mastered **Terracotta**[1] sculpture and carving in stone. The *cire-perdu* or **'lost-wax'** process for casting was learnt during the **Indus Valley Culture**[2]. Along with it, the process of making alloy of metals by mixing copper, zinc and tin which is called bronze, was discovered.

Introduction to Indian Bronze Sculpture

Bronze sculptures and statues of Buddhist, Hindu and Jain icons have been discovered from many regions of India. These sculptures belong to a period from 2nd century to 16th century. Most of these sculptures were used for ritual worship.

These sculptures were characterised for their graceful and aesthetic (attractiveness) appeal. During this period, the metal-casting process, was used for making articles for various purposes of daily use like utensils for cooking, eating, drinking, etc.

Method of Bronze Casting (Solid and Hollow)

Casting a bronze image is a difficult task and requires great skills. Sometimes an alloy of five metals i.e. gold, silver, copper, brass and lead is used to cast bronze images. For bronze casting, lost wax process is used. Solid as well as hollow form of image or sculpture can be made through this process.

1 **Terracotta** It is a type of fired clay of a brownish-red colour and unglazed, used as an ornamental building material and in modeling.

2 **The Indus Valley Civilisation** (IVC) Indus Civilisation was a Bronze Age Civilisation in the North-Western regions of South Asia lasting from 3300 BCE to 1300 BCE and in its mature form 2600 BCE to 1900 BCE.

The lost-wax process is used for making objects of metal in the regions of Himachal Pradesh, Odisha, Bihar, Madhya Pradesh and West Bengal. The tribal communities of present times also use the 'lost-wax' process for their art expressions. The lost-wax process involves several different steps which are

- First of all, a wax model of the image is made by hands from pure beeswax. The beeswax has been melted over an open fire and then strained through a fine cloth into a basin of cold water in which it get resolidified immediately.
- The wax is then pressed through a *pichki* or *pharni* which squeezes the wax into noodle-like shape. These wax wires are then coiled around to the shape of the entire image.
- The image is now covered with a thick coating of paste made of equal parts of clay, sand and cow-dung. On one side of opening clay pot is fixed and molten metal is poured into it. This metal is largely scrapping metal from broken pots and pans. The weight of the metal to be used should be ten times greater than wax. The wax is weighed before starting the entire process.
- When the molten metal is poured in the clay pot, the clay-plastered model is exposed to firing. As the wax inside melts, the metal flows down the channel and takes the shape of the wax image. The firing process is carried out almost like a religious ritual and all the steps take place in silence. The image is later carved with files to smoothen it and give it a finish.

Examples of Bronze Images in India

Dancing Girl

'Dancing Girl' from Mohenjodaro is the earliest bronze sculpture that belong to 2500 BCE. The limbs and torso of this female figurine are simplified in tubular (tube shaped) form.

Daimabad Man

A group of bronze statuettes have been discovered from archaeological excavation at Daimabad (Maharashtra) that belong to 1500 BCE. It consists of a 'Chariot', the wheels of which are represented in simple circular shapes. Along with chariot, the driver or human rider has been elongated (stretched out) and the bulls in the front are depicted in muscular forms.

Jain *Tirthankaras*

The bronze images of Jain *Tirthankaras* have been discovered from Chausa, Bihar during 2nd century CE. These images belong to the Kushana period. These bronze sculptures depict how the Indian sculptors had mastered the modeling of masculine human physique and simplified muscles.

The most remarkable example is the depiction of ***Adinath*** or ***Vrishabhnath***, who is identified with long hair locks (a curl of hair of the heads) dropping to his shoulders. Otherwise the *Tirthankaras* are distinguished by their short curly hair. Many famous Jain bronze images from Chausa in Bihar are now kept in the Patna Museum.

Bronze Images of Gujarat and Rajasthan

Gujarat and Rajasthan have been center of Jainism since early times. Many bronze images that discovered in Akota near Vadodara (Gujarat), established that bronze casting was practised in Gujarat or Western India between the 6th and 9th centuries. These bronze images were made using the lost-wax process. The images were embedded with silver and copper to bring out the eyes, crowns and details of the textiles on which the figures were seated.

Most of these images represent the Jain *Tirthankaras* like Mahavira, Parshvanath or Adinath. A new format was invented in which *Tirthankaras* are seated on a throne. They can be single or combined in a group of three or in a group of twenty-four *Tirthankaras*.

Female images were also casted representing *Yakshinis* or ***Shasanadevis***[3] of some prominent *Tirthankaras*. Their style was influenced by the features of both the Gupta and the Vakataka period bronze images. **Chakreshvari**[4] is the messenger of Adinath and Ambika is the messenger of **Neminath**[5].

Bronze Sculpture, Himachal Pradesh

Vishnu Images

There is growth of different types of iconography (collection of portraits) of Vishnu images in Himachal and Kashmir region. Four-headed Vishnu was worshipped in these regions. It is also known as ***Chaturanana*** or ***Vaikuntha Vishnu***.

The central face represents Vasudeva, while the other two faces are that of Narasimha and Varaha. The Narasimha *avatar* and Mahishasuramardini Durga images of Himachal Pradesh are among the very dynamic bronze images from that region.

Buddha Images

Many standing Buddha images of bronze with right hand in ***abhaya mudra***[6] were cast in North India, particularly in Uttar Pradesh and Bihar during the Gupta and post-Gupta periods, i.e. between the 5th, 6th and 7th centuries.

---

3 **Shasanadevis** They are divine female messenger of Jain *Tirthankaras*.

4 **Chakreshvari** The guardian goddess of *Yakshini*.

5 **Neminath** He is 22nd *Tirthankara* in Jainism. He attracts the most devotional worship among the Jains.

6 **Abhaya Mudra** It is a *mudra* (gesture) of reassurance and safety which eliminate fear and grants divine protection and bliss in many Indian religions. In this mudra, the right hand is held upright and the palm is facing outwards. This is one of the earliest *mudra* depicted on a number of Hindu, Buddhist, Jain and Sikh images.

In such sculptures, *sanghati* or the monk's robe (loose outer garment) is wrapped over the right arm to cover the shoulders. The other end of the drapery (hanging cloth) is wrapped over the left arm and the pleats are held by the extended hand of the same arm. The drapery falls and spreads into a wide curve and touch the ankle.

The Buddha's figure is made in a precise manner which shows the thin quality of the cloth. The whole figure is treated with refinement (purification) with certain fineness in the depiction of the torso. The Buddha figure appears youthful and proportionate in comparison with the Kushanas style.

Bronze Images of Buddha in Different Regions of India

- **Uttar Pradesh** In the bronze images of Buddha from Dhanesar Khera, Uttar Pradesh, the folds of the drapery are depicted as same as the Mathura style. The drapery are in a series of hanging down curves.
- **Sarnath** Sarnath-style bronze images of Buddha have foldless drapery. The outstanding example is Buddha image at Sultanganj, Bihar which is an enormous bronze figure. The polished style of these bronze images is the hallmark of the classical quality.
- **Maharashtra** Vakataka bronze images of the Buddha from Phopnar, Maharashtra are contemporary with the Gupta period bronze image. They show the influence of the Amravati style of Andhra Pradesh in the 3rd century CE. During this phase there was a significant change in the draping style of the monk's robe.

  In these images, Buddha's right hand in *abhaya mudra* is free so that the drapery holds on tightly to the right side of the body contour (shape). It results in a continuous flowing line on this side of the figure. At the level of the ankles of the Buddha figure, the drapery makes a visible curvilinear turn, as it is held by the left hand.

  The additional importance of the Gupta and Vakataka bronze images is that they were portable (movable). Monks carried them from one place to another for the purpose of individual worship and to install in Buddhist *viharas*. In this manner, the refined classical style spread to different parts of India and to Asian countries overseas.
- **Himachal Pradesh and Kashmir** These regions also produced bronze images of Buddhist deities and Hindu Gods and Goddesses. Most of these were created during the 8th, 9th and 10th centuries. These regions have a very distinct style than bronze images from other parts of India.
- **Bengal and Bihar Region** In Buddhist centres like Nalanda, a school of bronze casting emerged around the 9th century during the rule of the Pala dynasty in Bihar and Bengal regions. The sculptors at Kurkihar near Nalanda were able to revive the classical style of the Gupta period. A remarkable bronze image of these regions is of a four-armed Avalokitesvara, which is a male figure in graceful **tribhanga posture**[7].

---

7 **Tribhanga posture** Tribhanga is a standing body position or stance used in traditional Indian art and Indian classical dance forms like the Odissi, where the body bends in one direction at the knees, the other direction at the hips and then the body bends toward shoulders and neck.

Worship of female Goddesses was also adopted which represent growth of the **Vajrayana Buddhism**[8]. Images of Tara became very popular. Tara is shown seated on a throne along with a growing curvilinear lotus stalk (stem) and her right hand is in the *abhaya mudra*.

Development of Indian Bronze Sculptures in South India

During the medieval period, there was a significant development of bronze casting technique and making of bronze images of traditional icons in South India.

The bronze images were modelled and casted during the Pallava period in the 8th and 9th centuries, but some of the most beautiful and elegant statues were produced during the Chola period in Tamil Nadu from the 10th -12th century.

The technique and art of creating bronze images is still practised in South India particularly in **Kumbakonam**. The distinguished patron during the 10th century was the widowed Chola queen, Sembiyan Maha Devi. Chola bronze images are the most desired collection items by art lovers all over the world.

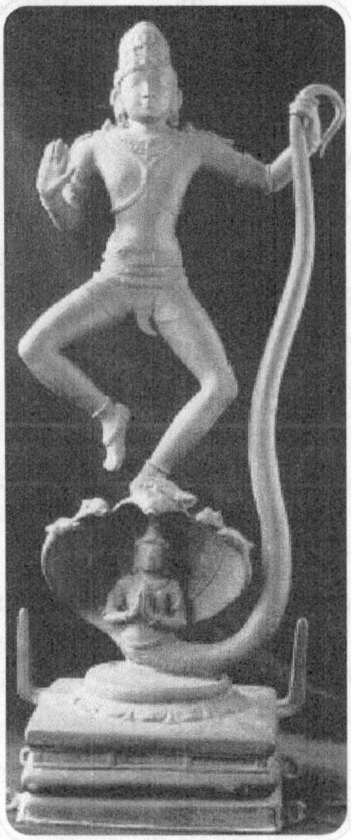

Kaliyadaman, Chola bronze, Tamil Nadu

Following images of bronze developed in South India

- **Shiva Seated in *Ardhaparyanka* Asana (One leg kept hanging)** This was developed in 8th century during Pallava period. In this bronze sculpture, the right hand of Shiva is in the ***achamana***[9] *mudra* gesture, suggesting that he is about to drink poison.
- **Shivas as Nataraja** The well-known dancing figure of Shiva as Nataraja was evolved and fully developed during the Chola period and since then many variations of this complex bronze image have been developed.
- **Shiva Iconography** A wide range of Shiva iconography was evolved in the Thanjavur (Tanjore) region of Tamil Nadu. The 9th century *Kalyanasundara Murti* is exceptional as it depicts *Panigrahana* (ceremony of marriage) ceremony by two separate statuettes.

  In this image, Shiva with his extended right hand accepts Parvati's (the bride's) right hand, who is taking a step forward and feeling very shy. The union of Shiva and Parvati is very divinely represented in the *ardhanarisvara murti* in a single image. Beautiful independent figurines of Parvati have also been modelled, standing in graceful *tribhanga* posture.

---

8 **Vajrayana Buddhism** Vajrayana Buddhism refers to Buddhist traditions associated with Tantra and Secret Mantra which developed in the medieval Indian sub-continent and spread to Tibet, East Asia, Mongolia and other Himalayan states.

9 **Achamana** It is a purification ritual that is believed to cure all physical and mental impurities.

- **Portrait Sculpture** During the 16th century which is known as the Vijayanagar period in Andhra Pradesh, the sculptors experimented with portrait sculpture in order to preserve knowledge of the royal patron for posterity (future generation).

  At Tirupati, huge standing portrait statues were casted in bronze depicting Krishnadevaraya with his two queens, Tirumalamba and Chinnadevi. The standing king and queens are depicted in praying posture, i.e. both hands held in the *namaskara mudra*. The sculptor has combined the likeness of the facial features with certain elements of idealisation. The **idealisation**[10] is further observed in the manner, the physical body is modelled to appear imposing as well as graceful.

Appreciation of the Bronze Image of Nataraja

Nataraja is a bronze statue of Shiva developed during Chola period. It represents Shiva in dancing position that depicts the end of **cosmic**[11] world.

In this bronze sculpture, Shiva has been shown balancing himself on his right leg and suppressing the *apasmara*, the demon of ignorance or forgetfulness with the same leg.

At the same time, he raised his left leg in **bhujangatrasita**[12] stance which represents *tirobhava* that is kicking away the veil of *maya* or illusion from the devotee's mind.

His four arms are extended and the main right hand is posed in *abhaya hasta* (*abhaya mudra*). The upper right hand holds the *damaru* (his favourite musical instrument) to carry the beat (*tala*).

The upper left hand carries a flame, while the main left hand is shown in **dola hasta**[13] gesture which connects with the *abhaya hasta* of the right hand.

His hair locks fly on both the sides touching the circular *jvala mala* or the garland of flames which surrounds the entire dancing figuration.

Name : Nataraja
Place : Thanjavur,Tamil Nadu
Medium : Bronze
Circa : 12th century AD (Chola Period)
Collection : National Museum, New Delhi

10 **Idealisation** It is the action of regarding or representing something as perfect or better than in reality.

11 **Cosmic** Cosmic means relating to the universe or cosmos especially as distinct from the Earth.

12 **Bhujangatrasita** It is a type of a dance step. It is believed that this dance step was learnt by Mahadeva from Tandu Rishi.

13 **Dola Hasta** Dola hasta is shown by using *pataka hasta* (all five fingers are held together without any gaps between the fingers) in both the hand facing down side with the arm stretched and elbows slightly bend.

EXAM PRACTICE

Multiple Choice Questions

1. During which civilisation or culture lost-wax method discovered?
   (a) Mesopotamian Civilisation
   (b) Indus Valley Civilisation
   (c) Egyptian Civilisation
   (d) Chinese Civilisation

Ans. (b) Indus Valley Civilisation

2. Which of the following is the earliest bronze sculpture that belongs to 2500 BCE?
   (a) Nataraja (b) Daimabad Man
   (c) Kaliyadaman (d) Dancing Girl

Ans. (d) Dancing Girl

3. Excavation at Daimabad is a bronze statue consisting of a chariot, a driver and a bull. To which period does this sculpture belong to?
   (a) 1500 BCE (b) 1600 BCE
   (c) 1700 BCE (d) 1800 BCE

Ans. (a) 1500 BCE

4. Jain *Tirthankaras* images that were discovered from Chausa Bihar was patronised by which dynasty?
   (a) Cholas (b) Kushanas
   (c) Pallavas (d) Satavahanas

Ans. (b) Kushanas

5. .... is the *Shasanadevi* of Adinath.
   (a) Ambika (b) Radhika
   (c) Chakreshvari (d) Padmavati

Ans. (c) Chakreshvari

6. Which deity is depicted in central face of *Chaturanana* or *Vaikuntha Vishnu* of Himachal and Kashmir region?
   (a) Narsimha (b) Vasudeva
   (c) Varaha (d) Buddha

Ans. (b) Vasudeva

7. Buddha image at Sultanganj Bihar is an example of which style?
   (a) Amravati (b) Sarnath
   (c) Mathura (d) Kushana

Ans. (b) Sarnath

8. Shiva seated in .... was developed in 8th century during Pallavas period.
   (a) *Abhaya mudra*
   (b) *Bhujangatrasita*
   (c) *Ardhaparyanka asana*
   (d) *Dola hasta gesture*

Ans. (c) *Ardhaparyanka asana*

9. Which theme is depicted in *Kalyanasundara Murti* that was evolved in Thanjavur region of Tamil Nadu?
   (a) *Panigrahana* ceremony
   (b) *Upanyana* ceremony
   (c) *Mundan* ceremony
   (d) *Nishkramana* ceremony

Ans. (a) *Panigrahana* ceremony

10. Which demon was suppressed by Shiva with his right leg in the sculpture Nataraja?
    (a) Danavas
    (b) Asuras
    (c) Apasmara
    (d) Mahishasura

Ans. (c) Apasmara

11. Match the following.

List I	List II
A. Dancing Girl	1. Dhanesar Khera
B. Jain *Tirthankaras* images	2. Chausa, Bihar
C. Buddha images with Mathura style drapery	3. Mohenjodaro
D. Buddha images with Sarnath style foldless drapery	4. Sultanganj, Bihar

Codes

(a) A-1, B-2, C-3, D-4
(b) A-2, B-4, C-3, D-1
(c) A-3, B-2, C-1, D-4
(d) A-2, B-3, C-1, D-4

Ans. (c)

12. Match the following.

List I	List II
A. Sculptors at Kurkihar	1. Pallava dynasty
B. Shiva seated in *Ardhaparyanka asana*	2. Vijayanagara Empire
C. Shiva in Nataraja	3. Pala dynasty
D. Krishnadevaraya	4. Chola empire

Codes

(a) A-1, B-2, C-3, D-4
(b) A-2, B-4, C-3, D-1
(c) A-3, B-2, C-1, D-4
(d) A-3, B-1, C-4, D-2

Ans. (d)

Assertion and Reason

Directions (Q. Nos. 13-15) There are two statements marked as Assertion (A) and Reason (R). Read the statement and answer the questions according to codes given below.

(a) Both A and R are true and R is the correct explanation of A
(b) Both A and R are true, but R is not the correct explanation of A
(c) A is true, but R is false
(d) A is false, but R is true

13. **Assertion** (A) The images of Jain *Tirthankaras* have been discovered from Chausa, Bihar during 2nd century CE.

Reason (R) Bronze statue from Dhanesar Khera, Uttar Pradesh represent Jain *Tirthankaras* in folds of the drapery similar to the Mathura style, i.e. hanging downwards.

Ans. (c) A is true, but R is false

14. **Assertion** (A) At Tirupati a life-size standing portrait statues were cast in bronze depicting Krishnadevaraya with his two queens, Tirumalamba and Chinnadevi.

Reason (R) During the 16th century known as the Vijayanagar period in Andhra Pradesh, the sculptors experimented with portrait sculpture in order to preserve knowledge of the royal patron for posterity.

Ans. (b) Both A and R are true, but R is not the correct explanation of A

15. **Assertion** (A) Nataraja represents Shiva in dancing position that depicts the end of cosmic world.

Reason (R) Shiva is performing Tandava which is a symbol of divine energy, harmony and rhythm. It represents five essential acts i.e. creation, preservation, destruction, veiling and grace.

Ans. (a) Both A and R are true and R is the correct explanation of A

Source Based Question

16. Read the source given below and answer the following questions.

In this bronze sculpture Shiva has been shown balancing himself on his right leg and suppressing the apasmara, the demon of ignorance or forgetfulness with the same leg. At the same time he raised his left leg in bhujangatrasita stance which represents tirobhava that is kicking away the veil of maya or illusion from the devotee's mind. His four arms are extended and the main right hand is posed in Abhaya hasta. The upper right hand holds the damaru his favourite musical instrument to carry the beat (tala). The upper left hand carries a flame, while the main left hand is shown in dola hasta gesture. This then connects with the Abhaya hasta of the right hand.

His hair locks fly on both the sides touching the circular Jvala mala or the garland of flames which surrounds the entire dancing figuration.

(i) Name the sculpture that is described in the above source.
(a) Nataraja (b) Daimabad Man
(c) Kaliyadaman (d) Dancing Girl

Ans. (a) Nataraja

(ii) Which dynasty patronised this sculpture?
(a) Pallavas (b) Palas
(c) Cholas (d) Satavahana

Ans. (c) Cholas

(iii) At which place this bronze sculpture was made?
(a) Thanjavur, Tamil Nadu
(b) Dhanesar Khera
(c) Chausa, Bihar
(d) Kurkihar near Nalanda

Ans. (a) Thanjavur, Tamil Nadu

(iv) What is Shiva performing in this bronze sculpture?
(a) Bharatanatyam (b) Kathak
(c) Odissi (d) Tandava

Ans. (d) Tandava

(v) Where is the collection of this sculpture available in India?
(a) National Gallery of Modern Art, New Delhi
(b) National Museum, New Delhi
(c) Kala Bhavana, Calcutta
(d) Government Museum and Art Gallery, Chandigarh

Ans. (b) National Museum, New Delhi

True or False

1. The process of making alloy of metals by mixing copper, zinc and tin which is called bronze.

Ans. True

2. Chakreshvari is the *Shasanadevi* of Neminath and Ambika is of Adinath.

Ans. False

3. In Buddhist centres like Nalanda, a school of bronze casting emerged around the 9th century during the rule of the Pala Dynasty.

Ans. True

4. *Chaturanana* or *Vaikuntha Vishnu* is a sculpture of four-headed Vishnu who was worshipped in regions of Bihar and Uttar Pradesh.

Ans. False

5. Shiva is performing Rasa-Lila in the famous bronze sculpture, Nataraja.

Ans. False

Very Short Answer Type Questions

1. Lost-wax process was widely used in the regions of Himachal Pradesh, Odisha, Bihar, Madhya Pradesh and West Bengal. With reference to this statement explain the meaning of lost-wax process.

Ans. Lost-wax process also called *cire-perdue* method of metal casting is a process in which a molten metal is poured into a mold that has been created by means of a wax model. Once the mold is made, the wax model is melted and drained away.

2. Write a short note on excavation at Daimabad.

Ans. A group of bronze statuettes have been discovered from Daimabad (Maharashtra) that belong to 1500 BCE. It consists of a 'Chariot', the wheels of which are represented in simple circular shapes. Along with chariot, the driver or human rider has been elongated (stretched out) and the bulls in the front are depicted in muscular forms.

3. Briefly explain the images of Jain *Tirthankaras* that belong to Kushana period.

Ans. The images of Jain *Tirthankaras* that belong to the Kushana period are found in Chausa, Bihar. These bronze sculptures depict how the Indian sculptors had mastered the modeling of masculine human body structures and simplified muscles. The most remarkable example is the depiction of Adinath, who is identified with long hair locks dropping to his shoulders. Otherwise the *Tirthankaras* are distinguished by their short curly hair.

4. Female images of *Yakshinis* and *Shasanadevis* were beautifully represented with the bronze images of Jain *Tirthankaras*. With reference to this statement define the figurines of *Shasanadevis*.

Ans. *Shasanadevis* are divine female messenger of some of the prominent Jain *Tirthankaras*. Their style was influenced by the features of both the Gupta and the Vakataka period bronze images. Chakreshvari is the *Shasanadevi* of Adinath and Ambika is of Neminath.

5. What is *Chaturanana* and where this sculpture is found?

Ans. *Chaturanana* is a sculpture of a four-headed Vishnu who was worshipped in Himachal and Kashmir regions. The central face represents Vasudeva, while the other two faces represent Narasimha and Varaha.

The bronze statues of Narasimha and Mahishasuramardini (Durga) are the most popular bronze statues of Himachal Pradesh.

6. Write a short note on *abhaya mudra*.

Ans. The *abhaya mudra* is a *mudra* (gesture) of reassurance and safety which eliminate fear and grants divine protection and bliss in many Indian religions.

In this *mudra*, the right hand is held upright and the palm is facing outwards. This is one of the earliest *mudra* depicted on a number of Hindu, Buddhist, Jain and Sikh images.

7. Write a short note on *tribhanga* posture.

Ans. *Tribhanga* is a standing body position or stance used in traditional Indian art and Indian classical dance forms like the Odissi, where the body bends in one direction at the knees, the other direction at the hips and then the other again at the shoulders and neck.

8. Briefly explain development of Indian bronze sculpture.

Ans. Indian bronze sculpture developed significantly during the medieval period. The bronze images were modelled and casted during the Pallava period in the 8th and 9th centuries. Chola bronze images are the most desired collection items by art lovers all over the world.

9. Appreciate the visual aesthetics and visual grandeur of the *Kalyanasundara* Murti of Shiva in precise manner.

Ans. *Kalyanasundara* Murti is exceptional depiction of *Panigrahana* ceremony by two separate statues. In this, Shiva with his extended right hand accepts Parvati's (the bride's) right hand, who is taking a step forward and feeling very shy. The union of Shiva and Parvati is very divinely represented in the *ardhanarisvara murti* in a single image. Beautiful independent figurines of Parvati have also been modelled, standing in graceful *tribhanga* posture.

10. What is represented in famous bronze sculpture Nataraja?

Ans. Nataraja represents Shiva in dancing position that depicts the end of cosmic world. In this, Shiva is performing tandava which is a symbol of divine energy, harmony and rhythm. It represents five essential acts i.e. creation, preservation, destruction, veiling and grace. Shiva is heavily ornamented wearing a pearl necklace, rings, anklets and chest bands and a crown.

Short Answer Type Questions

1. Do you think that the technique of bronze casting has been a continuous process? How did it evolve over a period of time? *(NCERT)*

Ans. Yes, the technique of bronze casting has been a continuous process and it has evolved over a period of time in the following ways

- Indian sculptors had mastered the bronze medium and the casting process as much as they had mastered Terracotta sculpture and carving in stone. The bronze sculptures are characterised by exquisite beauty and aesthetic appeal. The 'Dancing Girl' from Mohenjodaro is one of the earliest simplified figurines.
- The making of bronze sculptures reached a high stage of development in South India during the medieval period.
- Although bronze images were modelled and casted during the Pallava period in the 8th and 9th centuries, some of the most elegant and exquisite statues were produced during the Chola period.
- The well-known dancing figure of Shiva as Nataraja was evolved and fully developed during the Chola period and since then many variations of this complex bronze image have been modelled. A wide range of Shiva iconography was evolved in Thanjavur (Tanjore) region of Tamil Nadu during this period.
- The poses and the expressions on the faces of the bronze figures are very explicit. Apart from the *mudras* or the poses, the artisans have taken special care of the other details such as the weapons and the 'vahana'. Chola bronzes are created using the lost-wax technique. In artistic terms, it is known as 'Cire Perdue' which demands a high degree of skill.

2. In India sculpturing in stone and metal happened simultaneously. In your opinion what were the similarities and differences between both technically, stylistically and functionally? *(NCERT)*

Ans. Stone sculpting is a process where a stone is being carved or assembled so, that a three-dimensional shape can be formed in case of stone carving. Various rough natural stones are shaped by removal of certain portions of stones.

Metal sculpting is a process where various metals such as bronze, aluminium, copper, iron, gold as well as silver are used to make a variety of structures.

There are certain differences between sculpting in a stone and sculpting in a metal which are

- Technically and functionally, sculpting in a stone means giving direct form to a stone by removing certain portion of the stone, but in case of sculpting in a metal, first we need to create a clay form then we need to cast and mould it in bronze or in different metal.
- In case of sculpting of stone additive and subtractive styles are used, but in case of sculpting of a metal moulding style is used.

3. Briefly explain the images of Jain *Tirthankaras* that were found in Gujarat and Rajasthan regions.

Ans. For the bronze images of Jain *Tirthankaras* that were found in Gujarat and Rajasthan regions, refer to text on pg. 111.

4. Briefly describe the South Indian bronze sculpture in your own words.

Ans. For the South Indian bronze sculptures, refer to text on pg. 113 and 114.

Long Answer Type Questions

1. Write a detailed note on the method of bronze casting.

Ans. For the method of bronze casting, refer to text on pg. no. 109 and 110.

2. Evaluate the bronze images of Buddha which are found from different regions of Indian territory.

Ans. For description of the Buddha images of bronze from different regions of India, refer to text on pg. 112 and 113.

3. Why are Chola bronze sculptures considered as the most refined? *(NCERT)*

Ans. Chola bronze sculptures are considered as the most refined because lost-wax technique was used for the bronze sculpture. They are characterised by exquisite beauty and aesthetic appeal. They reached a high stage of development in South India especially during the Chola period.

Some of the most elegant statues were

- The 9th century *Kalyanasundara Murti* is highly remarkable for the manner in which *Panigrahana* is represented by two separate statuettes.
- The union of Shiva and Parvati is very ingeniously represented in the *ardhanarisvara murti* in a single image.
- The well-known dancing figure of Shiva as Nataraja was evolved and fully developed during the Chola period and since then many variations of this complex bronze image have been modelled.
- A wide range of Shiva iconography was evolved in Thanjavur (Tanjore) region of Tamil Nadu during Chola period.

In spite of being devoid of ornamentation, the Chola bronze sculptures are elegant, expressive and exquisitely beautiful. The poses and the expressions on the faces of the figures are very explicit. The Chola period was an age of continuous improvement and refinement of *Dravidian* art and architecture. The circumstances in which bronzes were cast during this period, and the contexts within which they are made, continue to have great relevance for our present-day understanding of art, poetry, science, history and society.

4. Explain the theme of the famous sculpture of Nataraja.

Ans. For the description of sculpture of Nataraja, refer to text on pg. 114.

CHAPTER 11

Aspects of Indo-Islamic Architecture

In this chapter

- *Introduction to Indo-Islamic Architecture*
- *Some Monuments of Indo-Islamic Architecture*

Introduction to Indo-Islamic Architecture

Muslims, through their migrations and conquests, included many features of local cultures and traditions and combined them with their own architectural practices. Thus in the field of architecture, a combination of many structural techniques, stylised shapes and surface decorations was introduced due to constant interventions of acceptance, rejection or modification of architectural elements. These architectural entities or categories showcasing multiple styles are known as **Indo-Saracenic** or **Indo-Islamic architecture**.

Hindus create manifestations of God in multiple forms as part of their religious faith, whereas Muslims thought of only Muhammad as their Prophet. Hence, Hindus decorated all surfaces with sculptures and paintings, whereas Muslims were not allowed to decorate the surfaces with any designs of living forms. They developed their religious art and architecture consisting of the arts of **arabesque**[1], geometrical patterns and calligraphy on plaster and stone.

Development of Indo-Islamic Architecture

- In the 7th and 8th centuries CE, Islam spread towards Spain and India. Islam came to India with Muslim merchants, traders, holy men and conquerors over a period of 600 years.

---

1 **Arabesque** It is form of artistic decoration consisting of surface decoration including rythmic linear patterns of crossing designs of leaves, flowers or plain lines.

- By the 8th century CE, Muslims began construction in Sind, Gujarat, etc. However, large-scale building activity began in early 13th century under the Delhi Sultanate that was established after the Turkish conquest of Northern India.
- By the 12th century, India was familiar with magnificent monumental constructions of Islamic architecture. Certain techniques and embellishments (decorations) were prevalent and popular such as trabeation (brackets, pillars and lintels) to support a flat roof or a small shallow dome.
- Trabeation was a style of architecture in which roofs, doors and windows were made by placing a horizontal beam across two vertical columns. Bracket is an architectural element which can be made of wood, stone, plaster, metal, etc. Lintel is a structural horizontal support used to span an opening in a wall or between two vertical supports. It is frequently used over windows and doors.
- Arches were made of wood and stone, but they were unable to bear the weight of the top structure. Therefore, the archuate (curved) form of construction was introduced in which arches could support the weight of the domes. Such arches needed to be constructed with **voussoirs**[2] and fitted with keystones. The domes are rested on **pendentives**[3] and **squinches**[4] to cover large spaces, so there are no pillars inside.

Types of Structures in Indo-Islamic Architecture

Architectural structures in the Indian sub-continent as well as around world were constructed by wealthy people. They are rulers and nobles and their families, merchants, merchant guilds, rural elite and devotees of a cult.

Many architectural structures were constructed over a period of time like mosques for daily prayers, the Jama Masjids, tombs, dargah, *minars*, hammams (a place of bathing), gardens, madrasas, sarais or caravansarais, Kos minars, etc. These were additions in the existing types of buildings in the sub-continent.

Categories of Styles in Indo-Islamic Architecture

The study of Indo-Islamic architecture is categorised into four styles which are

(i) The Imperial style (Delhi Sultanate)
(ii) The Provincial style (Mandu, Gujarat, Bengal and Jaunpur)
(iii) The Mughal style (Delhi, Agra and Lahore)
(iv) The Deccani style (Bijapur, Golconda)

These categories help in understanding the details of architectural styles in a better way.

Influences in Indo-Islamic Architecture

2 **Voussoirs** It is a wedge-shaped element, typically a stone which is used in building an arch or vault.

3 **Pendentives** Pendentive, in architecture is a triangular segment of a spherical surface, covering the upper corners of a room, in order to form a circular support for a dome at the top.

4 **Squinches** It is a straight or arched structure across an interior angle of a square tower to carry a superstructure such as a dome.

- In spite of the Islamic, Persian and Turkish influences, Indo-Islamic structures were greatly influenced by existing sensibilities of Indian architectural and decorative forms.
- Indo-Islamic structures also depends on the availability of materials, limitations of resources and skills and the sense of aesthetics (style) of the patrons.
- Among the provincial style of Indo-Islamic architecture, Bengal and Jaunpur have distinct style. However, the architecture of Gujarat have borrowed elements from regional temple traditions such as toranas, lintels in mihrabs, carvings of bell and chain **motifs**[5] and carved panels depicting trees, for tombs, mosques and *dargahs*.
- The 15th century white marble *dargah* of Shaikh Ahmad Khattu of Sarkhej is an example of provincial style which is greatly influenced by the form and decoration of Mughal tombs.

Decorative Forms in Indo-Islamic Architecture

These forms include designing on plaster through carving or **stucco**[6]. The decorative forms that were used in Indo-Islamic architecture were

- The designs were either left plain or covered with colours. Motifs were painted or carved in stone which include varieties of flowers, from the Indian sub-continent and outside regions, particularly Iran.
- The lotus bud fringe (margin) was used in the inner curves of the arches. Walls were also decorated with **cypress**[7], chinar, trees and flower vases.
- Many complex designs of flower motifs which are used for decorating the ceilings were also found on textiles and carpets.
- In the 14th, 15th and 16th centuries tiles were also used on the wall surfaces and the domes. They used blue, turquoise (sky blue to pale green), green and yellow colours.
- Techniques like tessellation (mosaic designs) and ***pietra dura***[8] were used for surface decoration especially in the **dado panels**[9] of the walls.
- Decoration form like ***lapis lazuli***[10] was used in the interior walls or on canopies. Some other decorative forms like arabesque, calligraphy, high and low relief carving and abundant use of **jalis**[11] were also adopted by architectures.

---

5 **Motif** Motif is a decorative image or design, especially a repeated one forming a pattern.

6 **Stucco** It is a fine plaster used for coating wall surfaces.

7 **Cypress** It is an evergreen coniferous tree with small rounded woody cones and flattened shoots bearing small scale-like leaves.

8 **Pietra dura** It is a pictorial mosaic work using semi-precious stones.

9 **Dado Panel** It is lower part of the interior wall when it is finished differently from the rest of the wall.

10 **Lapis Lazuli** It is a rich blue semi-precious stone. It was used as inlay in ornaments, jewellery, seals, etc.

11 **Jali** It is the term for a pierced stone or grid screen, usually with an ornamental pattern constructed through the use of calligraphy, geometery or natural patterns.

- The carving in high relief looks like three-dimensional. The arches were plain, squat as well as high and pointed. During 16th century, **Trefoil**[12] or multiple foliation arches were used. **Spandrels**[13] of the arches were decorated with **medallions**[14] or **bosses**[15].
- The roof include the central dome and other smaller domes, *chatris* and tiny minarets. An inverted lotus flower motif and a metal or stone pinnacle were placed above the central dome.

Dado panel on the wall, Agra

Pietra dura work, Agra

Materials used for Construction in Indo-Islamic Architecture

- The building walls were extremely thick and constructed using rough fragments of stones and bricks. These walls were then covered with *chunam* or limestone plaster or decorative stones.
- Some stones that were used for construction are quartzite, sandstone, buff, marble, etc. along with polychrome tiles.
- From the beginning of the 17th century, bricks were also used for construction and these imparted greater flexibility to the structures. In this phase, there was more dependency on local materials.

---

12 **Trefoil** It is an arch incorporating the shape or outline of a trefoil i.e. three overlapping circles.

13 **Spandrel** It is the roughly triangular area above and on either side of an arch bounded by a line running horizontally through the apex of the arch.

14 **Medallions** A piece of jewellery in the shape of a medal.

15 **Bosses** In architecture, a boss is a knob of wood, stone or metal.

Monumental Structures of Indo-Islamic Architecture

Forts

During medieval times, forts were built with **embattlements**[16] which symbolise the seat of power of a king. When such forts were captured by an attacking army, the defeated ruler either lost his complete power or his sovereignty because he had to accept the suzerainty of the victorious king.

Forts were constructed at great heights which gave them a good perspective of the region, strategic advantage for security, unrestricted and unhindered space to make residential and official complexes and creating a sense of awe (astonishment) in the people. Some examples of complex and strong forts are

- **Golconda Fort** In this fort, some complex structures like concentric circles of outer walls are included so that the enemy had to break these at all stages before entering the fort.
- **Daulatabad Fort** It was earlier known as Devgiri Fort. It had several strategic devices to surprise amaze the enemy such as staggered (in a zig-zag formation) entrances so that gates could not be opened even with the help of elephants. In the premises of Daulatabad Fort, there were two more forts which are located at higher elevation. These two forts were made in such a manner, that an enemy could not enter to the fort easily. In this complex pathway, a wrong turn could lead to the enemy soldier going in circles or his death by falling several hundred feet below.
- **Gwalior Fort** It was indestructible and impossible to compute because of its steep height. This fort had many habitations and use which surprised many rulers.

Gwalior Fort

16 **Embattlements** It is design at the top of old castle walls that looks like upside down teeth. It was used as a space for archers or sharpshooters to attack intruders.

For example, Babur did not find much standards in many things that he saw in Hindustan, but he was surprised to see the Gwalior Fort.

- **Chittorgarh Fort** It is the largest fort in Asia and was the seat of power for the longest time. It has many types of buildings including *stambhas* or towers to signify victory and bravery and also numerous water bodies. Many acts of bravery and courageousness are related to the principal people of this fort which provided the basis for many legends (epics).

Minars

Minars (another form of *stambha* or tower) are a common feature in the sub-continent. These *minars* are used for daily prayers or *azaan*. Its exceptional height symbolises the strength and power of the ruler.

Two most prominent *minars* of medieval times are the **Qutub Minar** in Delhi and the **Chand Minar** at Daulatabad Fort

- **Qutub Minar** It was built in the 13th century and is associated with most respected saint of Delhi, Khwaja Qutbuddin Bakhtiyar Kaki. It is a 234 ft high narrow tower divided into five storeys. It was built using red and buff sandstone with some marble in the upper storeys.
- **Chand Minar** It was built in the 15th century. It is a 210 ft high narrow tower divided into four storeys. Its front part which is now painted with peach colour, used to have **chevron patterning**[17] on the **encaustic tile**[18] work and prominent bands of Quranic verses. It looked like an Iranian monument. However, it was made by handwork of local architects along with the architects from Delhi and Iran.

Chand Minar, Daulatabad

Tombs

One of the most popular features of medieval India was the monumental structures over graves of rulers and royalty. Some well-known examples of such tombs are those of Ghyasuddin Tughlaq, Humayun, Abdur Rahim Khan-i-Khanan in Delhi, Akbar and Itmaduddaula in Agra.

17 **Chevron pattern** Chevron is an inverted 'V' pattern, with each side meeting at the point without interruption.

18 **Encaustic Tiles** These are ceramic tiles in which the pattern or figure on the surface is not a product of the glaze but of different colours of clay.

According to a remarkable scholar Anthony Welch, the idea behind the construction of the tomb was to provide a eternal paradise to the deceased as a reward for the true believer on the **Day of Judgement**[19]. As a result, the imagery for tomb construction became ideal.

With the introduction of Quranic verses on the walls, the tomb was placed within beautiful elements such as a garden or near a body of water or both. This can be seen in Humayun's tomb and the Taj Mahal, which follows the **charbagh style**[20]. Such structured and stylised monuments have been intended to signify peace and happiness in the next world as well as to showcase the greatness, glory and power of the person buried there.

Tomb of Itmaduddaula, Agra

Sarais

An interesting feature of medieval India was the sarais which surrounded cities and can be found in large numbers in Indian sub-continent. Sarais were primarily constructed on a square or rectangular layout and were intended to serve as temporary housing to Indian and foreign travellers, pilgrims, merchants, traders, etc.

Sarais were public spaces that were crowded with people from different cultural backgrounds. This resulted in cross-cultural interaction, influences and unification tendencies in cultural customs and at individual level.

---

19 **Day of Judgement** In Islamic eschatology (the theology concerned with death, judgement and final destiny of soul), the Day of Judgement is believed to be God's final assessment of humanity. i.e. life on Earth will come to an end.

20 **Charbagh Style** In this style of architecture, the main building is constructed at the centre of the quadrilateral garden, divided by walkaways or flowing water into four smaller parts.

Jama Masjid

Jama Masjids are large mosques that spread over huge spaces. Every Friday afternoon, congregational prayers were held in these mosques in which 40 Muslim male adults were required to be present. At the time of prayers, a *Khutba* (the sermon) was read out in the name of the ruler and his laws for his kingdom were also read out. In medieval times, a city had only one Jama Masjid which along with its surroundings became the focus of the lives of both Muslim and non-Muslim people. This is because of many commercial and cultural exchanges activities that took place here apart from religious and indirect political activity. These mosques were large with open courtyards, surrounded on three sides by cloisters (Walk-ways) and ***Quibla Liwan***[21] in the West. *Mihrab* and ***mimbar***[22] for ***Imam***[23] were also located in these mosques. People faced the *mihrab* while offering prayers as it indicated the direction of the *Kaaba* in Mecca.

Some Monuments of Indo-Islamic Architecture

One of the architectural features of medieval India was fusion of styles, techniques and decorations in public and private spaces of non-royal sections of the society. These included buildings for domestic usage, temples, mosques, *khanqahs* (hermitage of Sufi saints) and *dargahs*, commemorative gateways, pavillions in buildings and gardens, bazaars, etc. Some of the Indo-Islamic or Medieval architectures are

Name : Qutub Minar
Place : Mehrauli, Delhi, India
Medium : Stone (sand and marble)
Period : 13th century
Collection : Archaeological Survey of India

Qutub Minar

Qutub-ud-din Aibak, the **first Muslim ruler of Delhi**, commenced the construction of the Qutub Minar in 1200 AD, but could only finish the basement. His successor, **Iltutmish**, added three more storeys and in 1368, **Firoz Shah Tughlak** constructed the fifth and the last storey. Qutub means pole or column that symbolise justice and sovereignty. This tower was built for the purpose of calling people for prayer. The architectural features of Qutub Minar are

- This tower is located near Southern entrance gate called **Alai Darwaza** of Quwwat-ul-Islam Mosque which was built by Alauddin Khilji . An inscription over its Eastern gate provides information that it was built with material obtained from demolishing 27 Hindu temples.

21 **Quibla Liwan** The wall of mosque in the direction of Mecca.
22 **Mimbar** A stepped platform from where the *Khutba* was read.
23 **Imam** The person who leads a Muslim congregration in prayers.

- Its circumference at the base is 13.75 m and at the top is 2.75 m.
- A 7m high iron pillar stands in the courtyard of the mosque. The complex of tower also include the tomb of Zamin, the tomb of Iltutmish and major Smith's Cupola, etc.
- The tower has five distinct storeys each marked by a projecting balcony. The first three storeys are made of red sandstone.
- In the first and second storeys, stone tiles of pink colour were used, while in the third storey, tiles of dark shade of red colour were used. The fourth and fifth storey were made by using red sandstone and marble.
- All the five storeys and tower have unique designs. On the surface of the first storey, alternate, angular and circular groves are made vertically. The second storey has rounded groves and the third storey has only angular groves.
- The tower is ornamented by bands of inscriptions and by four projecting balconies supported by elaborately decorated brackets. The balconies have inscription and carvings from Holy Quran.

This tower is not only one of the finest monuments in India, but also in the world. The development of architectural styles from Aibak to Tughlak is quite evident in this tower. There is variation in relief work and even in the materials used for construction.

Gol Gumbad

Name : Gol Gumbad
Medium : Bricks and limestone
Collection : Archaeological Survey of India
Place : Bijapur, Karnataka
Period : 1626-1656 AD

It was built by **Muhammad Adil Shah** (1626-1656), seventh Sultan of the Adil Shahi dynasty (1489-1686) of Bijapur. Gol Gumbad is a prominent monument in spite of being unfinished. The tomb is a complex of buildings such as a gateway, a *Naqqar Khana*, a mosque and a *sarai* located within a large-walled garden.

Gol Gumbad is a fine convergence of many styles located in medieval India. Its structural particularities of dome, arches, geometric proportions and load bearing techniques suggest Timurid and Persian styles.

It is made of local material and is decorated with surface embellishments popular in the Deccan. The four towers at the corners are similar to the towers attached to mosques such as **Qila-i-Kuhna Masjid**[24] and the Purana Qila in Delhi.

The architectural features of Gol Gumbad are

- The Gumbad is a monumental square building with a circular drum at the top and above this a large dome is placed, giving the building its nomenclature.
- It is made of dark-gray basalt and decorated plasterwork.
- Each wall of the tomb is 135 ft long, 110 ft high and 10 ft thick. The height of the building is over 200 ft due to drum and the dome.
- The tomb has only one square chamber and the dome with a diameter of 125 ft. It covers a continous floor space of 18,337 sq ft which is the second largest in the world.
- The hemispherical masonry (stone work) dome above a square base was constructed with the help of pendentives. These pendentives not only give shape to the dome, but also transferred its weight to the walls below.
- The tomb chamber contains the burial place of the Sultan, his wives and other relatives. Their real graves lie perpendicularly below in a vault, accessed by stairs.
- New vaulting systems were consisted of arch nets or star shaped design plans in squinches. These vaulting systems were created to cover angles formed by intersecting arches.
- The building has an amazing **acoustical system**[25]. Along the drum of the dome there is a whispering gallery where sounds get magnified and echoed many times. The drum of the dome is decorated with foliation.
- At the four corners of the building, there are seven-storeyed octagonal spires or minaret-like towers. These towers have staircases leading to the top dome.
- A finely designed crown which is placed on the top of **corbels**[26] are the distinctive feature of this large building.

---

24 **Qila-i-Kuhna Masjid** Built by Humayun or Sher Shah between 1530 and 1545, it is located inside Purana Qila in Delhi.

25 **Acoustical system** It is a system which concerns with the production, control, transmission, reception and effects of sound.

26 **Corbels** It is structural piece of stone, wood or metal which is attached from a wall, to carry the weight imposed by the above balcony.

EXAM PRACTICE

Multiple Choice Questions

1. Indo-Islamic architecture is a mix of many structural techniques, stylised shapes and surface decorations. It is also known as ....

   (a) Indo-European (b) Indo-Turkish
   (c) Indo-Timurid (d) Indo-Saracenic

Ans. (d) Indo-Saracenic

2. In the 7th and 8th century AD Islam came to India with.....................

   (a) merchants (b) holy men
   (c) conquerors (d) All of these

Ans. (d) All of these

3. Name the style or technique that was popular to support a flat roof or a small shallow dome.

   (a) Trabeation (b) Squinches
   (c) Pendentives (d) Voussoirs

Ans. (a) Trabeation

4. Imperial style of Indo-Islamic architecture is also known as..........

   (a) Provincial style (b) Delhi Sultanate
   (c) Deccani style (d) Bijapur style

Ans. (b) Delhi Sultanate

5. White marble *dargah* of Shaikh Ahmad Khattu of Sarkhej was built during which century?

   (a) 15th century (b) 20th century
   (c) 18th century (d) 12th century

Ans. (a) 15th century

6. It is a rich blue semi-precious stone. The main source in the ancient world was the mountains of Badakshan, Northern Afghanistan.

   Which of the following material is described in the given lines?

   (a) Polychrome tiles (b) Jasper
   (c) Lapis lazuli (d) Quartz

Ans. (c) Lapis lazuli

7. Name the fort which has concentric circles on outer walls to protect it from enemy.

   (a) Daulatabad Fort (b) Golconda Fort
   (c) Gwalior Fort (d) Chittorgarh Fort

Ans. (b) Golconda Fort

8. .... were intended to serve as temporary housing to Indian and foreign travellers, pilgrims, merchants and traders.

   (a) Sarais (b) Tomb
   (c) Forts (d) Minars

Ans. (a) Sarais

9. Where is Qutub Minar located?

   (a) Agra, Uttar Pradesh
   (b) Bijapur, Karnataka
   (c) Mehrauli, Delhi
   (d) Jaipur, Rajasthan

Ans. (c) Mehrauli, Delhi

10. With which of the following saint was Qutub Minar associated?

    (a) Khwaja Moinuddin Chisti
    (b) Khwaja Qutbuddin Bakhtiyar Kaki
    (c) Sheikh Nizamat Ullah
    (d) Khwaja Pir Mohammad

Ans. (b) Khwaja Qutbuddin Bakhtiyar Kaki

11. Gol Gumbad is a mausoleum of which of the following ruler?

    (a) Qutub-ud-din-Aibak
    (b) Shah Jahan
    (c) Muhammad Adil Shahi
    (d) Iltutmish

Ans. (c) Muhammad Adil Shahi

12. Which of the following style is reflected in architectural style of Gol Gumbad?

    (a) Persian style and Gothic style
    (b) Persian style and Timurid style
    (c) European and Indian style
    (d) European and Persian style

Ans. (b) Persian style and Timurid style

13. Match the following.

List I (Sites)	List II State (Place)
A. Golconda Fort	1. Steep height and habitation
B. Daulatabad Fort	2. Staggered entrance
C. Gwalior Fort	3. Concentric circles on outer walls
D. Chittorgarh Fort	4. *Stambhas* to signify victory

Codes

(a) A-1, B-2, C-3, D-4
(b) A-2, B-4, C-3, D-1
(c) A-3, B-2, C-1, D-4
(d) A-2, B-3, C-1, D-4

Ans. (c)

14. Match the following.

List I	List II
A. Qutub Minar	1. Muhammad Adil Shah
B. Gol Gumbad	2. Qutub-ud-din Aibak
C. Alai Darwaza	3. Alauddin Khilji

Codes

(a) A-1, B-3, C-2 (b) A-2, B-3, C-1
(c) A-2, B-1, C-3 (d) A-3, B-2, C-1

Ans. (c)

Assertion-Reason

Directions (Q. Nos. 15-18). There are two statements marked as Assertion (A) and Reason (R). Read the statement and answer the questions according to codes given below.

(a) Both A and R are true and R is the correct explanation of A
(b) Both A and R are true, but R is not the correct explanation of A
(c) A is true, but R is false
(d) A is false, but R is true

15. **Assertion** (A) In the early 13th century large-scale building activity began under the Delhi Sultanate that was established after the Turkish conquest of Northern India.

Reason (R) During this period, Muslims absorbed many features of local cultures and traditions like trabeation, archuate, pendentives, squinches and combined them with their own architectural practices.

Ans. (a) Both A and R are true and R is the correct explanation of A

16. **Assertion** (A) In Gwalior Fort some complex structures like concentric circles of outer walls are included.

Reason (R) These concentric circles are used so that the enemy had to breach these at all stages before entering the fort.

Ans. (d) A is false, but R is true

17. **Assertion** (A) The Qutub Minar is a 234-feet- high tapering (narrow) tower divided into five storeys was built in the 13th century.

Reason (R) The monument Qutub Minar was associated with the Khwaja Moinuddin Chisti.

Ans. (c) A is true, but R is false

18. **Assertion** (A) Gol Gumbad is a prominent monument in spite of being unfinished.

Reason (R) Gol Gumbad is situated in Bijapur, Karnataka. It is the mausoleum of Muhammad Adil Shah the seventh Sultan of the Adil Shahi dynasty built by the ruler himself.

Ans. (b) Both A and R are true, but R is not the correct explanation of A

Source Based Question

19. Read the source given below and answer the following questions.

It is a fine convergence of many styles located in medieval India. Its structural particularities of dome, arches, geometric proportions and load bearing techniques suggest Timurid and Persian styles. It is made of local material and is decorated with surface embellishments popular in the Deccan.

The four towers at the corners are similar to the towers attached to mosques such as Qila-i-Kuhna Masjid and the Purana Qila in Delhi. The architectural features includes– The dome is a monumental square building with a circular drum at the top and above this a large dome is place, giving the building its nomenclature. It is made of dark gray basalt and decorated plasterwork. Each wall of the tomb is 135 ft long, 110 ft high and 10 ft thick. The height of the building is over 200 ft due to the drum and the dome. The tomb has only one square chamber and the dome with a diameter of 125 ft. It covers a continuous floor space of 18,337 sq ft which is the second largest in the world.

(i) Which of the following monuments has been discussed in the source?
(a) Taj Mahal
(b) Alai Darwaza
(c) Gol Gumbad
(d) Charminar

Ans. (c) Gol Gumbad

(ii) What is the material used in this monument?
(a) Bricks and limestone
(b) Bricks and soapstone
(c) Bricks and chunar stone
(d) Brick and sandstone

Ans. (a) Bricks and limestone

(iii) This monumnet was built by ....
(a) Shah Jahan
(b) Muhammad Adil Shahi
(c) Ahmad Shah Abdali
(d) Aurangzeb

Ans. (b) Muhammad Adil Shahi

(iv) Where is the monument located?
(a) Bihar
(b) Tamil Nadu
(c) Maharashtra
(d) Karnataka

Ans. (d) Karnataka

(v) In which year was the construction of this monument completed
(a) 1636 (b) 1626 (c) 1656 (d) 1646

Ans. (c) 1656

True or False

1. A *dargah* is a type of steam bath or a place of public bathing associated with the Islamic world.

Ans. False

2. Hammams were the place of congregation and worship.

Ans. False

3. The Provincial style of Indo-Islamic architecture include Mandu, Gujarat, Bengal, and Jaunpur.

Ans. True

4. Gwalior Fort had several strategic devices to amaze the enemy such as staggered entrances so that gates could not be opened even with the help of elephants.

Ans. False

5. Qutub Minar was built in 1193 by Qutub-ud-din Aibak.

Ans. True

Very Short Answer Type Questions

1. What do you understand by the term 'Indo-Islamic' or 'Indo-Saracenic' architecture? *(NCERT)*

Ans. Indo-Islamic or Indo-Saracenic architecture is a mix style that developed when Muslims include many features of local cultures and traditions like trabeation, archuate, pendentives, squinches and combined them with their own architectural practices.

2. What types of buildings were added in India in the 13th century? *(NCERT)*

Ans. In the 13th century, large-scale building activity begun under the Delhi Sultanate. Some new style like archuate form of construction to support the weight of the domes, voussoirs fitted with keystones and domes, resting on pendentives and squinches were added.

3. Name four styles of Indo-Islamic architecture. (NCERT)

Ans. The four styles of Indo-Islamic architecture are
(i) The Imperial style (Delhi Sultanate)
(ii) The Provincial style (Mandu, Gujarat, Bengal, Jaunpur)
(iii) The Mughal style (Delhi, Agra and Lahore)
(iv) The Deccani style (Bijapur, Golconda).

4. What decorative forms are used in Indo-Islamic architecture?

Ans. Decorative forms used in Islamic architecture include designing on plaster through carving or stucco. The designs were either left plain or covered with colours. Motifs were painted or carved in stone. These motifs include varieties of flowers, both from the sub-continent and outside particularly Iran.

5. What materials are used in construction of the monuments?

Ans. For construction of building walls of the monuments, rough fragments of stones and bricks were used which make them extremely thick. These walls were then covered with limestone plaster or decorative stones. Some stones that were used for construction are quartzite, sandstone, buff, marble, etc. along with polychrome tiles. From the beginning of the 17th century, bricks were also used for construction and these imparted greater flexibility to the structures.

6. What are the strategic devices used at Daulatabad Fort to protect it from enemies?

Ans. Daulatabad Fort had several strategic devices to amaze the enemy such as staggered entrances so that gates could not be opened even with the help of elephants. In the premises of Daulatabad Fort, there were two more forts which are located at higher elevation. These two forts were made in such a manner, that an enemy could not enter to the fort easily. One wrong turn in the complex pathway of the fort could lead to the enemy soldier going in circles or his death by falling several hundred feet below.

7. Appreciate the architectural style of Chittorgarh Fort which was known from its brave and courageous legends.

Ans. Chittorgarh Fort is the largest fort in Asia and was the seat of power for the longest time. It has many types of buildings including *stambhas* or towers to signify victory and bravery and also numerous water bodies.

8. What are *minars* in Indo-Islamic architecture?

Ans. *Minars* are a common feature in the sub-continent. These *minars* are used for daily prayers or *azaan.* Its exceptional height symbolises the strength and power of the ruler. Two most prominent *minars* of medieval times are the Qutub Minar in Delhi and the Chand Minar at Daulatabad Fort.

9. Write a brief note on the significance of Sarais and why they were constructed?

Ans. Sarais were the buildings that were intended to serve as temporary housing to Indian and foreign travellers, pilgrims, merchants, traders, etc. They were primarily constructed on a square or rectangular layout.

Sarais were public spaces that were crowded with people from different cultural backgrounds. This resulted in cross-cultural interaction, influences and unification tendencies in the cultural customs and at the individual level.

10. Which are the places where the dead are buried? How do these differ from each other? [NCERT]

Ans. Deads are buried in the tombs. The tombs differ from each other on the basis of size, design and complexity which included pyramids, mastabas (a type of Egyptian tomb) and rock-cut chambers. However, these differences were mainly due to the wealth and status of the owner, evolving religious beliefs or political circumstances.

Short Answer Type Questions

1. How did Indo-Islamic architecture evolve in India? *(NCERT)*

Ans. Indo-Islamic architecture evolved with the spread of Islam during 7th and 8th centuries CE. During this period, Muslims began construction in Sind, Gujarat, etc. It was only in the early 13th century that large-scale building activity began under the Delhi Sultanate that established after the Turkish conquest of Northern India.

By the 12th century India was familiar with magnificent monumental constructions. Certain techniques and embellishments were prevalent and popular such as trabeation (a type of beam) to support a flat roof or a small shallow dome. Arches were made of wood and stone, but they were unable to bear the weight of the top structure. Therefore, the archuate form of construction was introduced in which arches could support the weight of the domes. Such arches needed to be constructed with voussoirs and fitted with keystones. The domes are resting on pendentives and squinches which enable spanning of large spaces leaving the interiors free of pillars.

2. Which forms of secular architecture evolved during medieval times? What significance did these buildings have in the socio-cultural lives of contemporary people? *(NCERT)*

Ans. The Indo-Islamic style of architecture was developed during Medieval period.

Architecture would be considered secular if it can be accessed by believers of all religion. The Indo-Islamic architecture is one such form undoubtedly it had the influence of Persian and Turkish elements, still it was largely Indian in its outlook. It utilised the resources and labour locally. Sarais which were built by the Indo-Islamic rulers is a classic example of secularity. They were public structures which acted as accommodation to travellers. They have been utilised by people of all cultures and faiths.

The domes of the mosques represents royalty and socio-culture lives of the royals. The Islamic architecture affected the social cultural life of the contemporary people in various ways that is in case of mosque during prayer, people came together for praying purpose.

3. What is the structural classification of Indo-Islamic architecture?

Ans. Indo-Islamic architecture are classified in mosques for daily prayers, the Jama Masjids, tombs, *dargahs*, *minars*, *hammams*, gardens, madrasas, *sarais* or caravansarais, *Kos minars*, etc. These were some additions in the existing types of buildings in the sub-continent.

Architectural structures in the Indian sub-continent as well as around world were constructed by wealthy people. They are rulers and nobles and their families, merchants, merchant guilds, rural elite and devotees of a cult.

In spite of the Saracenic, Persian and Turkish influences, Indo-Islamic structures were heavily influenced by existing sensibilities of Indian architectural and decorative forms. It also depends on the availability of materials, limitations of resources and skills and the sense of aesthetics (style) of the patrons.

4. What was the significance of a fort in medieval India? What were the strategic devices adopted in the construction of forts to confuse or defeat the enemy? *(NCERT)*

Ans. The significance of a fort in medieval India was

- During medieval times, forts were built with embattlements which symbolise the seat of power of a king.
- When such forts were captured by an attacking army the defeated ruler either lost his complete power or his sovereignty because he had to accept the suzerainty of the victorious king.
- Forts were constructed at great heights to have a good perspective of the region, strategic advantage for security, unrestricted and unhindered space to make residential and official complexes.

Some of the strategic devices adopted in the construction of forts were

- In Golconda Forts, some complex structures like concentric circles of outer walls are included so that the enemy had to breach these at all stages before entering the fort.
- Daulatabad Fort had several strategic devices to amaze the enemy such as staggered entrances.
- The Gwalior Fort was indestructible and impossible to compute because of its steep height.

5. In spite of being unfinished how does Gol Gumbad symbolise the grandeur and majesty of Indo-Islamic architecture? *(NCERT)*

Ans. Gol Gumbad symbolise the grandeur and majesty of Indo-Islamic architecture as it has influence of *Dravidian* architecture. Gol Gumbad is in Bijapur and it got built in nearly 30 years for completing construction in 1656. The following features suggest that it is of Indo-Islamic architecture

- Gol Gumbad represent a circular dome which helps to support all the pillars.
- The walls and the base of the Gol Gumbad emits echo effect of sound.
- The dome-drum is seen as decorated with foliation. The cornice is heavily bracketed with corbels and that is regarded as an important feature of front.

Long Answer Type Questions

1. Write a brief note on the following
   (a) Influences on Indo-Islamic Architecture
   (b) Decorative forms in Indo-Islamic Architecture

Ans. (a) For description on influences on Indo-Islamic architecture, refer to text on pg. 123.

(b) For description on decorative forms in Indo-Islamic architecture, refer to text on pg. 123 and 124.

2. Comment on the structural style of *minars* in Indo-Islamic architecture by giving two suitable examples.

Ans. For the structural style of minars in Indo-Islamic architecture, refer to text on pg. 126.

3. Appreciate the visual aesthetics and grandeur of any building which was dedicated to Sufi Saint Bakhtiyar Kaki in Delhi Sultanate.

Ans. For description of Qutub Minar, refer to text on pg. 128 and 129.

4. What do you like about the aspects of Indo-Islamic architecture? Give a detailed explanation which justifies your choice.

Ans. The features I like in the Indo-Islamic architecture are

- The Indo-Islamic architecture encompasses a wide range of styles from various backgrounds that helped shape the architecture of the Indian sub-continent from the advent of Islam in the Indian sub-continent around 7th century.
- It has left influences on modern Indian, Pakistani and Bangladeshi architecture.
- Both secular and religious buildings are influenced by Indo-Islamic architecture which exhibit Indian, Islamic, Persian, and Ottoman Turkish influences.
- Indo-Islamic style provided spaciousness, massiveness to the Hindu architecture. Accurate style, which involved the use of beams and arches replaced the trabeation style which characterised Indian temples and other secular buildings.
- Arches, minarets and domes are the features of Indo-Islamic style that are largely used.
- The other distinguishing feature involved was the use of geometrical and arabesque designs and calligraphy on plaster and stone, keeping in mind the religious sensibilities of Muslims. In the later years, the technique of *pietra dura* was also introduced.
- Unlike the traditional Indian artisans who worked with mud for brick work, the artisans from Indo-Islamic style introduced the use of mortar as a cementing agent.

SAMPLE QUESTION PAPERS

(Painting, Graphics, Sculpture and Commercial Art)

SAMPLE
QUESTION PAPER
(Painting)

Time allowed : 2 hrs MM : 30 Marks

General Instructions

1. Section – A Attempt all Questions (Each Question will carry 1 Mark)
2. Section – B Attempt all Questions (Each Question will carry 2 Marks)
3. Section – C Attempt any two Questions (Each Question will carry 6 Marks)

Section A

1. Who made the first discovery of rock painting in India? **(1)**

(a) Archibold Carlleyle (b) Cockburn (c) Anderson (d) Mitra

2. **Assertion** (A) Pramanani principle is governed by certain laws which give capability of portraying something precisely.

Reason (R) Pramanani teaches the exact measurement, proportion and distance of subjects and objects. **(1)**

Codes

(a) Both A and R are true and R is the correct explanation of A
(b) Both A and R are true, but R is not the correct explanation of A
(c) A is true, but R is false
(d) A is false, but R is true

3. Archaeologists have discover thousands of seals from Indus Valley, mostly made of steatite and other materials like agate copper, terracotta, etc. For which purpose seals were used? **(1)**

(a) Commercial (b) Artistic (c) Spiritual (d) Educational

4. With whom among the following saints was Qutub Minar associated? **(1)**

(a) Khwaja Moinuddin Chishti (b) Khwaja Qutbuddin Bakhtiyar Kaki
(c) Sheikh Nizamat Ullah (d) Khwaja Pir Mohammad

5. **Assertion** (A) Hunting scenes predominate Mesolithic paintings. **(1)**

Reason (R) Pre-historic men only knew how to paint animals.

Codes

(a) Both A and R are true and R is the correct explanation of A
(b) Both A and R are true, but R is not the correct explanation of A
(c) A is true, but R is false
(d) A is false, but R is true

6. Who among the following was the author of the book 'Kamasutra'? (1)

(a) Vishvamitra (b) Valmiki
(c) Veda Vyas (d) Vatsyayana

7. Which among the following elements deals with accuracy and precision of measurement and structure in the painting? (1)

(a) Pramanani (b) Roopabheda
(c) Lavanya Yojanam (d) Bhava

8. Identify the place from which bronze figure of a bull found that is known for its massiveness and fury of the charge. (1)

(a) Lothal (b) Mohenjodaro
(c) Harappa (d) Rakhigarhi

Section B

9. "The six limbs forms the significant part of Indian painting."
With the context of the same statement, identify any two limbs of Indian painting. (2)

Or

"During the upper Paleolithic times we see a proliferation of artistic activities."
Identify the artistic art forms that evolved during the upper Paleolithic period.

10. "The richest paintings are reported from the Vindhya ranges of Madhya Pradesh and Kaimurean extensions into Uttar Pradesh."
Write in your language, the major reasons for discovery of paintings in large scale. (2)

Or

"Kerala painters during 16th to the 18th century evolved a pictorial language and technique of their own."
Write a short note on unique features of painting of Venugopal of Sri Rama Temple, Triprayar.

11. Prolific paintings of the Nayaka dynasty in the 17th and 18th centuries are visible in Thiruparankundram.
Write in your own words, how they were successful in depicting the beauty of women and Goddesses with reference to below mentioned painting. (2)

'Ladies attending Parvati'

Or

Though animals were painted in a naturalistic style, humans were depicted only in a stylistic manner. Describe this statement, with the reference to Bhimbetka paintings.

12. "The shape was manipulated by the pressure of the crafty fingers of the potter." Write in your words the distinctive painting features about the below mentioned object. (2)

'Painted Earthen Jar'

Or

Throw light on the large statues of Yakshas and Yakhinis that are found at many places like Patna, Vidisha and Mathura.

13. "The paintings of the upper Paleolithic phase are linear representations, in green and dark red, of huge animal figures." Evaluate the themes of paintings found in the upper Paleolithic period of prehistoric era. (2)

Or

The paintings, though from the remote past, do not lack pictorial quality, rather there is a charm of simple rendering of scenes of the environment in which the artists lived. Justify this statement by describing paintings of Bhimbetka.

Section C

14. The Gandhara, Mathura and Sarnath Schools that flourished in Indian sub-continent considered as the epitome of Indian art forms.

From your course of study, identify and explain the various features of these schools of art. Support your answer with reference to (6)

- Confluence of different traditions
- Hellenistic features
- Headless Kanishka
- Sensual and boldness

15. Analyse the given sculpture based on your observation and describe it through the following points.
    - Name the sculpture, its historical period, location, and the artistic style it belongs to.
    - Highlight the subject matter while describing the key figures depicted in the narrative panels, such as Queen Mayadevi's dream or the Ruru Jataka story.
    - Explain how the storytelling technique, including the use of space, posture, and the depiction of human and animal figures, enhances the visual appeal and conveys moral values that inspire dedication and righteousness. (6)

16. Write an essay about the Dancing Scene of Lakhudiyar rock painting. Your answer should include (6)
    - Mastery of skill of the primitive people's art forms.
    - Categories of Lakhudiyar Painting
    - Design pattern and colours

Answers

1. (a) Archibold Carlleyle
2. (a) Both A and R are true and R is the correct explanation of A
3. (a) Commercial
4. (b) Khwaja Qutbuddin Bakhtiyar Kaki
5. (c) A is true, but R is false
6. (d) Vatsyayana
7. (a) Pramanani
8. (b) Mohenjodaro
9. The six limbs of Indian painting were evolved during 1st century BC to 3rd century AD. These six limbs are linked together to form limbs of human beings. These six limbs are known as Shadangas in India. The six limbs of Indian paintings are Roopbheda, Pramanani, Bhava, Lavanya Yojanem, Sadrisyam and Varnikabhangam.

Or Various finely carved and painted pictures of animals found during the upper Paleolithic period. In India, the earliest paintings have been reported from the upper Paleolithic times. The subjects of their drawings were human figures, human activities, geometric designs and animal symbols.

10. The richest paintings are reported from the Vindhya ranges of Madhya Pradesh and Kaimurean extensions into Uttar Pradesh, because these regions are full of forests, wild plants, fruits, streams and creeks. These conditions made perfect place for Stone Age people to live and draw different art forms and shapes.

Or The Kerala painters evolved a language taking cues from contemporary traditions. In the painting of Venugopal of Sri Rama Temple, there are elements of Kathakali and Kalam-ezhuthu (ritual floor painting of Kerala), using vibrant and luminous colours like representing human figures in three-dimensionality.

11. In Lepakshi, near Hindupur, in present Andhra Pradesh, there are glorious examples of Vijayanagara paintings on the walls of the Shiva temple. The painting of 'Ladies attending Parvati' is exposed on surface of the temple. This fresco painting has particularly detailed in very bright dresses and colours.

Or The artists of Bhimbetka used many animals in a naturalistic form or style but humans were painted different stylistic ways. Women are painted both in the nude and clothed. The young and the old equally find place in these paintings. Children are painted running, jumping and playing. Community dances provide a common theme.

12. The Painted Earthen Jar was found in Mohenjodaro, which is made on a potter's wheel with clay. The most unique feature of this jar is its shape that was manipulated by the pressure of the crafty fingers of the potter. After baking the clay model, it was painted with black colour. High polishing was done as a finishing touch. The motifs are of vegetals and geometric forms.

Or The large statues of Yakshas and Yakhinis that are found at many places like Patna, Vidisha and Mathura are mostly in the standing position. One of the distinguishing elements in all these images is their polished surface. The depiction of faces is in full round with pronounced cheeks and physiognomic detail.

13. The paintings of the upper Paleolithic phase are linear representations. It is mainly done with green and dark red and of huge animal figures, such as bisons, elephants, tigers, rhinos and boars besides stick-like human figures. A few are wash paintings but mostly they are filled with geometric patterns. The green paintings are of dancers and the red ones are of hunters.

Or The Bhimbetka paintings, though belonged to the remote past but do not lack pictorial quality. Despite various limitations such as inadequate tools, materials, etc., there is a charm of simple rendering of scenes of the environment in which the artists lived. The men shown in them appear adventurous and rejoicing in their lives. The primitive artists seem to possess an inborn passion for storytelling. These pictures depict, in a dramatic way, both men and animals engaged in the struggle for survival.

14. During the 1st century AD onwards, Gandhara (now in Pakistan) and Mathura in Northern India emerged as important centres of art production. Buddha in the symbolic form got a human form in both this places. The sculptural tradition in Gandhara had the confluence of Bactria, Parthia and the local Gandhara tradition. The local sculptural tradition at Mathura became so strong that the tradition spread to other parts of Northern India.

The Buddha image at Mathura is modelled on the lines of earlier Yaksha images whereas in Gandhara it has hellenistic features. Early Jain Tirthankara images and portraits of kings, especially the headless Kanishka are also found from Mathura. Images of Vaishnava (mainly Vishnu and his various forms) and Shaiva (mainly the lingas and mukhalingas) faiths are also found at Mathura but Buddhist images are found in large numbers.

There is boldness in carving the large images. The faces are round and smiling, heaviness in the sculptural volume is reduced to relaxed flesh. The garments of the body are clearly visible and they cover the left shoulder. Images of the Buddha, Yakshas, Yakshinis, Shaivite and Vaishnavite deities and portrait statues are richly sculpted. In the 2nd century AD, images in Mathura get sensual, roundness increased. They become fleshier. The trend continues in the 4th century AD.

Sarnath and Kosambi also emerged as important centres of art production. Many Buddha images in Sarnath have plain transparent drapery covering both shoulders, and the halo around the head has very little ornamentation.

15. The Bharhut sculptures belong to the post-Mauryan period, dating back to the 2nd century BCE. These sculptures were discovered at Bharhut, Madhya Pradesh, and are now displayed in the Indian Museum, Kolkata. They represent an early phase of Buddhist art and follow a distinct style characterised by low-relief carvings, linearity, and the use of shallow depth, which gives the figures a flat appearance.

The subject matter of Bharhut sculptures mainly includes narrative panels depicting Jataka tales and events from Buddha's life. One such panel shows Queen Mayadevi's dream, where an elephant is depicted descending towards her womb, symbolising the birth of Siddhartha Gautama. Another panel illustrates the Ruru Jataka, where the Bodhisattva deer rescues a drowning man, who later betrays him by revealing his identity to the king. These panels effectively narrate Buddhist teachings through visual storytelling.

The artisans used space efficiently by clubbing multiple events within a single frame. Figures have stiff postures, but later carvings achieved more depth and realism. The depiction of human and animal figures conveys moral values like compassion, truth, and duty. Observing these sculptures inspires dedication, as they emphasise righteousness and selflessness through their artistic and narrative expression.

16. The rock shelters of Lakhudiyar is located in the Almora district of Uttarakhand. Lakhudiyar literally means one lakh caves. The Lakhudiyar paintings proves the mastery of skill of the primitive people's art forms. One of the interesting scenes depicted at Lakhudiyar rock painting is of hand-linked dancing human figures.

The Lakhudiyar paintings can be divided into three categories: man, animal and geometric patterns in white, black and red ochre. Humans are represented in stick-like forms. A long-snouted animal, a fox and a multiple legged lizard are the main animal motifs. Wavy lines, rectangle-filled geometric designs, and groups of dots can also be seen here. There is some superimposition of paintings. The earliest are in black; over these are red ochre paintings and the last group comprises white paintings.

SAMPLE
QUESTION PAPER
(Graphics)

Time allowed : 2 hrs MM : 30 Marks

General Instructions

1. Section – A Attempt all Questions (Each Question will carry 1 Mark)
2. Section – B Attempt all Questions (Each Question will carry 2 Marks)
3. Section – C Attempt any two Questions (Each Question will carry 6 Marks)

Section A

1. The Muslims ruler absorbed many features of local cultures and traditions of India. Which among the following was adopted them? (1)
   (a) Roof decorations (b) Wall painting
   (c) Surface decorations (d) Rock cutting shapes
2. **Assertion** (A) Large number of seals have been discovered from Indus Valley sites. (1)
   Reason (R) The discovery of seals shows that the people of Indus Valley were deeply spiritual in nature.
   Codes
   (a) Both A and R are true and R is the correct explanation of A
   (b) Both A and R are true, but R is not the correct explanation of A
   (c) A is true, but R is false
   (d) A is false, but R is true
3. Most of the art and architectural remains that survive from ancient and medieval India are (1)
   (a) religious in nature (b) semi religious in nature
   (c) religious and social in nature (d) secular in nature
4. Who among the following Chalukya king patronised Badami Caves and its paintings? (1)
   (a) Pulakesin I (b) Mangalesha (c) Kirtivarman I (d) Narsimha I
5. **Assertion** (A) The Mauryan pillars are different from the Achamenian pillars. (1)
   Reason (R) The Mauryan pillars are rock-cut pillars thus, displaying the carver's skills, whereas the Achamenian pillars are constructed in pieces by a mason.
   Codes
   (a) Both A and R are true and R is the correct explanation of A
   (b) Both A and R are true, but R is not the correct explanation of A
   (c) A is true, but R is false
   (d) A is false, but R is true

6. The most striking difference between Mauryan and Achamenian pillars is (1)
(a) pillar style (b) pillar motifs (c) pillar length (d) pillar material

7. Archaeologists in Harappa Civilisation have discovered thousands of seals, mostly made of .... (1)
(a) lapis lazuli (b) agate (c) steatite (d) bronze

8. The rock art of Bhimbetka has been classified into how many historical periods? (1)
(a) Three (b) Four (c) Five (d) Seven

Section B

9. Why provincial states like Gujarat was said to have a markedly regional character? (2)

Or

How it is been proved that Gujarat and Rajasthan have been strongholds of Jainism since early times through sculpture art form?

10. Give your observations and describe the subject matter and composition of any one of the Indian sculpture given below (2)

The Dancing Girl, Mohenjodaro

Or

The 'Chariot' Daimabad

11. Myths mentioned in the Puranas became part of narrative representation of the Brahmanical religion and its temples. Define and elaborate the technique, medium and depiction of Chatur Mukhlinga at Nachna-Kuthara. (2)

Or

Explain the three types of Brahmanical shrines or temples' that are found in many parts of Northern India.

12. Evaluate the Sarnath School of art with context of Mathura and Gandhara Schools. (2)

Or

The local sculptural tradition at Mathura became so strong that the tradition spread to other parts of Northern India. Explain this with the example of Railing Arts of Sangol.

13. How terracotta figurines show a very different delineation of the body as compared to the sculptures traditions in India? (2)

Or

The monumental rock-cut elephant at Dhauli in Odisha has modelled in round with linear rhythm. Explain.

Section C

14. Evaluate the tradition of art extended further down South in Tamil Nadu with regional variations during the regimes of Pallava and Pandya dynasties.
Appreciate the contribution in detail based on (6)
- Beginning of temple painting tradition
- Application of the rhythmic lines with increased ornamentation
- Sittanavasa ceiling painting

15. How the 'Pottery art forms' enable us to understand the gradual evolution of various design motifs as employed in different shapes, and styles? **(6)**

Support your answer with
- Types of plain pottery
- Technique in black painted ware
- Use of perforated pottery

16. Observe the given picture of prehistoric rock paintings from Lakhudiyar, Uttarakhand, showing hand-linked dancing human figures, wavy lines, and animal motifs.

Based on your study of prehistoric art, answer the following
- Identify the primary subjects depicted in the paintings.
- What types of animals are depicted in the Lakhudiyar rock paintings?
- Discuss the possible purpose of these paintings based on their themes and the context of prehistoric life. **(6)**

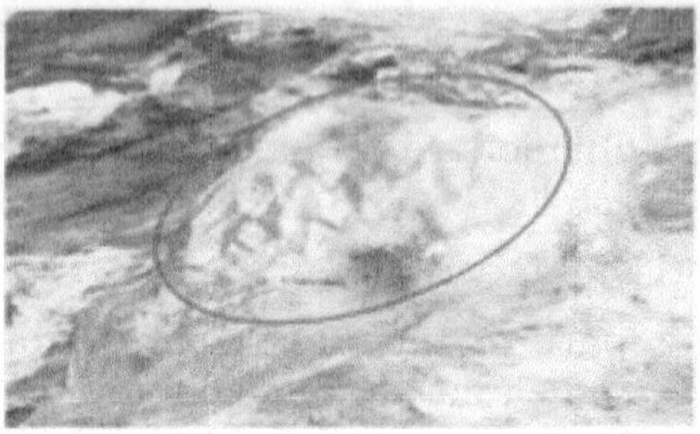

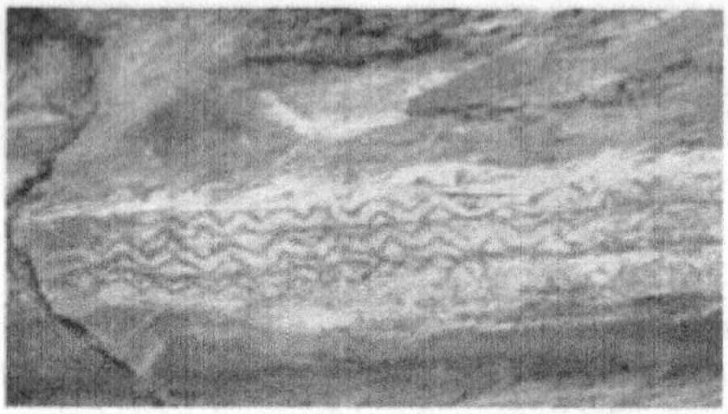

Answers

1. (c) Surface decorations
2. (c) A is true, but R is false
3. (a) religious in nature
4. (b) Mangalesha
5. (a) Both A and R are true and R is the correct explanation of A
6. (d) pillar material
7. (c) steatite
8. (d) Seven
9. The Gujarat was said to have a markedly regional character because its patrons borrowed elements from regional temple traditions such as toranas, lintels in mihrabs, carvings of bell and chain motifs, and carved panels depicting trees, for tombs, mosques and dargahs that they made.

Or

The hoard of bronzes discovered in Akota near Vadodara established that bronze casting was practiced in Gujarat or Western India between the 6th and 9th centuries. Most of the images represent the Jain Tirthankaras like Mahavira, Parshvanath or Adinath. A new format was invented in which Tirthankaras are seated on a throne; they can be single or combined in a group of three or in a group of twenty-four Tirthankaras. Stylistically, they were influenced by the features of both the Gupta and the Vakataka period bronzes.

10. **The Dancing Girl**
The 'Dancing Girl' from Mohenjodaro (now Pakistan) is the earliest bronze sculpture datable to 2500 BC. The limbs and torso of this female figurine are simplified in tubular form. It is one of the first and finest craft of dance form that originated in Indian sub-continent.

Or

The Chariot
The 'Chariot' is a group of bronze statuettes that have been discovered from archaeological excavation at Daimabad (Maharashtra) datable to 1500 BC. It significance is the 'Chariot', the wheels of which are represented in simple circular shapes while the driver or human rider has been elongated, and the bulls in the forefront are modelled in sturdy forms.

11. The Chatur Mukhlinga lies in the small sanctum (garbhagriha), which approximately 4.67 feet high Shivalingam with four faces (mukhlinga) with elaborate hair style. Three of these faces shown calm with meditating closed eye, smiling posture.
The fourth face of Shiva is shown as energised and in action, with wide open mouth, raised nostrils and slightly bulging open eyes in his form as Bhairava.

Or

The Brahmanical temples in Northern India usually had a principal image of a God. The shrines of the temples were of three kinds
(i) Sandhara type (without pradikshinapatha)
(ii) Nirandhara type (with pradakshinapatha)
(iii) Sarvatobhadra (which can be accessed from all sides).

12. The Sarnath School of art was more or less developed in the same period like Mathura and Gandhara Schools. Many Buddha images in Sarnath have plain transparent drapery covering both shoulders, and the halo around the head has very little ornamentation. On the other hand, the Mathura Buddha images continue to depict folds of the drapery in the Buddha images and the halo around the head.

Or

Mathura had local sculpture tradition which became so strong that the tradition spread to other parts of Northern India, especially in the stupa sculptures found at Sangol in the Punjab. It has very intrinsically details of human figures adorned with vegetables and even animal motifs as well.

13. The terracotta figurines making process began much earlier than the sculpture tradition in India. The terracotta figurines that mostly found in Harappa Civilisation is unevenly designed with no detailed attention had paid to its body dimensions and curves.
On the other hand, sculptures were made with skilled hands where much attention has been given to its artistic details.

Or

Depiction of a monumental rock-cut elephant at Dhauli in Odisha shows modelling in round with linear rhythm. It gives an illusion that an elephant comes out from the cave. The sculpture of Dhauli is famous for its Ashokan rock-edict. It is a remarkable example of execution of figure representation.

14. The tradition of art began in the South India with Pallava dynasty. The Pallava kings who succeeded the Chalukya kings in parts of South India, were patrons of arts. Mahendravarma I who ruled in the 7th century was responsible for building temples at Panamalai, Mandagapattu and Kanchipuram. The paintings in these temples too were done at his initiative, though only fragments remain. The Panamalai figure of a female divinity is drawn gracefully.

Paintings at the Kanchipuram temple were patronised by the Pallava king, Rajsimha. Faces are round and large. Lines are rhythmic with increased ornamentation when compared with the paintings of an earlier periods. Depiction of torso still remains like the earlier sculptural tradition but is elongated.

When the Pandyas came to power, they too patronised art. Tirumalaipuram caves and Jaina caves at Sittanavasa are some of the surviving examples. A few fragmented layers of paintings can be seen in Tirumalaipuram.

In Sittanavasal, the paintings are visible on the ceilings of shrines, in verandas, and on the brackets. On the pillars of the veranda are seen dancing figures with divinity in nature. The contours of figures are firmly drawn and painted in vermilion red on a lighter background. The body is rendered in yellow with subtle modelling.

15. A large quantity of pottery excavated from the different sites of Indus Valley Civilisations, enable us to understand the gradual evolution of various design motifs as employed in different shapes, and styles.

The Indus Valley pottery consists chiefly of very fine wheel-made wares, very few being hand-made. Plain pottery is more common than painted ware. Plain pottery is generally of red clay, with or without a fine red or grey slip. It includes knobbed ware, ornamented with rows of knobs.

The black painted ware has a fine coating of red slip on which geometric and animal designs are executed in glossy black paint. Polychrome pottery is rare and mainly comprises small vases decorated with geometric patterns in red, black, and green, rarely white and yellow. Incised ware is also rare. Perforated pottery includes a large hole at the bottom and small holes all over the wall, and was probably used for straining beverages. Pottery for household purposes is found in as many shapes and sizes as could be used for daily practical use. Straight and angular shapes are an exception, while graceful curves are in large numbers.

16. In the given picture of prehistoric rock paintings from Lakhudiyar, Uttarakhand, the primary subjects depicted are human figures, particularly dancing figures that are linked by their hands. There are also animal motifs such as a long-snouted animal, fox, and lizard. Additionally, geometric patterns like wavy lines are shown.

In the Lakhudiyar rock paintings, animals such as a long-snouted animal, a fox, a multiple-legged lizard, and other creatures are depicted.

The purpose of these prehistoric paintings was likely to capture important aspects of daily life. The themes, such as hunting, dancing, and animals, suggest that the paintings might have been created to document activities or events, like a successful hunt or religious rituals. These paintings could also have had spiritual or symbolic meanings, with animals representing strength, protection, or fertility. Since the people lived close to nature, the paintings might have been a way to connect with the world around them or ask for blessings from nature's forces. Additionally, the paintings could have been used to make their shelters more beautiful or to pass down stories and traditions to future generations.

SAMPLE QUESTION PAPER

(Sculpture)

Time allowed : 2 hrs MM : 30 Marks

General Instructions

1. *Section – A Attempt all Questions (Each Question will carry 1 Mark)*
2. *Section – B Attempt all Questions (Each Question will carry 2 Marks)*
3. *Section – C Attempt any two Questions (Each Question will carry 6 Marks)*

Section A

1. One of the best known artefacts from the Indus Valley is the Dancing Girl. It measurement is approximately (1)

   (a) three-inch-high copper figure
   (b) four-inch-high copper figure
   (c) five-inch-high copper figure
   (d) six-inch-high copper figure

2. **Assertion** (A) In the sculptures of Bharhut, narrative panels are shown with fewer characters. (1)

   Reason (R) Sometimes more than one event at one geographical place is shown together in the picture space while sometimes, only a single main event is depicted in the picture space.

   Codes

   (a) Both A and R are true and R is the correct explanation of A
   (b) Both A and R are true, but R is not the correct explanation of A
   (c) A is true, but R is false
   (d) A is false, but R is true

3. In this red sandstone figure, there are socket holes in the neck and shoulders for the attachment of head and arms. The frontal posture of the figure has been consciously adopted. Identify the object. (1)

   (a) Male Torso (b) Mother Goddess
   (c) Male Yogic (d) Bearded Priest

4. The figure of the bearded man, interpreted as a priest, is draped in a shawl coming under the right arm and covering the left shoulder. In which pattern his shawl is decorated with? (1)

   (a) Trefoil patterns (b) Zig-zag patterns
   (c) Square patterns (d) Oval patterns

5. **Assertion** (A) The mural paintings of Ajanta are very renowned and known for their artistic illustration. **(1)**

Reason (R) The paintings have large typological variate, clear lines, rhythmic movements and merging designs. Paintings are multicolour, with lot of emotions and facial expressions, make them realistic.

Codes

(a) Both A and R are true and R is the correct explanation of A
(b) Both A and R are true, but R is not the correct explanation of A
(c) A is true, but R is false
(d) A is false, but R is true

6. Name the most important among the following Indus Valley terracotta figures till the date. **(1)**

(a) Dancing Girl (b) Clay Cart (c) Mother Goddess (d) Mother Earth

7. The life-size standing image of a Yakshni holding a chauri (flywhisk) from Didarganj is good example of the sculptural tradition of the Mauryan period. At which place it is been preserved? **(1)**

(a) British Museum, UK (b) National Museum, New Delhi
(c) Patna Museum, Bihar (d) Indian Museum, Kolkata

8. Many standing Buddha images were cast in North India, particularly Uttar Pradesh and Bihar, during the Gupta and Post-Gupta periods with unique mudra or pose. Identify them among the following. **(1)**

(a) Dharmachakra mudra (b) Abhaya mudra
(c) Bhumisparsha mudra (d) Dhyana mudra

Section B

9. "The stambha or tower was the minar, a common feature of architecture in the Indian sub-continent". With this regard, give some details of the two most striking minars of medieval times **(2)**

Qutub Minar in Delhi

Or

Chand Minar at Daulatabad

10. "Monumental structures over graves of rulers and royalty was a popular feature of medieval India."

On the basis of the above statement identify the features of **(2)**

Tomb of Humayun

Or

Sarais

11. "Provincial style architecture of Mandu is regarded as too close to the structures of Imperial Delhi to make a bold statement of local traditions." **(2)**

With this regard, give your views by describing the

Jahaaz Mahal

Or

Hindola Mahal

12. The Mauryan Capital of Sarnath is the finest example of Mauryan sculptural tradition. Explain. (2)

Or

Give some valid point for the support of Gol Gumbad and explain why it is called a striking edifice in spite of being unfinished.

13. "The Kerala painters during the period from the 16th to the 17th centuries evolved a pictorial language and technique of their own."
On the basis of the above statement identify the features of Kerala paintings. (2)

Or

How Amravati Stupa developed along with Sanchi Stupa in the areas of Buddhist sculptures and architecture?

Section C

14. What do you understand by the lost-wax process? How it was flourished in Southern India? Explain the below mentioned points in detail (6)

- Origin of lost-wax process
- Stages and Technique of lost-wax
- Compositional material
- Different Metals for the use of lost-wax

15. Carefully observe the given picture of a rock-cut temple carved from a single monolithic rock. The temple features a towering vimana, a Nandi shrine, and intricate sculptures depicting mythological scenes. This structure is considered one of the greatest achievements in Indian rock-cut architecture.

Based on your study of temple architecture, answer the following

- Identify the name of the temple and the ruler under whose patronage it was built.
- Describe the key architectural features that make this temple unique.
- Explain the significance of monolithic rock-cut architecture in ancient India. (6)

16. Give the various stages of progression in Ajanta paintings and its unique features. (6)
Identify the below mentioned points in detail

- Themes of Ajanta
- Two layers of paintings
- Different stages of development

Answers

1. (b) four-inch-high copper figure
2. (a) Both A and R are true and R is the correct explanation of A
3. (a) Male Torso
4. (a) Trefoil patterns
5. (a) Both A and R are true and R is the correct explanation of A
6. (c) Mother Goddess
7. (c) Patna Museum, Bihar
8. (b) Abhaya mudra
9. The Qutub Minar was built in the early 13th century. Qutb-ud-Din Aibak laid the foundation of Minar in 1199 AD and it was completed by Iltutmish.

   The red sandstone tower of Qutub Minar is 72.5 m high, tapering from 2.75 m in diameter at its peak to 14.32 m at its base, and alternating angular and rounded goes up.

   Or

   The Chand Minar or the Tower of the Moon is a medieval tower situated in Daulatabad in Maharashtra. It was erected in 1445 AD by Sultan Alauddin Bahmani to commemorate his capture of the fort. The Chand Minar is considered to be among the finest specimens of Indo-Islamic architecture and it bears resemblance to the Qutub Minar of Delhi. It is 63 metres high and is divided into 4 storeys and 24 chambers. The tower also displays some indigenous Indian architectural features such as the brackets supporting its balconies.
10. Humayun's Tomb in Delhi is the first-of-its-kind opulent mausoleum built in India and also the first garden-tomb in the country. It was built by Humayun's first wife Begum Bega aka Haji Begum in 1572 AD. The grand tomb complex was designed by Mirak Mirza Ghiyas, a Persian architect. The huge tomb with a height of 154 feet and width of 299 feet is mainly built in red sandstone while white marble has been used for the double layered dome.

    Or

    The Sarais were known as ringed cities and were largely built on a simple square or rectangular plan and were meant to provide temporary accommodation to Indian and foreign travellers, pilgrims, merchants, traders, etc. In effect, sarais were public domains which thronged with people of varied cultural backgrounds.
11. The Jahaaz Mahal is an elegant two-storey 'ship- palace' between two reservoirs, with open pavilions, balconies overhanging the water and a terrace. Built by Sultan Ghiyasuddin Khilji, it was possibly used as his harem and as the ultimate pleasure and recreational resort. The detailing is brilliant and it has a built-in meticulous precision that follows an acoustic water supply pattern. The balconies are made in a way that it amplifies the sound and the delicate styles of carvings on the walls are gem of art work.

    Or

    The Hindola Mahal is a part of Royal Enclave group of monuments in Mandu. The Hindola Mahal represents the characteristic elements of simplicity, boldness, and well-proportioned. The Hindola Mahal looks like a railway viaduct bridge with its disproportionately large buttresses supporting the walls. Batter was used very effectively to give an impression of swinging (Hindola) walls.

12. The Mauryan pillar capital found at Sarnath popularly known as the Lion Capital is the finest example of Mauryan sculptural tradition. It is also our national emblem. The capital is carved with considerable care—voluminous roaring lion figures firmly standing on a circular abacus which is carved with the figures of a horse, a bull, a lion and an elephant in vigorous movement, executed with precision.

It shows considerable amount of mastery in the sculptural techniques. This pillar capital symbolising Dhammachakra Pravartana (the first sermon by the Buddha) has become a standard symbol of this great historical event in the life of the Buddha.

Or

Gol Gumbad is situated in Bijapur in the Bijapur District of Karnataka. It is the mausoleum of Muhammad Adil Shah (1626–1656 AD). Built by the ruler himself, it is known as a striking edifice in spite of being unfinished. It is built of dark grey basalt and decorated plasterwork. With the drum and the dome, the building rises to a height of over two hundred feet.

The tomb has only one square chamber and the dome, with a diameter of one hundred and twenty-five feet, it covers an uninterrupted floor space of 18,337 square feet, the second largest in the world.

13. The Kerala painters evolved a language taking cues from contemporary traditions, like Kathakali and Kalamezhuthu (ritual floor painting of Kerala), using vibrant and luminous colours, representing human figures in three-dimensionality.

Thematically too, paintings from Kerala stand apart. Most of the narrations are based on those episodes from Hindu mythology which were popular in Kerala. The artist seems to have derived sources from oral traditions and local versions of the Ramayana and the Mahabharata for painted narration.

Or

Like the Sanchi Stupa, the Amravati Stupa is one of the important stupa of ancient India. Events from the life of the Buddha and the Jataka stories are depicted. Though in the Amravati Stupa, there is evidence of construction activity in the 3rd century BC, it was best developed in the 1st and 2nd centuries AD.

Like Sanchi, the early phase is devoid of Buddha images but during the later phase, in the 2nd and 3rd centuries AD, the Buddha images are carved on the drum slabs and at many other places. Interior space in the composition is created by different postures of the figures such as semi-back, back, profile, frontal, semi-frontal, side, etc. Sculptural form in this area is characterised by intense emotions.

14. The Lost-Wax process is a technique used for making objects of metal, especially in Himachal Pradesh, Odisha, Bihar, Madhya Pradesh and West Bengal. In each region, a slightly different technique is used.

The legacy of Chola bronze casting dates back to many centuries in making bronze sculptures using the lost-wax process. The lost-wax technique is used to create sculptures in a variety of metals such as bronze, brass and other alloys.

The lost-wax process involves several different steps. First a wax model of the image is made by hand of pure beeswax that has been melted over an open fire, and then strained through a fine cloth into a basin of cold water. Here, it resolidifies immediately. It is then pressed through a pichki or pharni which squeezes the wax into noodle-like shape. These wax wires are then wound around to the shape of the entire image. The image is now covered with a thick coating of paste, made of equal parts of clay, sand and cow-dung. Into an opening on one side, a clay pot is fixed. In this, molten metal is poured. The weight of the metal to be used is ten times than of wax.

As the wax inside melts, the metal flows down the channel and takes the shape of the wax image. The firing process is carried out almost like a religious ritual and all the steps take place in dead silence. The image is later chiselled with files to smoothen it and give it a finish.

Casting a bronze image is a painstaking task and demands a high degree of skills. Sometimes, an alloy of five metals — gold, silver, copper, brass and lead is used to cast bronze images.

15. The temple shown in the picture is the Kailashnath Temple at Ellora, built under the patronage of the Rashtrakuta king Krishna I in the 8th century CE. It is one of the most remarkable rock-cut temples in India, carved entirely from a single monolithic rock.

The Kailashnath Temple is unique due to its Dravida-style architecture, featuring a towering vimana (temple tower), a separate Nandi shrine, and intricate carvings depicting various Hindu mythological scenes. The temple complex also includes pillared halls, subsidiary shrines, staircases, and detailed sculptures of gods, goddesses, and celestial beings. One of the most astonishing aspects is that the temple was carved from top to bottom, ensuring precision and grandeur.

Monolithic rock-cut architecture is significant because it showcases the skill, patience, and vision of ancient Indian artisans. Unlike other temples built by stacking stone blocks, this temple was excavated out of a massive rock, making it an extraordinary feat of engineering. Such temples also reflect the deep devotion and artistic excellence of the time. The Kailashnath Temple remains a symbol of spirituality, craftsmanship, and architectural brilliance, making it a treasure of India's cultural heritage.

16. The most famous cave site in India is Ajanta. It is located in Aurangabad district of Maharashtra state. Paintings of Ajanta have a lot of typological variations. The themes of the paintings are the events from the life of the Buddha, the Jatakas and the Avadanas. Some paintings such as Simhala Avadana, Mahajanaka Jataka and Vidhurpundita Jataka cover the entire wall of the cave.

The figures are heavy like the sculptures of Western India. The caves of the early phase also have paintings especially Cave Nos. 9 and 10. They belong to the 1st century BC. The figures are broad with heavy proportion and arranged in the picture space in a linear way in Cave No. 9.

The figures in Ajanta caves are painted with considerable naturalism and there is no over-stylisation. Events are grouped together according to geographical location. Tiered, horizontally-arranged figures appear as a convenient choice of the artisans. Separation of geographic location has been indicated by using outward architectural bands. Figures appear like the Sanchi sculptures which indicate how the lithic and painting traditions were progressing simultaneously.

The second phase of paintings can be studied from the images of the Buddha's painted on the walls and pillars of Cave Nos. 10 and 9. These Buddha figures are different from the figures painted in the 5th century AD.

The next stage of development is observed mainly in the paintings of Cave Nos. 16, 17, 1, and 2. The paintings of Cave Nos. 1 and 2 are very orderly and naturalistic, well integrated with the sculptures in the caves. Movements in the figures are very rhythmic.

SAMPLE QUESTION PAPER
(Commercial Art)

Time allowed : 2 hrs | MM : 30 Marks

General Instructions

1. Section – A Attempt all Questions (Each Question will carry 1 Mark)
2. Section – B Attempt all Questions (Each Question will carry 2 Marks)
3. Section – C Attempt any two Questions (Each Question will carry 6 Marks)

Section A

1. What does Lakhudiyar literally means? (1)

(a) Log paint (b) Cave paint
(c) One lac caves (d) One lac paints

2. **Assertion** (A) The art pieces in the domestic dwelling of the people perished. (1)

Reason (R) The domestic dwellings and the art pieces in them were made from material like wood and clay which became ruined over the time.

Codes

(a) Both A and R are true and R is the correct explanation of A
(b) Both A and R are true, but R is not the correct explanation of A
(c) A is true, but R is false
(d) A is false, but R is true

3. The rock-cut cave carved at Barabar Hills near Gaya in Bihar is known as (1)

(a) Barabar Caves (b) Lomas Rishi (c) Hathigumpha (d) Udaigiri

4. At which stupa in India, the depiction of the historical narratives such as the siege of Kushinara, Buddha's visit to Kapilavastu, visit of Ashoka to the Ramgrama Stupa are carved with considerable details? (1)

(a) Bharhut (b) Ratnagiri (c) Sanchi (d) Amravati

5. **Assertion** (A) New boundary wall has been constructed lately around the temples of Dravida style. (1)

Reason (R) With the passage of time, the population and size of town associated with temple would have increased.

Codes

(a) Both A and R are true and R is the correct explanation of A
(b) Both A and R are true, but R is not the correct explanation of A
(c) A is true, but R is false
(d) A is false, but R is true

6. The images of Jain Tirthankaras have been discovered from Chausa, Bihar, belonging to which period? (1)

(a) Mauryan
(b) Greek Roman
(c) Kushanas
(d) Guptas

7. The walls in all buildings during medieval period were extremely thick and were largely constructed of (1)

(a) sandstone
(b) limestone
(c) clay and rubble
(d) rubble masonary

8. The rock art of Bhimbetka has been classified into various groups on the bases of style, technique and (1)

(a) period (b) superimposition (c) usage of colours (d) projection style

Section B

9. Write a short note on copper tablets that found in Indus Valley Civilisation. (2)

Or

Find the major factors of Ashoka's pillar capitals with special reference to Sarnath Lion Capital.

10. Which types of sculptures have been found in Mathura Schools of Art? (2)

Or

The mural painting on interior and exterior walls of houses in villages or havelis is prevalent in different parts of the country. Justify your answer with various points.

11. What do you understand by iconography? Does it is based on or associated certain symbols and mythologies. (2)

Or

Find out the most striking features of Pashupati Seal of Harappa Civilisation.

12. Write some of the major strategic devices of the Daulatabad Fort. (2)

Or

Gwalior Fort

13. Why did pre-historic people draw various pictures? (2)

Or

The bead industry seems to have been well-developed in Harappan period. Explain.

Section C

14. Write basic forms and three different style of the Hindu temple architecture. (6)

Appreciate the contribution in detail based on

- Freestanding Temple
- Nagara/Dravida/Vesara
- Complex stage of temple building

15. Observe the given picture of a Harappan seal made of steatite. The seal depicts a human figure seated cross-legged with various animals surrounding it.
Based on your study of seals, answer the following
- Identify the name of the seal and the period to which it belongs.
- Describe the animals depicted on the seal and their possible symbolic significance.
- Explain the purpose of these seals, and how they might have been used in ancient times. **(6)**

16. Mention the importance of Stupas and Viharas in Indian architectural traditions. Justify your answer on the following parameters **(6)**
- Types of stupa/ viharas
- Major places of Stupas and Viharas
- Beginning of Sanchi

Answers

Section A

1. (c) One lac caves
2. (a) Both A and R are true and R is the correct explanation of A
3. (b) Lomas Rishi
4. (c) Sanchi
5. (a) Both A and R are true and R is the correct explanation of A
6. (c) Kushanas
7. (d) rubble masonary
8. (b) superimposition
9. The square or rectangular copper tablets, with an animal or a human figure on one side and an inscription on the other, or an inscription on both sides have been found in Harappa or Indus Valley Civilisation. The figures and signs are carefully cut with a burin. These copper tablets appear to have been amulets. Unlike inscriptions on seals which vary in each case, inscriptions on the copper tablets seem to be associated with the animals portrayed on them.

Or

The Lion Capital is located at Sarnath, near Varanasi. It is generally referred to as Sarnath Lion Capital. This is one of the finest examples of sculpture from the Mauryan period. It was built in commemoration of the historical event of the first sermon or the Dharmachakra Pravartana by the Buddha at Sarnath, the capital was built by Ashoka.

10. Images of Vaishnava (mainly Vishnu and his various forms) and Shaiva (mainly the lingas and mukhalingas) faiths are found at Mathura but Buddhist images are found in large numbers. It may be noted that the images of Vishnu and Shiva are represented by their ayudhas (weapons). There is boldness in carving the large images, the volume of the images is projected out of the picture plane. The faces are round and smiling, heaviness in the sculptural volume is reduced to relaxed flesh. The garments of the body are clearly visible and they cover the left shoulder.

Or

Today we can observe that mural painting on interior and exterior walls of houses in villages or havelis is prevalent. These paintings are usually made by women either at the time of ceremonies or festivals or as a routine to clean and decorate the walls. Some of the traditional forms of murals are pithoro in parts of Rajasthan and Gujarat, Mithila painting in Northern Bihar's Mithila region, warli paintings in Maharashtra, or simply paintings on the walls, in a village of Odisha or Bengal, Madhya Pradesh or Chhattisgarh.

11. The study of images of deities that falls within a branch of art history called 'iconography'. It consists of identification of images based on certain symbols and mythologies associated with them. While the fundamental myth and meaning of the deity may remain the same for centuries, its specific usage at a place might be influenced to its local or immediate social, political or geographical factors.

Or

The Pashupati Seal is the most remarkable seal that is generally identified as the Pashupati Seal by some scholars whereas some identify it as the female deity. This seal depicts a human figure seated cross-legged. An elephant and a tiger are depicted to the right side of the seated figure, while on the left a rhinoceros and a buffalo are seen. In addition to these animals, two antelopes are shown below the seat.

12. Daulatabad had several strategic devices to confound the enemy, such as huge entrances so that gates could not be opened even with the help of elephants. It also had twin forts, one within the other but at a higher elevation and accessed by a complex defence design arrangement. One wrong turn in the complex pathway could lead to the enemy soldier going in circles or falling to his death several hundred feet below.

Or

The Gwalior Fort in the state of Madhya Pradesh was invincible because its steep height made it impossible to scale. It had many habitations and usages. Babur, who did not find much merit in many things he saw in Hindustan, was said to have been surprised at the sight of the Gwalior Fort.

13. The pre-historic people may have drawn and painted to make their shelters more colourful and beautiful or to keep a visual record of their day-to-day life, like some of us who maintain a diary. It has been identified by the scientists that during this period, critical and creative ideas were began to function in the human brain.

Or

The bead industry seems to have been well-developed in Harappan period as it is evident from the factories discovered at Chanhudaro and Lothal. Beads were made of carnelian, amethyst, jasper, crystal, quartz, steatite, turquoise, lapis lazuli, etc. Metals like copper, bronze and gold, and shell, faience and terracotta or burnt clay were also used for manufacturing beads.

14. The basic form of the Hindu temple comprises the following factors in India Hindu temple architecture. The sanctum (garbhagriha), which was a small cubicle with a single entrance and grew into a larger chamber in time. The entrance to the temple which may be a portico or colonnaded hall that incorporates space for a large number of worshippers and is known as a mandapa.

Freestanding temples tend to have a mountain-like spire, which can take the shape of a curving shikhar in North India and a pyramidal tower, called a vimana, in South India.

The vahan, i.e., the mount or vehicle of the temple's main deity along with a standard pillar or dhvaj is placed axially before the sanctum.

Two broad orders of temples in the country are known as Nagara in the North and Dravida in the South. At times, the Vesara style of temples as an independent style created through the selective mixing of the Nagara and Dravida orders is mentioned by some scholars.

As temples grew more complex, more surfaces were created for sculpture through additive geometry, i.e., by adding more and more rhythmically projecting, symmetrical walls and niches, without breaking away from the fundamental plan of the shrine.

15. This seal is commonly known as the Pashupati Seal, and it dates back to around 2500-1900 BCE, from the time of the Indus Valley Civilisation.

The seal shows a variety of animals around the human figure, including an elephant, tiger, rhinoceros, and buffalo, along with an antelope at the bottom. These animals may have symbolic meanings, representing strength, power, and different aspects of nature. The elephant could symbolise wisdom and power, while the tiger might represent courage or fierceness. The rhinoceros and buffalo are possibly linked to fertility or agriculture, both important to the Harappan society.

The primary purpose of these seals was commercial. They were likely used to mark goods, ensuring they were identified and traded by their owners. These seals may have also served as amulets, worn by people as a form of protection or to display identity, similar to modern-day identity cards.

16. The popularity of Buddhism and Jainism gave huge importance for stupas and viharas, therefore these were constructed on a large scale. However, there are also examples of a few Brahmanical gods in the sculptural representations. It is important to note that the stupas were constructed over the relics of the Buddha at Rajagraha, Vaishali, Vethadipa and Pava in Bihar, Kapilavastu, Allakappa and Ramagrama in Nepal, Kushinagar and Pippalvina in Uttar Pradesh.

Stupa, vihara and chaitya are part of Buddhist and Jaina monastic complexes but the largest number belongs to the Buddhist religion. One of the examples of the structure of a stupa in the 3rd century BCE is at Bairat in Rajasthan. The great stupa at Sanchi was built with bricks during the time of Ashoka and later, it was covered with stone and many new additions were made. Subsequently, many such stupas were constructed which shows the popularity of Buddhism.

From the 2nd century BC onwards, we get many inscriptional evidences mentioning donors and, at times, their profession. The pattern of patronage has been a very collective one and there are very few examples of royal patronage.